he Po...

Also available from Continuum

The Essential Guide to English Studies
Peter Childs

How to Write Poetry
Fred Sedgwick

How to Read Texts
Neil McCaw

Literary Theory: A Guide for the Perplexed
Mary Klages

The Poetry Toolkit

The Essential Guide to Studying Poetry

Rhian Williams

continuum

Continuum
The Tower Building
11 York Road
London SE1 7NX
www.continuumbooks.com

80 Maiden Lane, Suite 704
New York
NY 10038

British Library Cataloguing-in-Publication Data
A catalogue record for this book is available from the British Library.

ISBN: 978-1-847-0-6048-8 (hardback)
         978-1-847-0-6049-5 (paperback)

Library of Congress Cataloging-in-Publication Data
A catalog record for this book is available from the Library of Congress.

Typeset by Fakenham Photosetting, Fakenham, Norfolk

Printed and bound in Great Britain by CPI Antony Rowe, Chippenham, Wiltshire

Acknowledgements

Many thanks to friends and colleagues for their generous help: Kirsty Bunting, Sara Clayson, Anna Fleming, Peter McDonald, Audrey and Cledwyn Martin, Rosie Martin, Emma Mason, Joseph Phelan, Chris Roche, Natalie Sandison, and Marion Thain. Thank you to Phil Brown for great conversation and, of course, poems. Love and thanks, as always, to the Williams family. Finally, and especially, to Tom Martin.

Copyright acknowledgements

Contents

Detailed contents

List of terms

abecedarian
accentual-syllabic
acephalous line
acrostic
allegory
alliteration
alliterative metre
amphibrach
anapaest
anaphora
anastrophe
antibacchius
antimetabole
antistrophe
aphorism
apostrophe ·
assonance
aubade
bacchius
ballad
ballad metre
ballad stanzas
ballade
blank verse
blazon
bob and wheel
bucolic
broadside ballad
Burns stanza
caesura
catalectic lines
chiasmus
closed couplets
conceit
concrete poems
consonance
counterpoint rhythm

couplets
courtly love
denouement
descriptive lyric
dramatic lyric
dimeter
doggerel
dramatic monologue
eclogue
elegiac quatrain
elegy
end-rhymes
end-stopped lines
enjambment
envoy
epic
epigram
epigraph
epitaph
epithalamion
epode
etymological puns
eye rhyme
falling metre
feet
feminine caesura
feminine lines
feminine rhyme
fixed French forms
form
free verse
haiga
haiku
heptameter
heroic couplets
heroic quatrain
hexameter

homonyms
homophones
homographs
hymnal measure
hypercatalectic lines
iamb
iambic pentameter
idyll
imperfect rhyme
in medias res
In Memoriam stanza
internal rhymes
inversion
irregular ode
kigo
kireji
light verse
limerick
line length
long hymnal measure
long measure
lyric
mad-song stanza
masculine caesura
masculine lines
masculine rhyme
meditation ode
metaphor
Metaphysical conceits
metaplasm
metre
molossus
monometer
motif
nonsense verse
octameter
ode
onomatopoeia
open couplets
ottava rima
outride
paranomasia
pararhyme

pastoral
pentameter
perfect rhymes
personification
Petrarchan conceits
Petrarchan sonnet
prose poetry
prosody
prosopopoeia
pun
quantitative metre
quatrain
refrain
rhyme
rhyme scheme
rhyming couplet
rime couée
rime royale
rising metre
romance
romance six
rondeau
Sapphic stanzas
scansion
scheme
sesta rima
sestina
Shakespearean sonnet
short hymnal measure
short measure
sibilance
simile
sonnet
Spenserian stanza
stanza
stich
stress
strophe
substitution
syllepsis
synaeresis
synaesthesia
synaloepha

syncope
tenor
tercet
terza rima
tetrameter
topos
tradition
tribach
trimeter
triolet
triple rhyme
triplets

trochee
trope
type
vehicle
Venus and Adonis stanza
vers de société
verse drama
verse novel
verse paragraphs
villanelle
zeugma

PART I: INTRODUCING POETRY

Part I Overview

Introduction

It's tempting to look for certainties in reading, even more so in studying. What is this? How will I recognize it again? Will it help me pass the exam? Such questions are often prompted by poetry when it appears as a subject for study. In an education system that values 'usefulness', the poem – writing that takes up a strange place on the page, uses odd language, and seems to hide rather than display meaning – is a disruption, perhaps a distraction: what is its point? Yet poetry is also something that escapes the classroom – it appears in cards, on billboards, on the Underground. It's echoed in songs and recited at weddings and funerals; it appears in dusty leather-bound books in libraries, in coloured paperbacks in gift shops, in manuscripts kept under lock and key. We hear it sung and spoken to us as children, and recite it again when we become parents. It's heard in assembly halls and read on toilet walls. It infuses our language: 'poetry in motion' describes a car, or an athlete. We might turn to poetry when we know what we feel but we don't know how to say it; when we read it we find more emotions, ones we didn't even know we felt. How can poetry be all of these things at once? How can poetry be something we study, but also something that makes us cry?

This book cannot answer all of these questions, if any at all. However, it does attempt to empower those who want (or have) to study poetry to articulate their own views on such questions, and to do so while also enjoying, valuing and engaging with poetry. This means finding a way in to the language of poetry because, for all of poetry's familiarity and ubiquity, it is also difficult. Poems seem to approach meaning, expression, even storytelling in strange ways. They seem to be arranged according to laws of their own: Why is that line the length it is? Why am I expected to believe that a face can 'launch' a thousand ships? In what sort of reality can the sun be addressed as a 'busie old foole'? With such devices poems give the impression that they have expectations of readers (surely, reader, you understand what this image means!) and even if poems don't give that impression, those who write about poems often will. Some discussions of poetry are replete with terms such as 'metre' or 'trope' or 'scheme' or 'genre', all of which can be very illuminating, but are confusing if their definition is assumed rather than stated. Other discussions of poetry dispense with this language altogether, and view poems in terms of historical context, politics, theory or setting. Such discussions are also engaging and vital to our understanding of poetry as alive – something that changes in different settings and at different times. But, you might wonder, where is the poetry in such a discussion? Where does it account for the fact that this writing is arranged as poetry? Where does

3

it acknowledge the effect (for the poet and the reader) of rhythm, or rhyme or pattern?

This book helps bring these two ideas together: it takes the technical terms implied in the first type of poetry commentary and provides working definitions for them. It then implies the fluidity of the second type of commentary by putting this definition into context with a short discussion of how such ideas have been used in Anglophone poetry (poems written in English). So a degree of definition is provided, but it emphasizes that these can shift and alter with each use and in different historical and political contexts. Hopefully, this approach will then allow you see a poem's political, social or historical engagement in the very details of its formal structure and rhythmic pattern. From there, the book encourages you to develop a vocabulary that not only describes this effect, but also allows it to be a part of your experience of the poem. Hopefully, these short essays will help to alleviate some of the confusion and fear that can arise either from poems or from criticism of poems and replace this with confidence and enjoyment. 'Working' definition is the point: these are intended as the first stage in your own 'work' of enjoying and studying poetry. Terms considered range from the generic ('epic', 'lyric') to different forms of poetry ('sonnets', 'limericks', 'ballads'), to the rhythm and metre of poetry ('iambic pentameter', 'alliterative metre') and finally through to wordplay used in poems ('metaphors', 'similes', 'chiasmus').

Such an arrangement of terms and definitions may suggest that the topic (poetry itself, or the different terms defined) is self-contained and 'out there', and that our relationship as students with that topic is simply to chase after it, to learn its rules and to be tested on them. However, this is precisely what this book encourages you to reconsider. For a start, although technical vocabulary and poetic devices can be confusing and even off-putting, this is not everyone's experience. Those who already enjoy reading and studying poetry may wish to use the book as a companion, a volume to have alongside poems and poetry, on hand to clarify an idea or simply satisfy curiosity: 'What is a sonnet, any way?'

Secondly, parts of this book introduce difficult ideas and concepts, but this is the source of the satisfaction or enjoyment that poetry can provide. Sometimes we look to poems to reflect our experiences – 'That's exactly what I was feeling' – and may even reject those that don't – 'I couldn't "relate" to that poem, so I don't value it.' But this limits your universe to your immediate experience. Reading poetry, just like reading novels or watching films or television, offers a route into other experiences, other historical periods, and – perhaps most excitingly – other ways of understanding and using language, communication and expression. However, those other experiences are not always immediately available when reading a poem. Understanding something of the traditions that a poem sprang from (or emerges within now) can help you access poems in ways that shift away from finding a world you already know and towards finding a world you did not know existed. You can begin to layer the different interpretations of a poem available: to move from 'What does this mean to me?' to 'How is this responding to convention?', to ask 'What does this reveal about the history of this form of writing?' or 'What does this image mean on the poem's own terms?', and finally to come back to the present moment and ask 'How has this poem influenced the conventions and ideas that shape our experiences today?' and 'How does it influence me now?' In a society that provides (or pretends to provide) instant gratification, spending an hour reading four lines of poetry that are difficult to understand might seem like an absurd deferral of pleasure or purpose, but time spent like this can equip us to participate in society in refreshing ways because it offers altered perspectives on familiar ideas and methods.

Moving on to thinking about how poetry sounds and feels, we can begin to see that all the innovative things that poetry does with language, rhythm, sound and pattern were important not only to the poet who wrote it; they are the source of our pleasure and understanding today. You might even understand a poem as much by feeling rhythms and hearing sounds as by following logic, yet how can you express that understanding to others? Think of some lines such as:

> A slumber did my spirit seal;
>   I had no human fears:
> She seemed a thing that could not feel
>   The touch of earthly years.
>
> No motion has she now, no force;
>   She neither hears nor sees;
> Rolled round in earth's diurnal course,
>   With rocks, and stones, and trees.
>
> William Wordsworth (1800), 'A slumber did my spirit seal'.

This short poem, known as one of Wordsworth's 'Lucy poems', is famously obscure and has prompted great streams of critical commentary seeking to unlock its secrets. Why is it so compelling? Partly, of course, we are intrigued by the 'she', and we may want to find out about the women Wordsworth knew in order to make sense of this reference. Yet, there is something more mesmerizing here than simply a story of a girl a poet may once have known. The aim of this book is to encourage you to stop and dwell on such poems, to feel for their rhythms, listen for their sounds and think about their poetic effect. You might begin to notice the repetition of sound: several 's' sounds quietly open the poem; 'ee's emerge towards line endings. The rhythm of the poem is gentle, comforting and strangely familiar. Even before we reach the lines that tell us that this figure is 'rolled round' in the natural world, our voice and body have become relaxed as they too roll over the rise and fall of the simple vocabulary arranged into on–off beats. We might say that the poem's use of **common hymnal measure** means the pace of this poem is familiar to our ear even if its content is confusing; its use of **alliteration** and **perfect rhymes** is complemented by **assonance** and **internal rhymes**, creating a range of aural stimulation that absorbs us just as the 'she' of the poem is absorbed into the natural world. And yet, while the poem creeps up on us with simple words and repeated sounds, it resolutely holds itself back and keeps its secrets: the poem compels because it teases us with gestures that draw us in and terms that block us out. When addressing a perplexing poem such as this, feeling for rhythms and listening for sounds can be a way into something strange. This book's section on **prosody**, in particular, addresses this aspect of understanding poetry and suggests ways into such puzzling poems. If a poem is completely confusing, start with listening for its sounds, marking its rhythms, thinking about its form. These starting points can open up a route to a more satisfying understanding. The vocabulary introduced here can then help you to express the effects you sense, and allow you to situate your experience within a range of other possible responses.

One anxiety that concentrating on forms, traditions, metres and so on can cause, however, is that it encourages you to think of poems as self-contained, historically unchanging and complete in themselves. But it is vital to see that things promoted as inevitable, unchanging, constant and 'real' are actually historically contingent, and open to interpretation. Even so, it is helpful to have a sense of what those constants could be. If you've spent all your reading life assuming that poems are things written with rhythm and rhyme, it's thrilling (or maybe alarming) to think that that doesn't have to be the case. It allows you to see that ideas come into currency within a set of circumstances, rather than appearing suddenly and complete. Accordingly, some of the ideas introduced here – such as the conventions used in **scanning** poems for example – are subject to debate in academic discussion and their usefulness is challenged or championed in different ways. To explain a convention is not to reify it or to make any claim to its constant truth. Indeed, the conventions considered here may dissolve at the touch of a poet's pen, and if not then, they may dissolve at the touch of a reader's eye as conventions and traditions are constantly made and remade; but this is not to deny their usefulness in terms of raising a debate, or marking out a territory for exploration.

Finally, what follows should suggest the exciting and flickering instability of poetry, its world of implied meanings, half meanings and received meanings. The relationship between a poem and a reader has been long debated and is almost impossible to define, but we may venture to say that poetry appeals to the dual pull that shapes all our experiences: the particular within the general. It acknowledges the allure of definition, but it seeks to express the lived experience that always qualifies it. As Shelley suggested, poetry is newly defined every time a poem is written, and every time a poem is read:

> A great poem is a fountain forever overflowing with the waters of
> wisdom and delight; and after one person and one age has exhausted

all of its divine effluence which their peculiar relations enable them to share; another and yet another succeeds, and new relations are ever developed, the source of an unforeseen and unconceived delight' (Shelley (1840), p. 269).

How to use this book

This book is divided into three parts: 'Introducing Poetry'; 'The Poetry Toolkit' and 'Practice'. In Part I you will find discussion of the broad traditions that have informed and influenced poetry written in English. Part II then features four chapters that explore and explain the technical vocabulary often used in studying poetry. This part encourages you to look carefully at the shape a poem forms on the page, to listen carefully for its sounds and rhythms, and to be aware of the patterns and conventions it uses. Further, it introduces practical techniques for marking, describing and analysing poetic patterns. It is designed to give you a vocabulary you can use to analyse poems and to express your views and experiences of them to others. In Part III the ideas, techniques and vocabularies defined and introduced throughout the book are put to practical use for some sustained close readings. Together with guidance on how to conduct your own close reading, two sample essays are provided that demonstrate how you might approach a sustained study of individual poems. Finally, the book turns over to you: you'll find four close reading exercises to try out, together with a list of primary sources for poems by all of the writers mentioned throughout this guide, and some recommendations for further reading in the field of poetry studies.

Although you may find it useful to read the book sequentially from start to finish, it is also designed for 'dipping into'. Each of the terms and ideas are given a succinct definition and discussions are presented as standalone 'essays', laid out clearly for ease of reference. You may simply want to read one of these essays to familiarize yourself with a particular term or tradition; however, they are also interlinked through the use of bolded terms. When you come across a term in **bold** text within any discussion this means it is explained fully elsewhere in the book: if you want to find that definition you can look up the term in the Index (as you may have noticed, this method is used in the Introduction). Other terms are defined in passing during discussion; these are *italicized*.

Each poetic example is given here with the date of its first publication, to give you a sense of the history of each poem. If a poem was first published some time after its author's death, the likely date of composition is given in squared brackets. At the end of the book the sources reading list will give full publication details in alphabetical order, according to the author's surname, together with a list of anthologies. Hopefully you will be inspired to pursue considerable further reading!

To sum up typographical conventions:

General

- Terms **bolded** within a discussion: fully discussed elsewhere in the book; find them in the Index.
- Technical terms *italicized* within a discussion: minor terms defined in passing.

Within poetic examples

- **Bolded** words or part-words within a poetic example: indicates a stress emphasis.
- *Italicized* words or part-words within a poetic example: draws attention to a rhyme.
- '|' indicates a line division in poetic quotations.
- '[ ]' mark feet divisions in scanned examples.

Reference

Shelley, P. B. (1840 [c. 1821]), 'A Defence of Poetry', in *Poems and Prose*, ed. T. Webb (1995) (London: J. M. Dent), pp. 247–78.

Types and traditions

Type
A class of writing distinguished by particular characteristics that become the pattern or model for subsequent writings.

Tradition
The handing down of beliefs, practices, customs and procedures from generation to generation.

Poetry, like all forms of writing, works within certain traditions and conventions. Just as when we visit the cinema our choice of film is partly dictated by its advertised category (thriller, horror, romantic comedy, musical, and so on), so our expectations of a poem are coloured by its traditional features. Sometimes this is obvious from the outset: 'Elegy in a Country Churchyard' (1751) by Thomas Gray, for example, lets us know immediately that it is a formal response to death (as is an '**elegy**'). We may then read on to find out how this poem fits with that tradition. On the other hand, we may need to make some inroads into Thomas Hardy's 'The Darkling Thrush' (1901) before we might suggest that it, too, is a form of elegy (as Jahan Ramanzani explores). Knowing something about what elegies tend to be about, their formal features and their usual outcomes will then help us to articulate what is strange and discomforting about Hardy's poem.

This chapter is concerned with types and traditions of poetry. Here we can start seeing how poetry both abides by rules and delights in breaking them. In the first instance, it is useful to identify whether a poem is telling a story, expressing an emotion, presenting an action, or whatever. Clarifying that point can free us up to experience that poem clearly. Of course, many poems do all these things and more at the same time, but the conventions to which a poem alludes can help us identify which, if any, of these dominate. The traditions considered here have been particularly significant for poetic production in English – of course, in prose and drama other conventions also exist – and they generally fall into narrative traditions and expressive traditions.

Narrative poetry is primarily concerned to present a story of any kind: those included here are epic, ballad, romance and, loosely, blank verse (considered in the chapter on form). Expressive poetry relies less on the passing of time and more on the experience of emotion and thoughtfulness: examples included here are lyric, elegy, some love poetry and pastoral. Yet all of these categories infuse each other constantly: stories are told with emotion and emotions take place over time. It is perhaps more useful to think in terms of stylistic traditions or modes of telling stories and expressing emotions: some are told with particular solemnity, some with lightheartedness and comedy.

During this discussion various *topoi* (singular *topos*) and *motifs* will become apparent. Topos means 'a place'; however, it has come to indicate a recurrent formulation or concept – a commonplace in fact – in a literary work (such as the notion that a hero is physically strong, for example). A motif is a dominant emblem that also recurs throughout a literary work, becoming a symbol of the work's central idea (it might be a physical motif, such as a sword or a gem, or an emotional motif, such as longing, or nostalgia).

Some of the traditions discussed here are not unfamiliar: 'epic' is often used to describe ambitious or grand-scale endeavours; any expression that is appealing to the ear or even just pleasingly whimsical has come to be thought of as 'lyrical'. Yet, perhaps especially if these terms are used in various settings, there are good reasons for finding out about their origins. It is vital to be aware of how modes, genres, topoi and motifs not only name particular literary conventions, but they also imply a set of attitudes and experiences. Types and traditions do not pop up out of nowhere; they emerge over time, and pick up various associations along the way. Their presence in a poem, therefore, not only indicates something about how the poem was composed, but also shapes our own response to that poem.

It's exciting then when a poem implies that it knows what it should be doing (demonstrating the heroism of a man of war, for example), but it deliberately upsets our expectations. This not only causes surprise in itself, but also encourages us to question whether we should have expected or welcomed the conventional outcome in the first place. So, a poem can underline the importance of convention but simultaneously jolt us into a more imaginative and thoughtful response to expectation. Clearly, it is useful to know something about those traditions in order to be alert to the poem's energetic approach to what it is expected and what it in fact delivers. In many intriguing ways, it is formal features (literally the shape, sound and size of the poem itself) that dictate the nature of poetic modes and genres: these will be considered in following chapters. This chapter, however, begins by uncovering some of the types and conventions that have shaped poetry as a tradition in Anglophone culture.

Reference

Ramanzani, J. (1991), 'Hardy's Elegies for an Era: "By the Century's Deathbed"', *Victorian Poetry* 29, 131–43.

Epic

A long narrative poem that follows the fate of an individual or tribe.

Traditionally the epic is associated with Classical Greece, and texts such as Homer's *The Iliad* and *The Odyssey* are typical. Yet this long, narrative form – addressing the trials, tribulations, heroisms and victories of a nation and its people – occurs in many world cultures and in all kinds of languages. Indeed, Adeline Johns-Putra's history of epic denies that any one definition can ever be satisfactory. Rather, the epic's grand ambition, which is to present the fate of different individuals within the history of a whole nation, or even cosmology, is remarkable for the many moves it makes between ideas: between the large- and small-scale, between nature and nurture, between the past and the present, and between the human and the superhuman. Epic speaks to the heart of nation-building and so is a rich source of the myths and values that a society adopts, accepts as natural and enjoys retelling. As such, it is often taken up for ambitious political and social reasons: in order to re-examine and redraw the social landscape writers seek to return to the foundation myths that underpin it. Epic writers across the world and across the centuries have sought to return to, and modify, those stories and modes with ambitious aims, and the tradition continues today. The epic, therefore, has identifiable features, but is also one that is endlessly rewritten. In order to measure the nature and extent of such rewritings, it's useful to begin with some points of comparison. Common features of epics include:

- a hero or demigod of national or cultural importance or supremacy
- an arduous journey or series of battles

- a cast of gods or supernatural powers who intervene in human action
- begins *in·medias res* (in the middle of things), so the narrative unfolds through a mixture of flashback and present-time action
- Near the beginning the poet will perform an invocation to address the muse and state the epic's argument, question or theme.
- The language is formal, serious and differentiated from everyday speech by a sense of ceremony.

As will be seen, epics tend to be written using language that stands apart from everyday speech, and this is emphasized by using particular **metres** and **prosody**. The details of these are considered in Chapter 3, but the metres used in epic include:

- dactylic hexameter: a relatively long line of six feet and the metre often used in Classical texts (see **quantitative metre**)
- **alliterative metre**: see the early northern-European epic, *Beowulf*
- **blank verse**: the most common form used in English epic
- **terza rima**: a three-line **stanza** form introduced by Dante in his *La Divinia Commedia*.

Epic style

The term 'epic' derives from 'epos', a Greek term for speech, and these poems were originally composed and transmitted orally rather than via print. This did not result in simplicity or colloquialism, as one might expect, but in grandeur and differentiation. In an oral culture that made many different demands on the ear, the epic distinguished itself with stately language and formulaic, alliterative metre. Events, ideas and expressions were then made to fit with the epic's established style. This sense of artistry continued with the development of literary epic (epics composed for the page) where the use of longer line length (which requires skill to sustain) or elaborate patterning continues the process of distinction that characterizes the epic's elevated ambition.

Traditional epics and the code of heroism

So-called traditional epics (composed orally – although eventually transcribed) include Homer's Greek tales of heroism in the Trojan wars (*The Iliad*) and in Odysseus' long journey back to Ithaca (*The Odyssey*). The former depicts super-human strength, passion (it opens with the rage of Achilles) and patriotic bonds between men on the battlefield; the latter emphasizes the heroic cunning and intelligence of its hero Odysseus in eventually outwitting the interventions of the gods who sought to thwart his quest. In both cases the epic is concerned to examine the nature of heroism (its code) and probe different notions of strength, whether intellectual or physical, under siege or in victory. The early northern-

European epic *Beowulf* (written in English and recently translated into modern English by Seamus Heaney, 1999) similarly explores the nature of heroism in a troubled society. In these cases, the fate of the nation is written out through the story of male action and development, so matching the male with the origin of that nation. For this reason, the epic has been considered a particularly 'male' or phallocentric genre: one that emphasizes the action and self-determination of the hero while assigning women secondary (albeit influential) roles of pawn (Helen of Troy), seductress (Calypso) or patient, waiting wife (Penelope). Indeed, one might suggest that masculinity itself – whether it is strong, violent, passionate, yearning, weak, loyal or betraying – is often the subject of the traditional epic even more so than the fate of a nation or tribe. Together with the epic's grand oratory (composed by men) a commonplace developed whereby nations were defined by masculine heroism and the equally heroic stamina of the epic composer who created awe-inspiring quantities of poetry to retell it.

Literary epics and the influence of Christianity

Epic tradition continued from the Classical initially with the move towards written (literary) composition and also, in Western tradition, the growing influence of Christianity. Epic writers sought to reconcile the epic's potent power to inculcate values through storytelling with the Christian emphasis on mercy, forgiveness and sacrifice. Further, writers needed to replace the cast of gods seen in Classical epic with the monotheism of Christianity, and its emphasis on subordination and obedience, rather than overt power struggle and violence. In the course of this development, arguably, comes Virgil's Latin *Aeneid* (c. 29 BCE). Although not a Christian text (it narrates the establishment of the Roman Empire), its hero, Aeneas, is forced to adapt the heroic code of old to develop an ideal more firmly attached to the nation: individual satisfaction and glory is sacrificed to patriotic leadership and rationality. Written in direct response to Virgil, Dante's Italian *La Divinia Commedia*, however, is explicitly Christian. This impulse is reconciled with epic tradition by more overt emphasis on **allegory** (as Johns-Putra discusses more fully): so the heroic quest represents a journey towards divine knowledge and the battlefield is evoked only in the abstract struggle between good and evil. Most famously, however, Milton took a direct approach to the question of a Christian epic by returning to the Garden of Eden to create a foundation story to rival Classical legend in *Paradise Lost*. Audaciously using the cultural apparatus of pre-Christian Classical civilization for Christian purpose, Milton's opening address to a 'Heav'nly Muse' (linked to Moses rather than the Classical muses) demonstrates his complex and sophisticated register (as is traditional in epic). He uses rhetorical devices such as **anastrophe** and multiple subordinate clauses to flesh out each element of his narrative with reverence and significance:

And chiefly thou O Spirit, that dost prefer
Before all temples th' upright heart and pure,
Instruct me, for thou know'st; thou from the first
Wast present, and with mighty wings outspread
Dove-like sat'st brooding on the vast abyss
And mad'st it pregnant: what in me is dark
Illumine, what is low raise and support;
That to the highth of this great argument
I may assert Eternal Providence,
And justify the ways of God to men.

John Milton (1667), 'Book I', *Paradise Lost*, ll. 17–25.

Notable here is Milton's ambition to write not for a particular nation, but for all men (humanity). Perhaps paradoxically, this large-scale project (rendered, as Milton points out in 'English heroic verse without rhyme') is overtly orchestrated by an individual poet. The extract given, together with later extracts, such as at the start of Book VII when the muse is invoked again for the second half of the epic, show the poet alone, save for the muse, and seeking to gain strength for his mighty task. The debate of heroism seen in early epics is here echoed in the struggle to remain on course for poetic heroism: 'still govern thou my song, | Urania, and fit audience find, though few' (Book VII, ll. 30–1). Of course this is framed by Christian piety and obedience; however, the question of individual poetic 'fitness' for epic fame flourished into a subject in itself for epic treatment.

The nineteenth-century epic and selfhood

Taking inspiration from Milton but radically repositioning the epic as quasi-autobiography, Wordsworth's *The Prelude*, eventually written in 13 books in 1805 but tinkered with until its posthumous (and first) publication in 1850, is a blank-verse poem that charts the development of the poetic mind. Picking up the epic's dynamic approach to narrative-through-flashback, it is a meditation on memory as a key to psychological development (and so fluctuates between the past and the present). Although it follows a narrative line, relating Wordsworth's life from his childhood, through adolescence, the travels of his young adulthood and finally his settling in Cumbria, it emerges as an epic that uses personal experience (as the only topic that the poet can address without presumption) to reflect on ideas of community, society and the individual within them. Perhaps surprisingly, given its centring on the self, Wordsworth introduces his epic argument in modest terms, having recently been revived by recollected thoughts of childhood:

> One end hereby at least hath been attain'd,
> My mind hath been revived, and if this mood
> Desert me not, I will forthwith bring down,
> Through later years, the story of my life.
> The road lies plain before me; 'tis a theme
> Single and of determined bounds; and hence
> I chuse it rather at this time, than work
> Of ampler or more varied argument.
>
> William Wordsworth (1805), 'Book I', *The Prelude*, ll. 664–71.

In 1856, Elizabeth Barrett Browning published a response to the Miltonic epic tradition and to the more immediate concerns of nineteenth-century society and the individual. *Aurora Leigh* takes up Wordsworth's cue that a poet's development is fit for epic treatment, but robustly repositions that poet as female. This novel-epic hybrid (see also the **verse novel**) uses Milton's epic structure of nine books (except that Barrett Browning's poem adds up to more lines) to address a contemporary setting more usually found in the novel. Thus it charts the struggle of the woman poet to occupy a position of cultural authority while attending to the immediate concerns of her society. As is boldly stated in Book 5, this poem installs overtly female imagery at the source of creativity:

> Never flinch,
> But still, unscrupulously epic, catch
> Upon the burning lava of a song
> The full-veined, heaving, double-breasted Age:
> That, when the next shall come, the men of that
> May touch the impress with reverent hand, and say
> 'Behold, —behold the paps we all have sucked!
>
> Elizabeth Barrett Browning (1856), 'Book 5', *Aurora Leigh*, ll. 212–18.

Admittedly Barrett Browning's attempt at overthrowing epic patriarchy does not always convince, as the swapping of a male voice for a female one sometimes feels cosmetic rather than extensively radical. Nevertheless, the experiment is testament to the desire among readers (it was very successful commercially) to see the continuation of the epic tradition, but to have its assumptions questioned and redrawn.

Questioning epic culture

Epic, perhaps inevitably given its self-imposed seriousness, is sometimes the subject of lampooning parody or burlesque. However, epics have also attracted earnest criticism of style and content. William Blake took issue with the premise of Milton's *Paradise Lost*, stating in his *Marriage of Heaven and Hell* (1789) that Milton was 'a true Poet and of the Devil's party without knowing it' (Plate 5).

Many critics have followed Blake in critiquing *Paradise Lost* for its handling of the difficult task of making paradise (an essentially static state) more attractive to readers than the dynamism of Satan's ostensibly more epic-heroic battles with God. Blake developed his theological and cultural disputes with Milton's poem into his own epic treatment, *Milton* (1804). Following in Barrett Browning's wake of relocating the female within epic tradition (itself an implied commentary on Milton's conventionally epic relegation of the female as secondary), Paula Burnett points to the Jamaican poet Jean Binta Breeze's 'A River Called Wise' (1993), which returned to epic's origins by being a performance piece composed for the female voice (although it has a male protagonist). Although not as long as traditional epics, its claim to the genre derives from its use of terza rima and its readdressing of the epic topic of heroic codes. Here, as Burnett asserts, it is the unsung heroism of women's work that drives the pulse of the poem, and the poet must take 'the chance you now have, to give those feet a voice'.

Read more

- A celebrated modern epic is Derek Walcott's *Omeros* (1990), written in a variation of terza rima. It takes an energetic and fresh approach to epic expectation. Who is the hero? Who is passive? How does its treatment of men and women rewrite epic assumptions? Consider its attitude towards St Lucia (its setting) and how the poem's events relate to national identity. Why does Walcott revisit this well-known epic story?
- In 1937 David Jones published *In Parenthesis*, a 'poem' that traces the fortunes of a British infantry unit fighting in France between 1915 and 1916. It flits between poetry and prose, using **free verse** passages to evoke the horror of immediate circumstances while intertwining these with episodes from English and Welsh epic writing and even echoing **romance** tales of quest and journey. In this treatment the epic protagonists, however, are not already known leaders of men or founders of civilization, but ordinary soldiers plucked from everyday existence and bracketed off (as the title suggests) into the realm of hyper-real experience and delirious bewilderment.
- Naturally, Classical epics have been translated many times into English. Some poetic translations to compare are Pope's *Iliad* (1715), Dryden's *Aeneid* (1697) and more recently Christopher Logue's *War Music* (1981–). Is it more effective to aim for a loose translation of the original's 'spirit', or to attempt an exact English rendering of its particular style and content? How do these translations differ? What attitudes towards their source do these translations demonstrate? Why might different societies prefer different translations of the same text?

References

Burnett, P. (1997), 'Epic, a Woman's Place', in *Kicking Daffodils: Twentieth-Century Women Poets*, ed. V. Bertram (Edinburgh: Edinburgh University Press), pp. 140–52.

Hainsworth, J. B. (2006), *The Idea of Epic* (Berkeley: University of California Press).
Johns-Putra, A. (2006), *The History of the Epic* (Basingstoke: Palgrave Macmillan).

Lyric

A poem in which a single speaker expresses thought and emotion.

You may reasonably ask, given the above, whether the definition of lyric is the definition of poetry itself – what poem doesn't express thought and emotion? Indeed, the lyric is the form of poetry that most people will think of when they think of poetry in general: it is expressive, and emotional, and spoken by one voice. In traditional classification – as influenced by Aristotle – the lyric is differentiated from the epic and the dramatic in terms of the presentation of 'speech'. Those two genres allow – to greater and lesser degrees – the exchange of voices across a poem, with one or another dominating at different times. The lyric, on the other hand, is a poem in which just one voice utters the expression of their thought process or emotional feeling. In this respect, the lyric is thought of as more 'direct' than other forms, because the speaker's expression is not framed by a narrator or put into context with other voiced opinions. However, lyrics do not always suggest isolation; often they address another person or object, using that as an occasion for expression, or meditation, or both. We tend to associate the lyric with passionate emotions, such as grief, love or faith, but they may also present a speaker engaged in more cerebral meditation as they trace the development of memory, or the articulation of a moral view, or the realization of a philosophical position, or a moment of perception. In other cases it is difficult to identify precisely the mood or emotion of a lyric, often because they can feel intensely private: although they are necessarily part of the public sphere, as they are printed or recited poems, they may rely on a hidden reference system that is difficult to access. Indeed, lyrics are especially intriguing because they present themselves as direct expressions of a single speaker's thought or emotion, and yet they are – of course – emotions and thoughts that have been shaped into poems. They, therefore, emerge from the interaction between intense feeling and convention, between emotion and tradition, between uniqueness and familiarity: they intriguingly express and encode emotions simultaneously. Given their open nature, lyrics are not really amenable to rules; without wishing to be prescriptive, therefore, these are some useful pointers to begin with:

- Lyrics are written in the first person, suggesting direct expression.
- Lyrics are conventionally non-narrative: rather than charting the passing of time or telling a story, they appear to capture a single, intense moment of feeling, or a changing series of such moments.

- Lyrics are often valued as apolitical, or non-judgemental expressions that stand apart from everyday discourse – whether they live up to this reputation or not is a matter of debate.
- The 'speaker' in a lyric poem is often said to be 'overtaken' by a particular emotion, although the degree of intensity involved naturally differs.
- Lyrics often appeal to the ear and have a musical quality; many use song-like **metres**.

History of the term

The word derives from 'lyre': a stringed instrument used in Classical civilization. Accordingly, lyrics are often associated with music, and so with music's sense of liberated feeling (although, as will be seen, lyrical liberation, just like musical liberation, is often the result of careful control and technical effect). So lyrics may evoke the image of a solitary singer accompanied by a lyre that charms the singer's feelings into expression. These origins are recalled in song-like metres and of course today we associate the term with song lyrics. However, as Hermes (the god of communication) is said to have created the lyre from a tortoise shell, animal hide and antelope horns, some suggest that this initial violence and wresting of materials from their original purpose has infused the lyric tradition, bringing with it notions of torment and despair.

Lyric ideology

In many ways the lyric has become the dominant poetic mode, particularly in latter centuries. Many cultural reasons exist to account for this emphasis on poetry as a mode connected to feeling and emotion rather than history, politics or narrative, not least the emergence of other cultural modes (novels, newspapers, film, television, the internet) that impact on areas traditionally associated with poetry. The result is that lyric (which often stands in for poetry itself) is left to serve various ideological purposes. These include notions such as:

- Feelings and emotions are intense and short-lived, and so lyric poems are relatively short.
- Lyrics present the utterance of a particular speaker, so you make sense of lyrics by identifying that speaker and the precise nature of the emotions and thought processes they go through.
- Lyrics have a particular emotive effect on their reader.
- Lyrics erase historical context in order to meditate on the precise nature of feeling itself (see Barbara Hardy's reading of the form, in which she suggests that lyric provides 'feeling, alone and without histories or characters' (p. 1)).

These ideas imply that the lyric is set apart from everyday experience and, for that reason, is recognizable and should be cherished; it is a safety net, because it holds on to a space for feeling and emotion in an otherwise material and commercial world. These ideas about lyric are vital to our understanding of and appreciation for lyric poetry, and yet they are also intensely scrutinized and questioned. Although lyric poetry is valued and enjoyed for being unique, set apart and self-sufficient (ideas which importantly informed poetry criticism in the twentieth century) readers and critics increasingly ask how those apparently 'natural', 'direct', 'unfettered' or spontaneous expressions can be historically contingent, circumstantial and essentially political.

Lyrics as short poems

Sappho, a Greek poet (usually depicted holding a lyre) is frequently associated with the origins of lyricism and her often-mournful poetry has dictated some of its traditions. Although apparently admired and celebrated throughout antiquity, Sappho's poetry only survived in fragments. Perhaps especially because of this (so we have only a tantalizing glimpse of her poetry's full extent) Sappho has proved particularly inspirational: she attracts not only many translators, but also many writers who seek to emulate the fleeting intensity that they find in the tiny pieces of verse that remain:

> Thou burnest us.
>
> Sappho [c. 650 BCE], 'Fragment 115' (trans. Henry Wharton, 1885).

Fragments such as this one not only suggest that lyricism is intense and burning with passion, they also suggest that lyrics should be short, even momentary. However, as is clear from Sappho's story, these fragments are the remains of her verse; the originals may, of course, have been much longer. Nevertheless, we can see that Sappho's example demonstrates how what is circumstantial (Sappho's poetry happened to be written on perishable material that has disintegrated into short fragments) comes to seem natural (the accepted idea that intense feeling does not last long). This reveals the importance not only of what is spoken or expressed, but also how it is said: does a feeling change when it is expressed in short bursts rather than long laments? This mixture of circumstance and reflection brings the lyric tradition alive: it takes complex things (such as emotions and feelings) and interrogates them in ways that are themselves complex, because they are scrupulous about how emotions become expressions.

Most obviously, poems can express fleeting intensity by being brief 'snapshots' of feeling: some would stipulate that a lyric is a short poem. Of course, because they are short, they are inevitably quick to read, so the reader as well as the poet is included in this short, intense experience. However, even as a short lyric seems to capture the precise length of the moment, so it also seems to slow it down enough for us to appreciate its significance.

in spite of everything
which breathes and moves,since Doom
(with white longest hands
neatening each crease)
will smooth entirely our minds

—before leaving my room
i turn,and(stooping
through the morning)kiss
this pillow,dear
where our heads lived and were.

E. E. Cummings (1926), 'in spite of everything'.

Cummings' lyric captures a moment in which the poet pauses in his daily routine to pay homage to the bed that he shared with his lover. We may at first be put off by its odd punctuation and lack of capital letters (this is an example of **free verse**). Yet it is just this idiosyncrasy that intimates the multiple feelings existing simultaneously in this moment, transforming it from a featureless part of the day to a moment of complex intensity. 'i turn,and', by squashing the words together, suggests quickness and anticipation. In it we see the direct, immediate expression of the lyric tradition (especially in the use of the first person) but also the desire to rush this moment in anticipation of the kiss that follows. Yet, the phrase in parentheses, '(stopping | through the morning)', holds back that quickness, stalling the moment both in the poem and in our reading; although this poem is short, its oddities mean that we must read it slowly. Within these retarding brackets is the idea of 'stopping' – stopping as a description of the poet as he stops his forward march into the day, but also of stopping time itself in order to hang on to this moment. Here the poet alludes to one of the ideas we associate with the lyric tradition: stopping time in order to capture single moments. The fact that we see this in brackets, and that it describes a moment in the day when the poet turns back (rather than endlessly progressing forwards), suggests that the lyric is suited to moments that stand apart from our regular, ordered experience. If we think of the speaker as going about his daily routine, probably heading for the door to enter the world of work and society, this turning back indicates a moment of private rather than public value: it is an action that will reap no financial reward (indeed, it holds him back from such goal-driven exercises), but promises great emotional value, in the moment itself, in its subsequent poetic expression and again in our reading experience. Indeed, the lyric itself – as a tradition – ideally emerges from precisely such in-between moments that defy the progress of clock-time.

Given all this emphasis on brevity, it is especially notable, therefore, when a poet seems to be sustaining a lyrical 'moment' across a much longer poem:

And now, with gleams of half-extinguished thought,
With many recognitions dim and faint,
And somewhat of a sad perplexity,
The picture of the mind revives again:
While here I stand, not only with the sense
Of present pleasure, but with pleasing thoughts
That in this moment there is life and food
For future years.

William Wordsworth (1798), 'Lines written a few miles above Tintern Abbey, on revisiting the banks of the Wye during a tour, 13 July 1798', ll. 60–7.

In fact, this poem repeatedly 'stretches' time by being mindful of the past preceding each moment of intensity and of the future when it might be recalled. In doing so, Wordsworth not only meditates on the feeling he has, but also on the method of its expression, implying that his reader should reconsider emotion and find it an experience that takes place over longer timescales, producing longer lyrics. Indeed, the precise nature of the feelings the poem explores are produced not only by the landscape lying before the poet but also by the poem's own lengthy, lilting metre. Whether a feeling or emotion exists before its expression, or exists because of its expression, is intriguingly blurred in such treatments. Often longer lyrics such as these are named *descriptive lyrics*. This poem is also styled as an address to the author's sister, Dorothy (see line 118 onwards); lyrics written to another person or object are sometimes called *dramatic lyrics*.

The lyrical speaker

As lyrics are written in the first person, we are encouraged to think of them as the 'true' expression of a particular subject. This convention has prompted much speculation and dictated the strategies sometimes used in reading and understanding lyric poems. Much of the energy invested in attempts to uncover the biographical history of figures such as Sappho, or indeed Shakespeare, is linked to the desire to sense the person behind the poems. If we find such a person, the logic dictates, we can then make sense of the poetry. Such a strategy can be distracting, however, if it overlooks the ways in which the poem itself (its arrangement of language, phrase, tone and pace) constitutes meaning independently. Lyrics use a series of conventions that allow a reader to 'make sense' of a poem even in the absence of any knowledge of its author and the idea of a voice 'behind' a poem can even be thought of as an effect of a poem rather than its premise. The idea that a poem is the natural expression of a single speaker might, therefore, usefully be thought of as a convention that is historically and ideologically situated (which is not to say that it is false, or that one is naive to accept it). An example by Felicia Hemans usefully illustrates some of the issues at stake here.

Goddess of the magic lay,
Ever let me own thy sway;
Thine the sweet enchanting art,
To charm and to correct the heart;
To bid the tear of pity flow,
Sacred to thy tale of woe;
Or raise the lovely smile of pleasure,
With sportive animated measure.

'Oh! Goddes of the magic lay,'
To thee my early vows I pay;
Still let me wander in thy train,
And pour the wild romantic strain.
Be mine to rove by thee inspir'd,
In peaceful vales and scenes retir'd;
For in thy path, oh! Heavenly maid,
The roses smile that never fade.

Felicia Hemans (1808), 'To the Muse'.

This poem promotes its lyricism by emphasizing feeling: the 'tear of pity' and 'smile of pleasure' are its badges of emotion, the outward signs of inner sentiment. Secondly, the opening **stanza** lists ways in which poetry is said to act on the reader/listener: our heart is charmed and 'corrected' by the enchanting art, our eyes release tears on hearing tales of woe, and we are pleased by the measured yet animated way in which poetry organizes its expression. So the poem defines the lyric as something expressed by the poet, but also as a tradition experienced in particular ways by the reader. Moving on, we read the exclamation marks as signs of feeling that go beyond expression: they create the effect of little gasps of awe, or delight, again promoting the poem as the record of direct sound. The scene outlined here – a poet roaming free across 'peaceful vales' in raptured inspiration – then consolidates its lyricism by depicting its typical conditions: a single, inspired speaker, out of doors, free from constraint, pouring forth their 'wild romantic' strains of poetry. In many ways, then, by making lyricism a solitary art (or, at least, one that involves only the poet and her muse), it charts the individual's ultimate escape from social intercourse. Here we might be tempted to see the lyric's disinterestedness as 'opting out'.

Yet, in order to feel the tone of this poem's complex perspective on lyricism, we need to step back a little and realize that, even if we see this as opting out, the mood of the poem is about wanting to opt in to something. The overarching frame of this lyric moment is not, as we might assume, the confident voice of the accepted poet: rather it is an appeal. It repeatedly pleads to stay under the auspices of the muse ('Ever let me own thy sway'; 'Still let me wander in thy train'), which rather suggests that the speaker sees their position as poet as precarious. By foregrounding the actions you need to take in order to be a poet – primarily, addressing the muse and then giving yourself over to their influence – the poem emphasizes the process of becoming a poet: the role is adopted rather than natural. Rather than indicating that poetic expression is all about spontaneous, artless speaking, it outlines the conditions that need to be in place for poetic expression to occur.

The poem's final line, 'The roses smile that never fade', draws this to a neat conclusion by hinting at a natural world (of roses) that is strangely unnatural because they never fade. Just as these oddly preserved roses are a synthetic version of the natural, so the roaming poet-figure evoked in the poem, while seeming to be the spontaneous, natural figure that we associate with lyric poetry, is actually a role adopted and sustained by hard poetic graft. When we think that this was written in 1808, and written by a woman, we might then be tempted to reflect on the politics of being a poet in the early nineteenth century: we might wish to politicize the apparently apolitical realm of the lyric. This is because what we take to be natural in fact implies certain social, economic, cultural and political conditions that can exclude certain groups (whether by gender, or sexuality, or class, or race, or whatever) from the apparently 'natural' position of the poet. Perhaps this woman seeks to hold onto the poet-position because it is under threat in wider culture? Indeed, the poignancy of some lyrics comes not from the expression of feeling, but the sense of being excluded from expression itself.

More hopefully, recognizing that lyricism is a convention allows you to think about how different speakers and different social groups bend and shape that convention to their purpose, so finding ways to speak. Of course, the conventions of lyricism also alter with different historical settings as well as social groupings. Although certain conditions may traditionally shape lyricism, its concentration on feeling, thought and emotion, after all, are experiences that everyone undergoes; in that sense, it is an inclusive tradition.

The lyric and society

The emphasis we saw Hemans' poem put on the emotional response anticipated in the reader actually raises the question of lyric's political potential. While lyrics may not necessarily make direct demands of their reader (they often feel disinterested), they are nevertheless aware that the emotions they express should inspire sympathetic feeling. As we are encouraged to cry, or smile, or sigh, or yearn along with the poet, so we are brought out of our individual experience and pressed into a socializing act of shared emotion. Lyrics, then, can have a kind of emotional-political influence, whereby they seek to effect change by appealing to the humanizing capacity of feelings and sentiments: see Emma Mason's discussion of Hemans' method in this regard, where she describes the lyric as 'lift[ing] the reader out of the discursive and into emotion' (p. 26). This marshalling of lyrical effect for political (or religious) purpose was emphasized by Romantic poets, but can be seen earlier, as for example in Milton's political sonnets. 'On the Late Massacre in Piedmont' (1673) suggests a cry of despair, and evokes the moans of the dying, thereby raising the emotion of the reader in order that they are drawn into consideration of the more abstract religious-political background to the massacre.

Lyric and print

Finally, as we touch on the historical and cultural conditions that surround and shape the lyric tradition, we come to the effects of print culture. As we have seen, the lyric is associated with music, with directness, with naturalness and with a speaker's expression. All of these notions seem compatible with poetry as a spoken form: when you encounter poetry directly from the horse's mouth, so to speak, it is relatively unproblematic to accept a poem as a speaker's 'true' expression. When that expression is translated into print, however, and encountered through silent reading, the poem's association with a speaking voice becomes uncanny. Throughout lyric history the idea that the lyric is both a spoken expression and a material, silent, object (a poem on the page) has provoked intense reflection and meditation on the nature of feeling and expression: see the discussion of **concrete poems**, **epitaphs** and **acrostics** for particularly scrupulous considerations of poetry's dual identity. Shakespeare's *Sonnets* (1609) are celebrated for their preoccupation with themselves as 'monuments' as well as expression. During the nineteenth-century expansion of print culture, the implications for lyric poetry were also intensely considered (see Matthew Rowlinson's essay summarizing these changes). Most prominently, the **dramatic monologue** unravels our assumption that lyric poetry involves the direct expression of a single voice.

When a lyric is printed the precious qualities associated with that form are potentially threatened by their association with the mechanics of print: it embodies one of the 'distressing' contexts in which 'the tenderest, most fragile forms must be touched by, even brought together with precisely that social bustle from which the ideals of our traditional conception of poetry have sought to protect them' (Adorno, p. 56). Such threats, however, seem only to add another frame of complexity and thoughtfulness to the lyric's interrogation of the relationship between emotion and expression. To finish then with an example that, while seemingly conventional, in fact pushes the limits of what we can describe as 'lyrical'.

Tennyson first published 'Mariana' in a volume of 1830 titled *Poems, Chiefly Lyrical*. Yet, immediately it's apparent that the poem is not written in the first person. It builds on a reference to Mariana in Shakespeare's *Measure for Measure*, in which characters refer to a woman abandoned by her fiancé and left to reside 'dejected' in a moated grange. However, in Tennyson's handling, a poem that might be dramatic (it might tell Mariana's story) in fact seems lyrical as, although it is written in the third person, it is absorbed in emotional expression.

With blackest moss the flower-plots
  Were thickly crusted, one and all:
The rusted nails fell from the knots
  That held the pear to the gable-wall.
The broken sheds looked sad and strange:
  Unlifted was the clinking latch;
  Weeded and worn the ancient thatch
Upon the lonely moated grange.
    She only said, 'My life is dreary,
      He cometh not,' she said;
    She said, 'I am aweary, aweary,
    I would that I were dead!'

Alfred Tennyson (1830), 'Mariana', ll. 1–12.

We can identify certain formal features that gesture towards the lyric, most overtly in the final four lines that break out into speech and use a **refrain**, written in **ballad metre** that evokes singing, emphasized by its tight **rhyme scheme**. This interjection of lamenting speech encourages us to reread the stanza's apparently descriptive passage as a lyrical expression, alerting us to the **personification** of despair in 'sad' sheds, a 'lonely' grange and 'worn' thatch. In such a setting the metre, rhyme and refrain produce a strangulating effect that closes in on this abandoned, trapped woman. Each stanza holds a **rhyming couplet** in its centre (here 'latch' and 'thatch') around which alternate rhymes reverberate, making the couplet the eye of a storm. It is striking how the content (which describes a mournful stasis as nothing is moving and everything has decayed) is repeated in the sound and form of the poem, so becoming the mood of the poem.

Together these features intimate what it is about Mariana that has captured Tennyson's imagination: not the story of how she came to be trapped, or when she might escape, but the precise quality of her emotional experience of entrapment, heartache and depression. Therefore, the poem doesn't really go anywhere; like the endlessly returning rhymes and refrain, it stays still, immersed in the experience of abandonment. As such, Tennyson's poem takes the lyric's non-narrative nature to a startling extreme as its over-riding quality is a lack of progression. Yet, it is oddly at a remove from the directness we associate with lyricism. In this case, the lyrical quality comes from a kind of collaboration between Mariana's predicament and Tennyson's poetic intervention: it implies that Mariana 'speaks' through Tennyson, and perhaps Tennyson also expresses melancholic emotion through Mariana. The poem seems aware of how print – a silent mode – can leave this two-voiced impression intact (rather than making one dominate through a male or female speaking voice). The layers and filters between emotion and expression suggested here then allude to the broader process of filtration and mediation that is involved in translating a felt emotion and a spoken expression into a written, printed one. So, just as a printed lyric both is and isn't the 'voice' of a subject, so the poem ends up being both highly expressive and also distanced and removed from direct expression. Further, this 'collaboration' between male and female voices encourages readers to think about how relationships between the sexes might be played out in a lyric setting, and which (if either) holds lyrical authority.

Although Tennyson's lyric engages with a longstanding tradition that often emphasizes 'timelessness', we can see that its features also make 'Mariana' very much of its time: it meditates on the lyric as an emotional 'echo-chamber'; it hints at how voices are increasingly mediated into print; and it gently probes the relationship between gender and poetry at a time when women poets were increasingly dominating the poetry market.

The lyric, therefore, is a simple expression of intense feeling, but it is also an exquisitely insightful cultural mode, and one that offers sensitive tools for effecting social, emotional and cultural commentary and change.

Read more

- Due to their broad application, lyrics and lyricism may be found throughout literary tradition. Indeed, lyricism infuses many other genres, making 'hybrid' forms.
- 'Lyric elegies': the lyric's expression of intense feeling means many have been written to express grief and mourning. The lyric form adds to, and sometimes alters, the formal category of mourning poetry, **elegy.** See Tennyson's *In Memoriam A. H. H.* (1850); Milton's *Lycidas* (1637); Sylvia Plath's 'Daddy' (1965); Geoffrey Hill's 'September Song' (1968).
- 'Love lyrics': of course, love has long proved the inspiration for lyrical expression. Again, many of these combine generic categories, such as Christopher Marlowe's 'The Passionate Shepherd to his Love' (1599), which is both lyrical and **pastoral**. Letitia Landon's 'Sappho's Song' (1824) explicitly alludes to a Sapphic tradition of unrequited love (allowing Landon to style herself as a lyric poet in Sappho's image). Many of W. B. Yeats' love lyrics in *The Wind among the Reeds* (1899) reflect both on the present moment of painful, yearning love and on the love lyric tradition that extends for centuries before it.
- 'Religious lyrics': the lyric's delineation of a precious order of experience makes it particularly apt for expressing the elusive quality of faith, or indeed doubt. Examples of religious lyrics include George Herbert's 'Home' (1633) or 'A Better Resurrection' (1857) by the great lyric poet Christina Rossetti.
- Finally, many lyrics are allied to longstanding formal traditions, as are introduced in the next chapter. It is significant that this 'natural' expression is so frequently found in relatively strict traditional arrangements: in particular see the **ode**, the **sonnet**, the **haiku** and the **fixed French forms**.

References

Adorno, T. (1974), 'Lyric poetry and society', trans. Bruce Mayo, *Telos* 19, 56–71.

Hardy, B. (1977), *The Advantage of Lyric* (London: The Athlone Press).

Mason, E. (2006), *Women Poets of the Nineteenth Century* (Tavistock: Northcote House).

Rowlinson, M. (2002), 'Lyric', in R. Cronin, A. Chapman and A. H. Harrison (eds), *A Companion to Victorian Poetry* (Oxford: Blackwell).

Ballad

A poem, originally sung, that uses regular rhythms and rhymes to tell a story.

In many ways a simple form that uses repetition and rhyme to aid the memory, the ballad nonetheless has a complex and colourful cultural history. Importantly, it emerged within oral culture – that is, societies that relied on the human voice to transmit news, educate, warn of danger, entertain, develop values and traditions, and establish themselves by telling stories of their own past. In such a setting, a song which could be picked up easily, and which drew listeners in by using **refrains** or choruses to punctuate tales of horror, bawdiness, love, corruption, deceit, loyalty, defeat or victory unsurprisingly became a popular means not only of establishing particular social groups, but also spreading values and ideas from group to group. So, the ballad is associated with collective singing and with the solitary figure of the minstrel travelling across the country spreading news by song. The main features and associations of the ballad form are:

- simple but fixed formal features
- simple, even objective, delivery that emphasizes the story rather than the author
- simple, often dialect, language
- political and social radicalism
- content ranging between folklore, ghost stories, moral tales, love stories, military exploits and political commentary.

Formal features

Given the ballad's musical heritage, and its need to be easily learnt and recognized, the form naturally gathered particular rhythmic patterns that became stock features of the form. The typical ballad uses **ballad metre.**

Ballad metre
Four-line stanzas (**quatrains**)
Lines 1 and 3 have four **stresses** each (**tetrameter**).
Lines 2 and 4, which usually **rhyme**, have three stresses each (**trimeter**).

The folk ballad 'Lord Thomas and Fair Annet', a tale of compromised love and eventual death, demonstrates the form in this stanza. It incidentally also demonstrates the ballad tradition's use of recurring imagery. The rose here later reappears tragically on Fair Annet's grave (the stresses are bolded):

> He **had** a **rose** in**to** his **hand**,
>   He **gave** it **ki**sses **three**,
> And **reach**ing **by** the **nut**-browne **bride**,
>   Laid it **on** fair **Ann**ets **knee**.

Anon, 'Lord Thomas and Fair Annet' (1767), ll. 85–8.[1]

Many ballads in fact vary from this regularity, but they do tend to feature **rising metre**, using a mixture of **iamb** and **anapaest** feet, short lines, all types of rhyme, repetition (of single words or whole phrases in refrain), and short **stanzas**. These terms can be followed up in the chapter on prosody. At this point, just note that the ballad uses features that aid the memory by their simplicity, brevity, repetition and natural-seeming stress patterns, designed to fit easily with musical accompaniment. The term 'ballad' derives from the Latin *ballare*, 'to dance', suggesting some ways in which the tradition developed, and emphasizing its strong rhythm.

Despite this tendency towards 'naturalness', even spoken simplicity comes under some pressure when it is made to conform to rhythm and rhyme, as seen in line 86 of 'Lord Thomas'. The ballad tradition actually features many poetic devices such as **inversion**, **synaeresis** and **synaloepha**. The various indigenous languages of Britain also converge in ballads, as when Scottish or Irish ballads, while written primarily in English, still retain the use of older Celtic constructions or dialect words and phrases. Collections of ballads for the modern reader often feature copious footnoting to explain terms that have now fallen out of use. The ballad's formal simplicity, therefore, unravels on closer inspection into a varied and engaging history of language and communication.

The ballad's appeal

Ballad metre tends to sound familiar to Western ears, being reminiscent of children's rhymes and religious song (ballad metre is close to **common metre** used in hymns). Although the form is old, its rhythms have become so associated with storytelling that they put us into a state of anticipation and readiness, simply through sound. What we anticipate, generally, is a story with purpose; we are waiting for the 'moral' of the tale. We hope that whatever upset occurs during the ballad, some kind of order and resolution will be reaped in the end and taken on into the future. The power of the ballad, however, comes from how that anticipation and gradual unfolding of purpose is controlled (or, as discussed below, denied).

The use of repetition and sing-song rhythm seems at first to be a distancing device: rather than racing to its conclusion, the ballad indulges in the present moment of telling, relishing in the pleasurable sounds of regular rhythm and rhyme. For example, note the use of refrain 'Follow my love, come over the strand' in Thomas Deloney's 'The Maidens Song', which also uses repetition to end each stanza with either 'Northumberland' or 'Scotland'. These devices build up to the eventual, rather dubious 'moral' with which it ends:

> All you faire maidens be warned by me,
>> Follow my love, come over the strand:
> Scots were never true, nor never will be,
>> To Lord, nor Lady, nor faire *England*.
>
> Thomas Deloney (1626), 'The Maidens Song', from *Iohn Winchcomb
> (Iack of Newbery)*, ll. 137–40.

Yet holding off the main point adds to the story's eventual power: the circling returns to familiar words and phrases and the establishment of rhythm enacts a deepening of emotional engagement, encouraging the listener to sympathize with the protagonists' plight, or become enjoyably outraged by salacious bawdiness, or increasingly indignant (or delighted) at a villain's audacity, or terrified by the relentless shape-shifting of ghosts and ephemera. As such, the ballad eventually delivers its *denouement* (the final unravelling or catastrophe of the story) at a moment when the audience is at a pitch of engagement. In this way, the ballad became an important social and political form – its appeal to the collective ears and hearts of listeners offers a direct route to the emotive roots of social values.

The ballad and society

The ballad's role as the spreader of stories, news and scandal makes it extremely sociable. Rejecting a rarefied atmosphere of solitary inspiration, the ballad is robustly oriented towards gatherings of people, most likely united by circumstances. Often that gathering would be for entertainment, and many ballads relate tales of love and minor intrigue, or humorous ribaldry. Equally, the ballad may entertain by inducing controlled fear among its listeners: ghosts, spectres and supernatural happenings are common, raising the adrenalin while staying within the recognized realm of storytelling and familiar tradition. However, these apparently benign features cover a radical and often subversive form. Most overtly this is revealed in the subcategory known as the broadside ballad, discussed below. However, ballad tradition in general engages energetically with received ideas of right and wrong, especially in terms of social order. This partly derives from its association with lower social classes, which drives its implicitly disapproving or mocking attitude towards dissolute aristocracy and overlords: of course Robin Hood is one of the stock figures of English ballad tradition. The ballad also breaks down social order, as hinted in 'Margaret's Ghost', by concentrating on death, or sex, as social leveller:

> Her face was like an April morn,
>   Clad in a wintry cloud:
> And clay-cold was her lily hand,
>   That held her sable shrowd.
>
> So shall the fairest face appear,
>   When youth and years are flown:
> Such is the robe that kings must wear,
>   When death has reft their crown.
>
> David Mallet (1767), 'Margaret's Ghost', ll. 5–12.[2]

The ballad's storytelling eye for a tug at the heartstrings or trigger to the passions can also celebrate non-conventional couplings or actions. For example, in 'Lord Thomas', mentioned above, we are left with an emotive image that evokes mourning and celebration of a love that actually contravenes social order (the lovers die in quick succession but are remembered by the growth of intertwining rose and birch trees). Just as the ballad existed outside conventional literary culture, so it often endorsed a kind of 'common' morality unchecked by convention.

Yet, the ballad form is unusual in how it convinces its audience of these alternative social values. Rather than using a didactic tone, or even featuring direct expressions of feeling (emotions are described, usually in others, rather than expressed, as would be found in the **lyric** tradition), ballads are noted for their objectivity. The ballad minstrel (or, as is often the case, mariners) travelled around relating events and reactions easily and comprehensively. This slightly impassive mode – where the balladeer is a channel for a story rather than its 'author' per se – shaped the ballad as a form that does not overtly direct response. Rather the reader or listener is leant on to make judgement of the story (although this can be a collective reaction), which is often all the more affecting for its lack of embellishment or rhetorical design.

Ballads and print: Percy's Reliques

As has been emphasized, the ballad is strongly associated with oral tradition and ballads are still sung today. However, this oversimplifies a culture that actually engaged with print culture throughout its history. Scholars have in recent years recovered a print history that was obscured (rather than non-existent) because it did not fit with recognized print culture: see the Bodleian Library's 'Broadside Ballads' project, for example. Early on, ballads were written by hand on single sheets of paper to effect quicker, larger-scale distribution. These sheets were rarely signed by an author, rarely dated, and often quickly replaced with new ballads, or simply destroyed through everyday wear and tear. However, in 1767 the antiquarian Thomas Percy made a radical intervention with his *Reliques of Ancient English Poetry*, which gathered together definitive versions of popular songs, poems and ballads. As Nick Groom describes, Percy's *Reliques* became vital to English ballad tradition: as well as preserving materials that might otherwise have been lost, it fixed ballads onto the page, allowing them to become the subject of editorial, social-historical and political scrutiny. Ballads became 'exhibits in the cultural museum of Englishness' (Groom, i: 56). Although, to an extent, this neutralized some of the ballad's radicalism and, indeed, salaciousness (in opposition to the broadside tradition discussed below). Percy's *Reliques* nevertheless facilitated a new appreciation for ballads among the reading classes, directly influencing the Romantic interest in the form headed by Wordsworth and Coleridge in their *Lyrical Ballads* (1798). It also introduced an air of nostalgia which would become important in the subsequent century: rather than evoking the often-disquieting contemporary society (where ballads had political force) the form could now represent an ironic escape from current complexities to a so-called simpler age of collective identity and simple morality.

Broadside ballad: A ballad printed on one side of a single sheet of paper (a 'broadside'), providing alternative satirical words – usually lampooning a contemporary event or person – for a well-known tune.

The broadside ballad gains great power from being associated with an already-popular tune, and by being relatively quick and cheap to produce and distribute. They were also often well illustrated with woodcut drawings to catch the eye. As they were pasted up on walls (aiding the memory) they occupied potent position within public space. Although some broadsides featured relatively innocuous ballads, the opportunity for reaching public consciousness through this powerful combination of narrative and melody associated the tradition with savage commentary and invective. Indeed, Groom describes the ballad as 'dangerously incendiary' (i: 18), citing the case of the execution of Admiral Byng in 1757, partly brought about by popular discontent voiced in 'Tantarara Hang Byng', sung through the streets of Westminster by a hundred balladeers. This radical tradition is also seen in broadside ballads such as 'The Sufferings of the British Army in the Camp before Sebastol' (featured in the 'Broadside Ballads' project), a searing attack on the political and military leadership of the Crimean War. The tradition continues today, albeit often in a more humorous form, with modern descendants perhaps including the satirical songs featured in *Spitting Image* produced by Central Television in the 1980s.

Ballad hybridity and beyond

Lyrical Ballads – the volume by Wordsworth and Coleridge published first in 1798 – brought the category of 'ballad' under implied pressure from its twinned genre of lyric (and, of course, vice versa). The title of their volume neatly indicates the complexities it explores, such as the relationship between literate and illiterate cultures, the politics of literary form, bourgeois idealization of the ballad, the robustness of received morality in a changing society and the relationship between emotion and formulated expression. This results in a series of 'uncanny' ballads – that is, ballads that appear to conform to expectation, but actually undermine our instinctive search for meaning. Coleridge's *The Rime of the Ancient Mariner* (conforming to the strong tradition of seafaring narrators), for example, is a ballad without a clear moral message. Wordsworth's contributions, such as 'The Thorn', or 'We are Seven' scrutinize the role of the minstrel/narrator figure of ballad tradition by bringing his objectivity or rational response into painful and moving conjunction with the experiences of damaged, bereaved or rejected rural dwellers. As such the two used the ballad to re-examine late eighteenth-century society, which had so embraced Percy's *Reliques*, from the perspective of its complex literary culture.

This experimental and hybrid approach is seen elsewhere, for example, in the work of Letitia Landon, which seeks to unpick expectations of femininity. 'Lines of Life' uses the simplicity and naivety of ballad metre to relate, with disarming coolness, the artfulness of the woman whose public persona is entirely fabricated and manufactured:

> I teach my lip its sweetest smile,
>   My tongue its softest tone;
> I borrow others' likeness, till
>   Almost I lose my own.
>
> Letitia Landon (1829), 'Lines of Life', ll. 13–16.

Landon, along with others such as Emily Dickinson, thus also complicate relationships between the ballad and society, the ballad and print culture, the ballad and silence or singing, and the ballad and the individual voice. The ballad culture that we inherit in the twenty-first century, therefore, is in fact rich, varied and complexly self-reflective: simple in premise, perhaps, the poem that uses rhythm and rhyme to tell a story in fact emerges as an incisive cultural probe.

Read more

- Oscar Wilde's *The Ballad of Reading Gaol* (1898): a great commercial success. Consider why his use of this form, rather than the more elaborate ones he employed in his early poetry, appeared to be a more acceptable vehicle for this by-then-notorious dandy figure.
- Deryn Rees-Jones' narrative poem, *Quiver* experiments with different forms to tell its murder mystery. Note the ballad-metred 'A Dream', and its allusion to the ghostly, time-shifting ballad tradition: 'Last night I saw the future's ghost' (Deryn Rees-Jones (2004), 'A Dream', l. 1).
- *The Oxford Book of Ballads* (1969), ed. J. Kinsley (Oxford: Clarendon Press): its ambition is to produce a text 'closer to the true ballad event, the singer's song' (p. vii) using original spelling, no author names in the main text and musical scores. Consider how its presentation directs a reader's understanding of the ballad tradition.
- Military ballads: there is a strong tradition of using ballads to relate military victories and defeats, some of which have been adopted as national songs ('Rule Britannia!', for example, or 'Heart of Oak'). Why might the ballad be suited to sea tales and, perhaps rather differently, to jingoism?
- The Bodleian Library's 'Broadside Ballads' project can be accessed at www.bodley.ox.ac.uk/ballads/ballads.htm.
- Percy's *Reliques* are available in this facsimile edition: Thomas Percy (1996), *Reliques of Ancient English Poetry*, three volumes, with an introduction by Nick Groom (London: Routledge/Thoemmes Press).

Notes

1. Textual source: spelling modernized from the text in Percy's *Reliques*, Vol. 2.
2. Text from Percy's *Reliques*, Vol. 3.

Love poetry

Poetry that formulates the experience of love into traditional patterns and motifs.

Naturally love of every kind and degree inspires poetry as it does all of life, but this section does not consider different types of love, or indeed different poetic treatments of love. Any and all of the forms and genres in this book may feature loving, erotic, sensual, passionate, caring or yearning expressions of love felt between men and women, men and men, women and women, parents and children, brothers and sisters, friends, teachers and pupils, the mortal and the divine, the patriot and their country and so on. Yet poetry has also developed some formulaic expressions and organizations of love that have importantly shaped not only subsequent poetic treatments but also the experience of love undergone every day. Certain tropes and associations may seem 'natural', but they may be traced back to literary practice and, although in many cases these will have begun as formulaic treatments of love between men and women (in accordance with prevalent social customs), they have been innovatively and intriguingly reapplied to other loving relationships in various literary experiments. It is useful to be able to identify these older formulaic conventions in subsequent literary treatments so as to enhance your enjoyment of a poem (which may then be seen in dialogue with a great range of poetic expression), but also to gauge the poem's wider effect beyond the immediate circumstances of the love described, interrogated or celebrated. The conventions of love poetry considered here are:

- romance: a formulaic love narrative
- courtly love: a code of address and behaviour for aristocratic lovers in mediaeval lyric and romance
- blazon: a poem celebrating parts of the beloved's body
- aubade: a poem set at dawn
- epithalamion: a wedding poem.

Romance: A tale in verse that details the chivalric world of knights and ladies, often in a supernatural setting.

The romance genre began in mediaeval France (particularly associated with Provence), where it effectively became an alternative to the other narrative poetic genre, **epic**. Whereas epics' otherworldly happenings reference gods or religious deities, the romance tale is set in a more domestic context and details the business of knights and ladies at court. However, their exploits are shaped by the mysterious interventions of supernatural beings, spirits, spells, strange disappearances, mirages, hauntings and seemingly immortal creatures. The purpose of such settings, apart from their entertainment and wonder value, is to create circumstances in which human endeavour is put under extraordinary pressure (because magical events twist the usual course of events), so bonds between people can be tested, examined and celebrated at their extremes. The primary focus of the romance's plot may well be the pursuit of a heroine by a chivalrous hero, but the romance's intense interest in bonds and promises will often find those between men and men as important as those between hero and heroine. Like all genres, the romance demonstrates a set of expected features, but these are manipulated and refigured in individual treatments, to reflect different social contexts, and implicitly to direct politico-cultural development. Features of the romance tale include:

- Settings within a chivalric age (usually the Dark Ages) notable for highly developed manners.
- Often set at the court of a king or the household of a noted aristocrat.
- Imprecise timescales – time may slow down or speed up in different parts of the tale.
- A central oath of allegiance declared by a knight for a heroine; this is often mirrored (or complicated) by another oath of allegiance on the part of the knight to a king or overlord.
- The heroine should maintain a cool distance, withholding her love for the knight until his worth is proved.
- Elaborate displays of masculine strength and endurance demonstrated by jousting tournaments, hunting scenes, slaying of mythical beasts (especially dragons), arduous journeys, which refer metaphorically to the knight's desire to keep to a bond of allegiance.
- Lovers may be parted and reunited several times as natural and supernatural forces malign to obstruct their path to union.
- Wondrous events on a supernatural scale frame the human story.
- Codes of behaviour in terms of love, honour, loyalty, obedience and manners.
- The tale may be offered as an **allegory** of a contemporary concern.

Romance is a strong prose as well as poetic tradition and many modern manifestations of the genre are seen in novels (or *romans* in French, demonstrating their romance roots) or, more recently, cinema, often based on King Arthur and the knights of the Round Table, as told in Thomas Malory's *Morte D'Arthur* (1470). However, many influential romances were written in verse, such as *Sir Gawain and the Green Knight* (see **alliterative metre**) and interpretations of the tales of Arthur were produced in verse in the nineteenth century by writers such as Alfred Tennyson and William Morris. The romance tale has, in recent years, also been reconsidered as a vital genre for romantic poetry (see Stuart Curran and Jacqueline M. Labbe). Having said this, verse romances (or metrical romances as they are also known), constitute the smaller part of romance tradition.

As in the epic, cultures reflect on social, political and cultural values through romance tales that are distant from yet mirrors to contemporary life. Helen Cooper notes that a romance typically depicts a state of order that is suddenly disrupted. This is followed by a period of trial and tribulation, but the tale will finally deliver a 'symbolic resurrection and better restoration' (p. 5). So, in its early incarnation, romance serves as social endorsement and conservative reassurance: things will turn out right in the end. However, within that broader framework values are tested and reconstructed, allowing the tale to reflect hierarchies in social values. In *Sir Gawain and the Green Knight*, for example, one might argue that the focus is on restoring male bonding rather than those between men and women, as you might expect from a romance. The quest is undertaken by Gawain in order to protect King Arthur, who therefore occupies the heroine position. This is layered by a series of bonds into which Gawain enters with the Green Knight. In this context, the erotic subplot between Sir Gawain and his host's lady acts as a disruption that threatens Gawain's status as loyal knight within a male triangle.

This process of adoption and adaptation occurs on a broader scale throughout the history of romance as different elements of the typical arrangement are emphasized in different historical periods and under different writers (Cooper points to the 'far away and long ago' convention as making 'it especially easy for [romances] to be appropriated for interpretations that fit the immediate historical or cultural moment of subsequent new readers', p. 4). Merely with reference to King Arthur romances one might find Gawain celebrated in one tale (implying strength, heroism and male bonds of loyalty) and Launcelot proving the source of fascination to another (again implying heroism, but also an erotic disruptiveness as he is associated with Arthur's wife Guenevere). Not just the attitudes of the relative authors are implied by these shifts in emphasis; the move from Tennyson's depiction of 'Guinevere' as guilt- and grief-ridden, to Morris' depiction of her as defiant and sensual indicate broad changes in audience expectation as well as indicators of different agendas on the part of the poet.

In any case, the romance instigates certain patterns of behaviour that then colour the depiction of love in other cultural forms. Most notably the genre established codes for gender that insist on men as strong, questing and loyal and women as passive and delayers of gratification (or else erotically dangerous threats to male society). Love is generally treated as a state of anticipation rather than gratification; interactions between the sexes and between different hierarchies within the sexes are governed by linguistic codes that emphasize politeness, formulaic convention and mannered speech rather than unshackled emotional outbursts. Love is often allegorized into a commentary on philosophy, monarchy or social values, meaning that its individual significance is mapped onto (or even dissolved into) the experience of the social group. However, these expectations may be present at some level within a romance poem without necessarily becoming enacted. Indeed, the implication that a poem knows how it should proceed as a romance but then fails to is intrinsic to its cultural as well as aesthetic importance. In her readings of Romantic poets' engagements with the conventions and expectations of romance, Labbe suggests that violent and deathly imagery in these relatively late metrical romances points to the acts of violence that they enact on the expectations of the romance genre. The happy ending may be refused, the heroine may demonstrate a too-quick desire for erotic fulfilment (which instigates various crises), the hero fails to fulfil the expectations of gender, or else the poem reconfigures strength as aesthetic power (so implying that the poet's own art involves such strength). The mannered speech (which would seem to be so apt for metrical arrangement) may also break down into a series of cries of anguish or desire. In Keats' 'mini-romance' tale, it is more a refugee from (than a hero of) romance who appears at its start:

> Oh what can ail thee, knight-at-arms,
>   Alone and palely loitering?
> The sedge has withered from the lake,
>   And no birds sing.
>
> John Keats (1820), 'La Belle Dame Sans Merci', ll. 1–4.

The tale's **ballad stanzas** and spare detail imply at a structural level that this romance tale does not have the strength to expand into the long-line, long-length narratives of romance allegory or philosophical-meditative treatments. Rather the hero relates his tale in elusive fragments that the reader must assemble into something like the familiar romance structure. This might lead us to speculate that the lady in this case actively pursued the knight with erotic purpose, effectively committing a crime against genre (to use Labbe's terms, p. 3), spelling disaster not only for the protagonists, but also for the successful telling of the tale itself. Indeed, Keats' poem implies that the romance genre is more of a ghoulish nightmare than an ideal template; one that traps its protagonists within its conventions (ll. 37–40):

> I saw pale kings and princes too,
>   Pale warriors, death-pale were they all;
> They cried, 'La belle dame sans merci
>   Hath thee in thrall!'

Courtly love: A set of conventional behaviours and linguistic formulation used in romances and romance-derived love poetry.

'Courtly love' refers to the formulaic conventions used in romance to characterize a knight's love for and behaviour towards a heroine. More broadly it characterizes love between men and women in formal love poetry. It is a phrase that encapsulates the trials and tribulations that a knight or would-be lover endures as a sign of his strength of feeling, and is a convention in which women are understood as distant, cool and indifferent to the male's passionate plight. This fires the lover's determination to win the 'lady's heart and fashion ever more elaborate ways of expressing the lady's superiority (the **blazon** is important to this convention). Courtly love often sees the male lover adopt a 'low' perspective while the female beloved occupies a high pedestal position. This hierarchical and formal relationship is then carried out through self-consciously mannered and elaborate language as the female is referred to as 'a lady'. The lady's beauty and appearance is praised, and attributes such as her voice, posture and particularly her manners, dainty movements, coy blushes and even the way she eats or her

gracious response to human suffering (although notably not the lover's pain!) are
the subject of polite enthusiasm. Sidney's sonnets to Stella are typical:

> Cupid, because thou shin'st in Stella's eyes,
>   That from her locks, thy day-nets, none 'scapes free,
>   That those lips swell, so full of thee they be,
> That her sweet breath makes oft thy flames to rise,
> That in her breast thy pap well sugared lies,
>   That her grace gracious makes thy wrongs, that she,
>   What words so e'er she speaks, persuades for thee,
> That her clear voice lifts thy fame to the skies;
>   Thou countest Stella thine, like those whose powers,
> Having got up a breach by fighting well,
> Cry, 'Victory, this fair day all is ours!'
> O no, her heart is such a citadel,
>   So fortified with wit, stored with disdain,
>   That to win it, is all the skill and pain.

> Philip Sidney (1591), '12', *Astrophil and Stella*.

One purpose of framing human emotion in these elaborate and fixed formulations is to raise the experience of love out of the earthly and fleshly and into the
realms of the ideal and spiritual, hence the importance of keeping a distance
between the two protagonists. Interestingly courtly love often describes a
relationship between a lover and a married woman, making their love technically abstract and impossible (although of course implying the possibility of
the actual). It also promotes the idea that such spiritualized love is the 'grand
passion' and defining experience of the lover, so raising it to an ontological or
metaphysical status.

> **Blazon:** The poetic 'dissection' of a beloved's body into metaphoric parts
> for celebration.

In a blazon a poet will list all the separate parts of a beloved's physical appearance
that are delightful and attractive and use evermore elaborate and flattering
similes and metaphors to describe their intense beauty and dazzling effect. The
Song of Solomon in the Old Testament demonstrates this convention: here the
various parts of the two lovers are repeatedly listed, and the effect is almost as
though the absent beloved is brought to life before the lover by force of these
spell-like lists. In poetry it was often used in mediaeval romance tales and then
in the **sonnet** tradition, especially by English writers such as Spenser and Philip
Sidney. In this example, Spenser likens each part of his beloved to a different
flower in an abundant garden, only to suggest that her final element, her odour,
surpassed all comparison:

Coming to kisse her lyps (such grace I found)
Me seemd I smelt a gardin of sweet flowres
That dainty odours from them threw around
For damsels fit to decke their lovers bowres.
Her lips did smell lyke unto gillyflowers,
Her ruddy cheeks like unto roses red;
Her snowy browes lyke budded bellamoures,
Her lovely eyes like pincks but newly spred,
Her goodly bosome lyke a strawberry bed,
Her neck lyke to a bounch of cullambynes;
Her brest lyke lillyes ere theyr leaves be shed,
Her nipples lyke yong blossomd jessemynes.
Such fragrant flowres doe give most odorous smell,
But her sweet odour did them all excell.

Edmund Spenser (1595), 'Sonnet 64' from *Amoretti.*

Here the comparison of this extended simile (that the beloved is a garden of flowers) suggests her natural as well as her superlative beauty. Other blazons may use gems and precious stones to suggest each part of the beloved. Shakespeare's 'Sonnet 130', on the other hand, resolutely begins an 'anti' blazon ('My mistresses' eyes are nothing like the sun', l.1) in order to perform a blazon that registers the uniqueness of the speaker's love through describing each part of her body without embellishment: 'black wires grow on her head' (l. 3). Here Shakespeare rejects the clichéd tone of the blazon's reliance on **Petrarchan conceits**.

Although the blazon is overtly a flattering and glorifying convention, it has been critiqued: it is contended that the (usually female) object of the speaker's love is reduced to a series of parts (or by implication possessions), but denied a coherent status outside the speaker's perception. The blazon thus indicates the larger objectifying power of the lover's gaze and the dismantling of female identity in its grip. This poem, published by 'Michael Field', the pseudonym for two women writers, Katharine Bradley and Edith Cooper, implies the possessive impulse of this apparently loving convention by envisaging the lover as an explorer who would map (and so have power over) the beloved's body. As the poem closes, this is articulated as an equally aesthetic and erotic desire, but the poem admits that enumerating the parts of a beloved's body does not mean that the lover possesses that body:

There is balmy air I trow
On the uplands of thy brow,
But the temple's veinèd mound
Is the Muses' sacred ground;
While the tresses pale are groves
That the laurelled godhead loves.
There is something in the cheek

Like a dimple still to seek,
As my poet timidly
Love's incarnate kiss would flee.
But the mouth! That land to own
Long did Aphroditè moan,
Ere the virgin goddess grave
From the temptress of the wave
That most noble clime did win;
Who, retreating to the chin,
Took her boy's bow for a line,
The sweet boundary to define,
And about the beauteous bays
Still in orbèd queenship plays.
I have all the charact'ry
Of thy features, yet lack thee;
And by couplets to confess
What I wholly would possess
Doth but whet the appetite
Of my too long-famished sight:
Vainly if my eyes entreat,
Tears will be their daily meat

Michael Field (1893), 'Love's Sour Leisure', ll. 7–34.

Aubade: A poem that heralds the dawn, traditionally spoken by lovers.

The aubade – which comes from the mediaeval French tradition – is a poem that is spoken or sung at dawn, either by one of a pair of lovers or by a third party who warns the lovers of the breaking day. It may be a delicate and subtle poem that suggests the rising sun moving gradually across its lines, heralding a new horizon, a fresh perspective and the growing fertility of the day. Walter Pater considered it to have a special quality of redemption and salvation as it coincides with 'something of relief from physical pain with the first white film in the sky' (p. 304), a notion that he pointed to in this example that dwells particularly on the infused light and warmth of the day:

Pray but one prayer for me 'twixt thy closed lips,
Think but one thought of me up in the stars.
The summer-night waneth, the morning light slips,
Faint and gray 'twixt the leaves of the aspen, betwixt the cloud-bars,
    That are patiently waiting there for the dawn:
        Patient and colourless, though Heaven's gold
    Waits to float through them along with the sun.
    Far out in the meadows, above the young corn,
        The heavy elms wait, and restless and cold

> The uneasy wind rises; the roses are dun;
> Through the long twilight they pray for the dawn,
> Round the lone house in the midst of the corn.
>   Speak but one word to me over the corn,
>   Over the tender, bow'd locks of the corn.

William Morris (1858), 'Summer Dawn'.

However, more usually in the aubade the sun and the dawn are considered an interruption to the union of the lovers who must now part. It may suggest innocence and youthfulness attached to the early part of the day, but it gains particular sensuality and eroticism from how it acknowledges the couple as lovers: to be together at dawn they must have spent the night together. In Donne's famous example, the dawn is a far from welcome interruption to this sensual pleasure, and so the sun is addressed with angry contempt:

> Busie old foole, unruly Sunne,
>   Why dost thou thus,
> Through windowes, and through curtaines call on us?
> Must to thy motions lovers seasons run?

John Donne (1633), 'The Sunne Rising', ll. 1–4.

Aubades do not always stand alone; often they appear within longer poems as narratives pause to enact this traditional love song. A famous example is that spoken by Romeo and Juliet at the only dawn they do share (see *Romeo and Juliet* (1597), III: 5, ll. 1–11).

The aubade then is a form that holds together the thrill of consummation with the pain of imminent separation and the convention's two-sided attachment to sunrise allows poets simply to use the image of the rising dawn and from it evoke a poignant layering of emotion, even without extending it to a formal poem in the conventional mode.

Epithalamion: A poem written for a wedding.

In some ways the counterbalance to the **elegy** (although much less frequently attempted) the epithalamion (the plural is epithalamia) engages with poetry as celebration; after all we rely on poetry to commemorate joy as well as to comfort sorrow. The term derives from the Greek, 'before the bedchamber', which is where these poems were sometimes sung. The epithalamion is generally a celebration of the couple's love and a hope for their future posterity, the perfection of which is reflected in the form's frequently delicate and well-balanced arrangements of sound and symbol. Although the epithalamion's overt optimism can sit uncomfortably with ideas of marriage as a state involving subjugation or obligation, on the whole the epithalamion is an optimistic commemorative form that is as much a testament to a community and its rituals as it is to an individual couple and their future lives. Elements that often occur in the epithalamion include:

- a progressive narrative that traces the progress of the wedding day, and the transformation of its protagonists from individuals into a fused couple
- a typical narrative would move from an invocation to the muses, to dressing of the bride, the ceremony, the bride's entry to the marital home, a wedding feast with singing and dancing and finally the preparations for the wedding night
- a sense of abundance and wealth seen in the natural world, or in gems and jewels
- echoes of ritual, renewal and longstanding patterns of commitment
- prediction of future fertility and generations of children who will reflect their parents' goodness
- the combination of contemporary colour and detail with longstanding religious or pagan practice.

Edmund Spenser set a high standard with his example written for his own wedding by manufacturing line and **stanza** forms for each of the hours of his wedding day, combining with them the various cycles that came together in a day of commemorative and sacramental ritual. Ancient pagan belief, religious doctrine and the contemporary Irish setting combine into a dance between past and present, as can be seen in this section, which invites revellers to imbibe in celebration with the couple. The poem combines religious sanctity, Bacchic excess, communal feasting and dancing, and nature's ringing endorsement:

> Make feast therefore now all this live long day,
> This day for ever to me holy is,
> Poure out the wine without restraint or stay,
> Poure not by cups, but by the belly ful,
> Poure out to all that wull,
> And sprinkle all the postes and wals with wine,
> That they may sweat, and drunken be withal.
> Crowne ye God Bacchus with a coronal,
> And Hymen also crowne with wreaths of vine,
> And let the Graces daunce unto the rest;
> For they can doo it best:
> The whiles the maydens doe theyr carroll sing,
> To which the woods shall answer and theyr Eccho ring.

> Edmund Spenser (1595), 'Epithalamion', ll. 248–60.

This sense of the wedding day and its epithalamion as a central fixed point through which many different people, rituals and patterns pass can be touching and moving, and reflects the public declaration of love that is at the centre of a wedding celebration. Even Philip Larkin, in 'Whitsun Weddings' (1964) admits something of the spectacular within the provincial as he snobbishly observes several couples begin their married lives simultaneously-yet-separately in the carriages of a train. David Jones' two wedding poems written in 1940 for his friends Harman Grisewood and Margaret Bailey ('Prothalamion' – meaning in anticipation of a wedding – and 'Epithalamion'), didn't have the luxury of an immediately hopeful setting (this was a wartime wedding) yet the epithalamion's traditional long-view on human experience prompts Jones' complex and thrillingly wide-ranging meditation (which reads almost as a chant or incantation) on folklore, religion, myth and symbolism. This seems, eventually, to create a soothing sense of salvation focused in the image of the bride (in this poem a culmination of a series of female figures from across history) emerging 'bright in this darkness, and constant' (l. 235).

This striking image of Margaret Bailey converted into celestial overseer demonstrates the process of transformation understood at the heart of the marriage ceremony, and therefore of the epithalamion. Especially in more elaborate and traditional epithalamia, the poem operates as a controlled commentary that guides the couple toward the moment when they will be altered from two individuals into one pair ('mystically joyn'd, but one they bee;', John Donne, 'Epithalamion made at Lincolnes Inne', l. 39). Although the groom is clearly present and celebrated, the notion of intrinsic change tends to be focused in the figure of the bride whose move from virgin to wife is given symbolic potency, making hers the keynote experience of the poem. While for Bailey this works as an intangible beatification, in many epithalamia this process is carried out by the bride's female attendants who dress her for the ceremony, so realizing the bride's move into the symbolic rather than the earthly. The significance of this process of enrobing is understood by Donne ('Conceitedly dresse her, and be assign'd, | By you, fit place for every flower and jewell', ll. 19–20), but his poem has a perhaps prurient, even morbid, fascination with the sexual transformation to which this symbolic process points. In a reverse move, therefore, Donne relates the *un*dressing of the bride, and she, encouraged by flirtatious slyness, transforms back from the untouchably symbolic into the tangibly material, available to the touch of her groom, but also, the poem hints disconcertingly, the touch of death:

> Thy virgins girdle now untie,
> And in thy nuptial bed (loves alter) lye
>   A pleasing sacrifice; now dispossesse
> Thee of these chaines and robes which were put on
> T'adorne the day, not thee; for thou, alone,
>   Like vertue'and truth, art best in nakednesse;
>   This bed is onely to virginitie
> A grave, but, to a better state, a cradle;

> John Donne (1633), 'Epithalamion made at Lincolnes Inne', ll. 73–80.

Of course epithalamia have tended to address heterosexual bonds, but examples also exist that point abstractedly to same-sex coupling. Tennyson's elegy, *In Memoriam A. H. H.* (1850), frequently uses images of marriage and widowhood to indicate the intensity and sincerity of grief felt for a lost male friend, a tendency that seems ambivalently answered by the poem's final movement, which is an epithalamion for the author's sister. Such a finale to an elegy indicates the symbolic weight of the epithalamion as a public celebration of stability and futurity, acting as a social salve for the pain addressed throughout the poem. Yet this lip-service treatment of the form as religious and social conservatism sits uncomfortably with the poem's complex engagements with wavering religious belief and intense love between young men. Gerard Manley Hopkins' unfinished 'Epithalamion', written on the occasion of his brother's marriage in 1888, begins conventionally with a call to action and an effusive rendition of the bounty of nature, but the traditional epithalamion's celebration of natural abundance here colours the poet's sensual memories of male bodies, bringing them together in a crucible that has marriage as its cue ('What the delightful dean? | Wedlock. What the water? Spousal love', ll. 46–7), but which takes thrilling liberty with how that transpires.

Finally, Katherine Phillips' touching epithalamion for her sister shies away from the ostentation of epithalamia, characterizing that tradition as a male one centred on possession of the bride as trophy and symbol rather than woman. In a rather reassuring antidote to the sometimes vicarious idolizing (or even pawing) of the female body in epithalamia, this poem resolutely enacts a female tradition of careful and earnest protection of a woman's intellectual experience of marriage:

> We will not like those men our offerings pay
> Who crown the cup, then think they crown the day.
> We make no garlands, nor an altar build,
> Which help not Joy, but Ostentation yield.
> Where mirth is justly grounded these wild toyes
> Are but a troublesome, and empty noise.
>
> But these shall be my great Solemnities,
> *Orinda*'s wishes for *Cassandra*'s bliss.
> May her Content be as unmix'd and pure
> As my Affection, and like that endure;
> And that strong Happiness may she still find
> Not owing to her Fortune, but her Mind.
>
> Katherine Philips (1667), 'To My Sister Mrs C. P. on her Marriage', ll. 1–12.

Read more

- *Romance*: Famous verse romances include Chaucer's 'The Knight's Tale' [c. 1380–1387], 'The Squire's Tale' and 'The Franklin's Tale' [both c. 1392–1395] (from *The Canterbury Tales*); Edmund Spenser, *The Faerie Queene* (1590–1609); Coleridge, *Christabel* (1816); John Keats, 'The Eve of St Agnes' (1820); Morris, 'The Defence of Guenevere' (1858).
- *Courtly love*: See Chaucer's *Troilus and Criseyde* [c. 1382–1386], Petrarch's *Song Book* and Dante's *La Vita Nuova* (1290–1294) for early and very influential treatments of courtly love.
- *Blazon*: Henry Howard, Earl of Surrey, used a blazon – although one that divides up the body in order to praise its intellectual rather than erotic potential – in his elegy for Thomas Wyatt. As it is occasioned by the death of Wyatt the blazon extends to the subject's bones and finally, its 'ghost' ('Epitaph on Sir Thomas Wyatt', 1542).
- *Aubade*: Kenneth Patchen's 'As we are so wonderfully done with each other' (1942) reveals itself as an aubade with the striking metaphor, 'A waterglass on the bureau fills with morning' (l. 9). The poem ends, however, on a note that turns inwards to the loving union as the poet closes the poem up against the intrusive light. Philip Larkin's 'Aubade' (1977) finds the poet very much alone, disarmingly addressing death and mortality rather than a lover.
- *Epithalamion*: Although apparently an arcane and ancient form, many epithalamia were written in the twentieth century. Examples include, Dannie Abse, 'Epithalamion'; D. H. Lawrence, 'Wedding Morn'; Dylan Thomas 'On the Marriage of a Virgin'; Philip Larkin 'Wedding Wind'. How do they fashion this ancient form for new cultural conditions? How much are they public poems of celebration, or how much are they occasions for private memories? Is it significant that so many epithalamia are written by men?

References

Cooper, H. (2004), *The English Romance in Time: Transforming Motifs from Geoffrey of Monmouth to the Death of Shakespeare* (Oxford: Oxford University Press).

Curran, S. (1986), *Poetic Form and British Romanticism* (New York: Oxford University Press).

Labbe, J. M. (2000), *The Romantic Paradox: Love, Violence and the Uses of Romance, 1760–1830* (Basingstoke: Macmillan).

Pater, W. (1868), 'Poems by William Morris', *Westminster Review*, n.s. 34, 300–12.

Elegy

A poem of lamentation and mourning for the dead.

In Classical culture the term elegy (from 'elegos', a mournful poem, and 'elegn' a flute reed) referred to any poem that featured elegiac **couplets** and, in performance, was accompanied by a pipe called an aulos. This regular and rather formal style was suited to serious and sombre subjects, often lamentations about love (see Ovid's *Amores* and, later, John Donne's *Elegies*). With time, however, the term became restricted to its present use: a poem written at a time of death to express grief, memorialize the deceased and orchestrate a period of mourning. Each of these impulses has a complex literary significance and the elegy is a genre that works to meet many demands. Central to its dynamic is how it brings together the public with the private: to write an elegy is to make a public display of what is often a very private emotion or relationship. Some elegies lean more towards the public sphere, and are formal responses to the death of a public figure. These elegies act as monuments to the deceased and as a focus for public strife and disorder – while they often enumerate the virtues of the lost figure they must also emphasize the impulse to move forward and generate a sense of renewal and progress. The more private elegy also attends to a desire to be healed in the wake of bereavement; however, the elegy may focus more painfully on the emotional experience of grief in the individual, often overlapping with the expressive genre of the **lyric**. Elegies importantly developed within the **pastoral** tradition and some of their most enduring features derive from that genre's idealizing attitude towards the natural world. Although many elegies struggle to live up to elegiac expectation (grief is often a much more complicated and disordered affair than the neat patterns of tradition), it is often the very absence of expected features that adds to their poignancy, anger or bitterness. To begin with some common features of the elegy:

- Calls to a muse, figures from Classical myth, or previous famed elegists.
- The natural world reflects the elegist's grief and implicitly 'joins in' with mourning the lost figure.
- Nymphs (in pastoral tradition) or religious deities may be accused of neglecting or failing to care for the deceased.
- Processions of mourners and lists of flowers follow or deck the hearse.
- The elegist is often 'diverted' from speaking of the dead and reflects on other pressing issues of the day.
- Final consolation.

Elegiac forms

Traditional elegiac metre, following Classical example, uses alternate lines of **hexameter** (six **feet**) and **pentameter** (five feet). Later the **elegiac quatrain** became associated with the genre, as used in Thomas Gray's 'Elegy written in a Country Churchyard' (1751). The poem of mourning and lamentation, however, appears in all formal styles.

The elegy and the dead: remembrance

Perhaps the greatest (and gravest) service the elegy undertakes is to the dead figure. As both a memorial and a monument, the elegy comes to stand in for the dead figure who is now absent. Responsibility falls to the elegist, therefore, to secure the subject's reputation. Partly this is undertaken simply by the very act of elegizing the dead, which absorbs that figure (along with the elegist) into a longstanding literary tradition, implicitly comparing them with those previously thought worthy of remembrance. Naturally this often results in idealization and celebration. The use of established and extravagant **metaphors**, such as when the subject is likened to the day and their death to the night, expresses the heightened emotion of the elegist while simultaneously evoking a sense of collective mourning through shared imagery and echoing phrase. Alluding to allied traditions, such as love poetry, also works to give a kind of collective recognition to the dead. Douglas Dunn, for example, describes an essentially private and domestic scene that remembers the life he shared with his wife using the language and style of **courtly love**, so performing the intertwining of public and private that characterizes the elegy and using that tradition to express the elevated regard in which she was held:

> My lady loved to cook and dine, but never more
> 　Across starched linen and the saucy pork
> Can we look forward to *Confit de Périgord*.
> 　How well my lady used her knife and fork!
> Happy together – ah, my lady loved to sport
> 　And love.
>
> Douglas Dunn (1985), 'Dining', ll. 9–14.

In other cases it is idiosyncrasy that presses to be remembered: the ancient tradition of listing in elegies (of mourners or of abundant flowers used to deck the hearse) might be reformulated as lists of attributes or memories of the dead in an urgent impulse to accumulate and retain that which has been lost. Paul Muldoon's 'Incantata' (1994), for example, is an exhaustive, almost chanted enumeration of fragmented memories that provoke both love and frustration in the mourner. Very commonly, however, the final act of praise is drawn as a reinvestment of love and energy as the figure is transformed into a symbol of strength or goodness, as at the end of Milton's influential pastoral elegy 'Lycidas', in which Lycidas is raised as 'genius' or deity:

> Now, Lycidas, the shepherds weep no more;
> Henceforth thou art the genius of the shore,
> In thy large recompense, and shalt be good
> To all that wander in that perilous flood.

John Milton (1637), 'Lycidas', ll. 182–5.

Although, as discussed below, elegies often voice religious doubt, they can also segue into praise for God as they anticipate the protection and care God will provide for the deceased, who emerges as this 'chosen' one. A rather idiosyncratic example of the connection between elegy and religious fervour, which engages with notions of sacrifice and faithful ecstasy, is Gerard Manley Hopkins' *The Wreck of the Deutschland* (1875) written, according to the head-note 'to the happy memory of five Franciscan nuns' who had drowned in a sea storm.

The elegy and the living: grief and consolation

Simply the act of writing or commissioning an elegy goes some way towards consolation since to remember is to deny the annihilation that threatens us all. However, the process of reaching such consolation is naturally fraught with difficulty and often failure, so elegies are as much about charting the experience of the bereaved as they are about remembering the dead. That experience might amount to little beyond a cry of grief or it might be a long and convoluted journey that does not easily fit with expectation or desire (see Thomas Hardy's bitter and loving elegies for his wife, *Poems 1912–13*). Yet uniting these experiences is a compulsion on the author's part to shape their experience into elegy. For some the act of writing – its systematic filling up of time – can provide succour, especially as the formal demands of elegy can establish order at a time of confusion and upset. See Lyric V of Tennyson's *In Memoriam A. H. H.*, for example:

> But, for the unquiet heart and brain,
>   A use in measured language lies;
>   The sad mechanic exercise,
> Like dull narcotics, numbing pain.

Alfred Tennyson (1850), 'Lyric V', from *In Memoriam A. H. H.*, ll. 9–12.

Similarly, Oxlie's elegy for her friend, the poet William Drummond, claims that her bereaved temperament is unfit for poetic purpose at this time ('From an untroubled mind should Verses flow; | My discontents make mine too muddy show;', ll. 7–8), yet she produces a series of careful, ordered couplets

49

in a pastoral memorial that glorifies the deceased (a consolation in itself) by suggesting that the natural world – indeed the sun itself – grieves its loss:

> Senseless things do see thee moane,
> Stones do weep, and Trees do groane,
> Birds in aire, Fishes in flood,
> Beasts in field forsake their food,
> The Nymphs forgoing all their Bow'rs
> Teare their Chaplets deckt with Flow'rs;
> Sol himselfe with misty vapor,
> Hides from earth his glorious Tapor,
>   And as mov'd to heare thee plaine
>   Shews his griefe in show'rs of raine.
>
> Mary Oxlie (1656), 'To William Drummond of Hawthornden', ll. 44–52.

As nature seems to join with the elegist in despair, so it can also offer consolation through its cycles of renewal and regeneration. It is common to find images of natural fertility to counteract the elegy's solemn and impoverished occasion, as when Spenser criticizes himself for mourning one who has moved on to a place of beautiful Elysian abundance:

> No daunger there the shepheard can astert:
>   Fayre fieldes and pleasaunt layes there bene,
>   The fieldes ay fresh, the grasse ay greene:
>   O happy herse,
> Make hast ye shepheards …
>
> Edmund Spenser (1579), 'November' from *The Shepheardes Calender*, ll. 187–91.

However, the elegy is most psychologically and socially 'useful' when it leads the elegist (and the reader) towards a cure, either by transforming the dead figure into a symbol that can absorb the griever's energies, or by staging a scene of social regeneration, such as the marriage at the end of *In Memoriam A. H. H.* Rituals and traditional performances can help avoid unrest and promote the continuation of social order (as explored by Dennis Kay), while also binding the elegist and the deceased into a longstanding ceremony. Peter Sacks, meanwhile, draws attention to how the elegy's traditional move towards cure parallels the process of gradual psychological recovery that Sigmund Freud describes in his essay 'Mourning and Melancholia' (1915). John Donne's *Anniversaries* arguably also move towards a consolatory image, although his are concentrated in religious meditation and complex theological scrutiny. These finally recognize the deceased as 'the Proclamation' of God's authority and the elegist as 'The Trumpet' of that realization (John Donne (1612), 'The Second Anniversary', ll. 526–8).

However, this is not to suggest that consolation is easily gained, or easily achieved in elegy. In the case of *In Memoriam A. H. H.*, for example, the narrative line towards recovery was imposed by preparation for publication rather than faithfully indicating the course of emotional change in the author: some of its most seemingly pained lyrics, while printed at the start, were written towards the end of its composition (see Christopher Ricks, pp. 331–41). Consolation itself, of course, might also be a disturbing and poignant acceptance of despair and mortality, as in King's moving elegy for his wife, 'The Exequy'. Opening with a lament for how 'lazily time creeps about | To one that mourns' (ll. 16–17), over the course of the poem King actually speeds up time's progress (propelled by the poem's energetic rhyming **tetrameter**), taking dubious consolation from how this brings him closer to his own death, and so reunion with his wife:

> Stay for me there; I will not fail
> To meet thee in that hollow vale.
> And think not much of my delay;
> I am already on the way,
> And follow thee with all the speed
> Desire can make, or sorrows breed.
> Each minute is a short degree,
> And every hour a step towards thee.
>
> Henry King (1657), 'The Exequy', ll. 89–96.

For some, however, even this ambivalent consolation rings hollow: many elegies are an exercise in denial and anger.

The elegy and the living: anger and dispute

As Spenser wrote, 'Silence augmenteth grief, writing encreaseth rage' ('Another of the Same' in *Astrophel* (1595), l. 1). The pressure to remember the lost figure as virtuous can produce the opposite effect when experience fails to live up to expectation: elegies may be used to settle scores (an especially complex impulse since the dead can no longer defend themselves). Sylvia Plath's 'Daddy' (1965), for example, directs bitter invective at a figure who seems to represent a generalized oppressive patriarchy. Anger may also be directed at the griever themselves for indulging in selfish emotion, especially in a Christian culture that encourages the bereaved to accept death as a move towards God. However, the elegy's historic association with social purpose and religious ceremony (the elegist is often called upon to speak for a community of mourners in a funeral setting) also means that social (and religious) values can come under fire from the angry (and fearful) griever. Tennyson's *In Memoriam A. H. H.* is famous for its moments of doubt, interrogation of scientific knowledge, and for its bitter recognition that nature is not consolatory, as elegiac tradition would suggest, but viciously 'red in tooth and claw' (Lyric LVI, l. 15). Owen's 'Anthem for Doomed

Youth' is a deeply resentful and ironic allusion to the elegiac tradition as this poem turns on the precise absence of ceremony as so many soldiers die:

> What passing-bells for these who die as cattle?
> —Only the monstrous anger of the guns.
> Only the stuttering rifles' rapid rattle
> Can patter out their hasty orisons.
>
> Wilfred Owen (1920), 'Anthem for Doomed Youth', ll. 1–4.

In the modern, more secular age (as Jahan Ramanzani explores) a strain of uncertainty towards elegiac consolation has persisted, especially in the face of deaths on unprecedented scales, such as in the Jewish holocaust. Indeed, the claim that elegy can serve the dead cracks under such sustained pressure in poems such as Geoffrey Hill's 'September Song' (1968), for example, which admits that its purpose seems only to serve the living.

Self-elegy

As Hill suggests, it is difficult to escape the fact that elegies exist among the living. More pressingly, the elegist cannot escape their shaping presence in their poems, nor, in many cases, would they want to. Hopkins implied, indeed, that self-mourning is part of the human condition, replying to his question, 'Margaret, are you grieving | Over Goldengrove unleaving?' that 'It is the blight man was born for, | It is Margaret you mourn for.' ('Spring and Fall' (1883), ll. 1–2, 14–15). While this philosophical and psychological point haunts much elegiac writing, the self-elegy developed as a subcategory in response to all-too-real necessity among women writers facing the sobering prospect of giving birth in earlier centuries. As described by Germaine Greer (p. 11), the task of writing a poem of lilting and controlled rhythm could prove soothing to the anxious would-be mother (although the comfort, admittedly, is meagre). Bradstreet's example, however, also uses the opportunity to exert a small pressure of control on her potential successor when she movingly relinquishes her duty of care to her children:

> And when thy loss shall be repaid with gains
> Look to my little babes my dear remains.
> And if thou love thy self, or loved'st me
> These O protect from step Dames injury.
>
> Anne Bradstreet (1678), 'Before the Birth of one of her Children', ll. 21–4.

Elegies for other poets

Finally, one of the commonest forms of elegy is that written to another poet, sometimes known as literary elegies. While clearly offering a chance to idealize and recognize the talents of the lost figure, such an elegy is also a way for the elegist to gain cachet by association. Ben Jonson demonstrated his canny eye for literary posterity when he secured a place for his actually rather arch elegy for Shakespeare ('To the Memory of My Beloved, The Author, Mr William Shakespeare, and what He Hath Left Us' (1623)) at the front of the first folio edition of its subject's works. Rossetti's complex memorial to Letitia Landon ventriloquizes the earlier poet's voice, as though to speak that which Landon suppressed. Its potentially mawkish **refrain**, 'My heart is breaking for a little love', acknowledges cherished assumptions about women, but it also adopts a critical distance on that attitude, using repetition to emphasize the art, and even manufacture, of female persona. At its end, Rossetti demonstrates the power an elegist can wield by absorbing Landon into her own brand of reserved faithfulness rather than reward her with worldly affection:

> I deck myself with silks and jewelry,
> I plume myself like any mated dove:
> They praise my rustling show, and never see
> My heart is breaking for a little love.
>   While sprouts green lavender
>   With rosemary and myrrh,
> For in quick spring the sap is all astir.
>
> [...]
> Yet saith a saint: 'Take patience for thy scathe;'
> Yet saith an angel: 'Wait, for thou shalt prove
> True is best is last, true life is born of death,
> O thou, heart-broken for a little love.
>   Then love shall fill thy girth,
>   And love make fat thy dearth,
> When new spring builds new heaven and clean new earth.'
>
> Christina Rossetti (1866), 'L.E.L', ll. 22–42.

This poem emerges from a broader tradition in nineteenth-century women's writing of using the elegy to establish and characterize a female tradition (as Labbe suggests). This in itself mirrors a male ritual of literary elegies, noted examples being Spenser's for Sidney (*Astrophel*), Thomas Carew's for Donne ('An Elegy upon the Death of Dr John Donne', 1633), Shelley's for Keats ('Adonais', 1821), Swinburne's for Charles Baudelaire ('Ave Atque Vale', 1868) and Auden's for Yeats ('In Memory of William Butler Yeats', 1940), the latter also an act of remarkable impersonation as Auden performs Yeats' voice and tone, creating a ghostly and uncanny sense that the dead poet is 'risen again' through a rather wry spirit medium.

The variety and longevity of elegy seen here underlines the strength of the elegiac impulse. Indeed, it is a genre with particularly deep investment in poetry as a cultural force. At a time of death poetry appeals most acutely – as therapy, as consolation, as guard against annihilation, as route to immortality.

Read more

- The eighteenth century saw a revival of elegiac writing that extended the parameters of elegy, engaging with class and remembrance (Thomas Gray's 'Elegy Written in a Country Churchyard', 1751), and even species and remembrance (William Cowper, 'Epitaph on a Hare', 1784), although the latter has a Classical precursor in Catullus' lament for Lesbia's sparrow. How democratic is elegy? What subjects may be fit for elegy and why?
- How might elegy be political? Consider the elegy's polemic power, demonstrated, for example, by the case of Lucy Hutchinson, who wrote a series of angry elegies to clear her husband (John Hutchinson) of involvement in a Monarchist plot (*Elegies*, 1664). Compare this with the politics found in public elegy, for example in Andrew Motion's 'Remember This: An Elegy on the Death of Her Majesty Queen Elizabeth the Queen Mother' (2002).
- Having considered the importance of ceremony, compare this with the informality of elegies by, for example, W. S. Graham, such as 'Dear Bryan Wynter' (1977) that asks the deceased, 'Anyhow how are things?' (l. 12).

References

Greer, G. (1988), 'Introduction', in G. Greer, S. Hastings, J. Medoff and M. Sansone (eds), *Kissing the Rod: An Anthology of Seventeenth-Century Women's Verse* (London: Virago Press), pp. 1–31.

Kay, D. (1990), *Melodious Tears: The English Funeral Elegy from Spenser to Milton* (Oxford: Clarendon Press).

Labbe, J. M. (2000), 'Re-Membering: Memory, Posterity and the Memorial Poem', in M. Campbell, J. M. Labbe and S. Shuttleworth (eds), *Memory and Memorials, 1789–1914* (London: Routledge), pp. 132–46.

Ramanzani, J. (1994), *Poetry of Mourning: The Modern Elegy from Hardy to Heaney* (Chicago: University of Chicago Press).

Ricks, C. (ed.) (1987), *The Poems of Tennyson*, 2nd edn, three volumes (London: Longman).

Sacks, P. M. (1985) *The English Elegy: Studies in the Genre from Spenser to Yeats* (Baltimore: Johns Hopkins University Press).

Pastoral

Conventional, Classically influenced poetry that idealizes rural life and contrasts it with corruption in the city.

Traditionally, pastoral poetry is associated with the Classical world (it began with Theocritus's *Idylls*) and was importantly developed by Virgil in his *Eclogues*; even when written centuries later it tends to refer to Classical figures and settings. Originally pastoral poetry entertained sophisticated courtly audiences with tales of rural simplicity, and presented potentially rather twee scenes of shepherds (*pastor* being Latin for shepherd), usually at rest from their labours (often reclining beneath a tree) speaking in unrealistically elaborate and arcane language about their work, their landscape and their loves. The tradition rests on recognizing such a scene as ideally harmonious and full of simple pleasure, in contrast to the faraway corruption of urban space. Of course, the paradoxes are multiple … Pastoral poetry idealizes rural labourers, but it only occurs when such labourers are not working; it celebrates the simplicity of the rural space, where older value-systems reign incorruptible, yet this is expressed in highly stylized, self-conscious language that assumes familiarity with Classical civilization on the part of the shepherd and the reader. Pastoral poetry, then, is an odd hybrid between the rustic and the urbane. For some this is problematic, leading to accusations that it is too quick to believe its own beautified rhetoric. It has been derided for being overly idealistic in its depiction of rural life, blind to the harsh realities of living off the land, and superannuated in its investment in a Classical culture that is divorced from the very world (shepherding) it takes as its subject. It also suffers from the whiff of synthetic fashion associated with the mythic play-acting of aristocrats such as Marie Antoinette, dressed in shepherdess garb in her petit palace. But this is to underestimate the potential of the tradition's often-shrewd use of poetic convention in 'artless' rural scenes. The contradictory dynamic that necessarily underpins this somewhat strange tradition puts at its centre a process of reflection and detachment that makes pastoral suitable for surprisingly acute commentary, and for drawing upon emotions that are derived from contradiction, such as nostalgia, regret, hopefulness and joy in what is precious often because it is so precarious. The tradition has seen many treatments, from the typical to the caustically critical and in recent times pastoral has received new attention with the growth of modern eco-consciousness and its attendant literary treatments. To begin with the traditional features of pastoral:

- set in Arcadia: originally referring to the mountainous region in Greece, it now names any idealized rural setting
- inhabited by shepherds and shepherdesses, often carrying musical pipes

- intensely verbal: labourers are depicting in conversation rather than at work
- implied criticism of the distant urban space
- a retreat: either a move back in time as readers are encouraged to 'remember' an ideal past, or a geographical retreat as protagonists move from urban to rural space
- a return: either a relocation back to urban space or, as Terry Gifford suggests (Chapter 4), a moral or refreshed perspective is 'returned' to the audience/reader following exposure to the pastoral scene.

Formal features of pastoral poetry:

- elegant phrasing arranged into fixed forms such as **couplets**
- *eclogue*: a short poem on rural life and pastoral themes delivered either as a monologue by a shepherd, or as a dialogue between two or more shepherds
- *idyll*: a short poem that describes a picturesque rustic scene; the term now also refers to the space itself
- *bucolic*: from the Greek *boukólos* (herdsman), an adjectival synonym for pastoral but 'bucolics' are also pastoral poems
- archaic or deliberately 'artificial' language
- poems arranged in groups according to cycles (for example, a calendar year with a poem for each month, or a seasonal arrangement of four poems).

The pastoral and convention

In some considerations, pastoral is defined by strict convention, meaning that all of the above features must be present for it to be 'pastoral': Leo Marx summed this up by suggesting, 'No shepherd, no pastoral' (quoted in Gifford, p. 1). Spenser provides a typical example of the pastoral as shepherd poem here, where the narrator is approached by a 'straunge shepheard', and they both recline to play music:

> He sitting me beside in that same shade,
> Provoked me to plaie some pleasant fit,
> And when he heard the musicke which I made,
> He found himselfe full greatly pleasd at it:
> [...]
> He pip'd, I sung; and when he sung, I piped,
> By chaunge of turnes, each making other mery,
> Neither envying other, nor envied,
> So piped we, untill we both were weary.
>
> Edmund Spenser (1595), 'Colin Clouts Come Home Again', ll. 68–79.

(Note how Spenser uses spellings that were old-fashioned and 'quaint' even at the time of writing.) Most pastorals pick and choose from convention according to other considerations: the retreat–return movement is often more prominent in a polemical or moralizing pastoral. This dynamic can be acutely radical – the rural space is one of 'misrule' with a stock pastoral character being the 'Shepherd King', his grandeur hidden beneath humble clothes. This radical approach extends to contemporary debate outside the poem as pastoral's built-in outsider's perspective on urban corruption allows poets to produce sophisticated commentary on current affairs. Further, pastoral's playfulness and self-conscious artifice becomes an excuse for speaking 'out of turn', meaning that while the poems appear conventional, they actually often pose ideological challenges to contemporary audiences who may otherwise assume that the city equals progress.

Verbalism dominates pastoral poems that contrast their simple setting with complex philosophical debate, usually in the tradition of dialectic (the exchange of arguments) that uses conversation to work out what constitutes and defines Arcadia (the ideal, effectively).

Frequent references to Classical civilization – for example using shepherd names such as Thyrsis or Lycidas – characterize nostalgic approaches that evoke an Arcadian Golden Age (a period that pre-dates the emergence of human strife). A period (or a poet) that is anxious about contemporary life might, for example, evoke such an ideal past to use as a comparison and a nostalgic reassurance. The nature of the shepherd figures also varies: sometimes the treatment is very literal and refers to caring for a flock; other times the shepherd is evoked as a symbol of an ideal man. This latter approach is common in pastoral **elegies**, such as those by Matthew Arnold (*Thyrsis*, 1866) or John Milton (*Lycidas*, 1637), where the transformation of a dead friend into a shepherd figure adds to the poignancy and significance of the loss. The conventions can be absorbed into Christian culture through converging Arcadia with the Garden of Eden, and making shepherding a **metaphor** that holds together Christ as the carer (the 'good shepherd') and the cared for (the 'Lamb of God').

The movements between these different approaches to pastoral convention indicate the cultural work that a particular poem is performing: pastorals reflect as much on society outside their world as on their internal dynamics. So whether a pastoral poem champions literary culture in a state driven by commerce, or critiques a society in thrall to the pleasures of the city for its neglect of rural space and values, it does so with a sophisticated eye on how its artificial and highly literary performance of rural idealization filters and directs contemporary debates about authenticity, civilization and good living.

The pastoral and authenticity

As Marlowe's famous poem of invitation to a life of country pleasure winningly demonstrates, pastoral poetry is a consciously artificial, synthetic 'version' of rural life, seen here in miniature as the shepherd's manufacturing enthusiasm leads him to leap quickly from the authentic shepherding-garb of wool and straw to the otherworldly visual delights of gold and warm amber:

A gown made of the finest wool
Which from our pretty lambs we pull;
Fair lined slippers for the cold,
With buckles of the purest gold;

A belt of straw and ivy buds,
With coral clasps and amber studs:
And if these pleasures may thee move,
Come live with me, and be my love.

Christopher Marlowe (1599), 'The Passionate Shepherd to His Love',
ll. 13–20.

Clearly, a shepherd is as unlikely to access 'coral clasps' as he is to spend time fashioning pretty verses in lilting couplets (although shepherds' unlikely poetic abilities are often attributed to nymphs' refined teaching). Yet the poem's delight in replacing transient fibres (wool, straw) with enduring minerals (gold, amber) wryly acknowledges the poem's broader purpose: by rendering the authentic and humble as synthetic and elevated the poem draws attention, delight, celebration and lastingness to otherwise overlooked virtues of simple and harmonious human interaction. Raleigh's reply to Marlowe's poem, however, demonstrates that this might be reversed, pointing out that what appears authentic (the pastoral tradition's investment in shepherds as eminently trustworthy) is often far from it, as this shepherd's ulterior designs are as prettified and synthetic as his clothes and verses:

If all the world and love were young,
And truth in every shepherd's tongue,
These pretty pleasures might me move
To live with thee and be thy love.

Walter Raleigh (1600), 'The Nymph's Reply to the Shepherd', ll. 1–4.

Rather than desiring the alchemy of wool into gold, the nymph wishes for the delight that would blossom if 'youth [could] last and love still breed' (l. 21): an altogether more sobering desire that alludes to human decay and fading passion. The dynamic played out between these two poems demonstrates the pastoral's over-arching idealism: the wish to render humanity – a muddled, capricious, deceiving, fallen entity – as benevolent, sociable, beautiful and loving. To an extent this works, with the pastoral serving as a remedial space (city dwellers can be saved by exposure to the pastoral) and as reassurance that parts of civilization remain uncorrupted. However, it is also the source of pastoral's poignancy: for all its investment in rural scenes as somehow perfect, they are usually framed by the knowledge (just as the Garden of Eden is invaded by knowledge) that theirs represents a desire for – rather than a realization of – order and harmony.

In the idealized pastoral setting, however, nature is often 'hyper-real'; that is, its colours are vivid, its scents heady, even its decay is elegantly drawn out. As in Pope's handling, the flowers shine, the very roses breathe, the lamb dances:

> Sing then, and Damon shall attend the strain,
> While yon' slow oxen turn the furrow'd plain.
> Here the bright crocus and blue violet glow;
> Here western winds on breathing roses blow.
> I'll stake yon' lamb, that near the fountain plays,
> And from the brink his dancing shade surveys.
>
> Alexander Pope (1709), 'Spring: the First Pastoral, or Damon', ll. 29–34.

The artifice of the poet's depiction is evident, but this does not signal naivety. As Pope suggested, the aim of the pastoral tradition is 'not to describe our shepherds as shepherds at this day really are, but as they may be conceiv'd then [in the Golden Age] to have been' (p. 120): immediately the reality of the scene is obscured by the ideal extrapolated from that scene. It follows that the natural world depicted is clearly framed by the intervention of the poet ('we must therefore use some illusion to render a Pastoral delightful' (p. 120)), who performs in ways akin to the rural labourers who intervene in nature's rhythms: here the natural world is domesticated, trimmed to size, cultivated and the harmony reached after hinges on symbiosis between human activity (shepherding, farming, harvesting) and nature's activity (decay and regeneration). Nature is not only acknowledged as a human construct; it is subject to the whims of a shepherdess' fluctuating emotions ('All Nature mourns, the skies relent in showers, [...] | If Delia smile, the flowers begin to spring', ll. 69, 71).

It is not so much that pastoral renders the natural world inauthentic, than that its overt artifice draws sophisticated attention to the interfaces between experience and its articulation. Pastoral asks us to consider why one version of the natural world is accepted as authentic and another is rejected as artificial. However, in terms of the authenticity of rural labour there is a more dynamic debate: some would treat shepherding as **allegory** and others reclaim this activity as a reality. The labouring poet John Clare's *The Shepherd's Calendar* (echoing Spenser's pastoral of the same name) segues fascinatingly between traditions – on the one hand flagging up the storytelling 'literary' culture of the farmer's wife, other times exposing the brutal gap between the literary ideal of a life hampered only by the dramas of love and the reality of a life in grinding poverty, subject to acts meted out by the powerful (whether governmental or divine) to the meek and dispossessed:

Now, musing o'er the changing scene,
Farmers behind the tavern-screen
Collect; – with elbow idly press'd
On hob, reclines the corner's guest,
Reading the news, to mark again
The bankrupt lists, or price of grain;
Or old Moore's annual prophecies
Of flooded fields and clouded skies;
Whose Almanac's thumb'd pages swarm
With frost and snow, and many a storm,
And wisdom, gossip'd from the stars,
Of politics and bloody wars.

John Clare (1827), 'January' from *The Shepherd's Calendar*, ll. 7–18.

Rather than reclining beneath a tree, these 'shepherds' have retreated to the tavern. The shadow of pastoral's elegance and sophistication is cast in Clare's sustained handling of **tetrameter couplets**, but the earlier high-artifice of Spenser's metrical variations and use of interlaced **rhymes** have not survived, and along with the fading of language that is overtly separated from everyday life (Spenser delighted in archaism) the ideal of complete retreat that characterized pastoral has disappeared. This community is not immune to the savagery of far-off life: wars and politics infiltrate the rural scene, and serve to reflect rather than contrast the misery of rustic labour. R. S. Thomas, much less sympathetically, also sought to reveal the man beneath the symbol of pastoral shepherding in his recurring character, Iago Prytherch, a figure characterized by stasis, although this is the stasis of mindlessness rather than ideally preserved timelessness: 'Motionless, except when he leans to gob in the fire' ((1955), 'A Peasant', l. 12). Thomas' purpose would seem to be to confront literary culture with its own fastidiousness, yet the poetry veers towards the discomforting effects of objectification just as dangerously as does the traditional, idealizing pastoral.

Read more

- Spenser's *The Shepheardes Calendar* (1579) is often read as an elaborate allegory of contemporary religious debates, engaging with his family's Reformist Puritan sympathies: why might such commentary be encoded into the 'simple' pastoral mode?
- How do the poems making up Wordsworth and Coleridge's *Lyrical Ballads* engage with pastoral tradition? Can such treatments still be termed pastoral?
- In recent years the rise of a newly acute form of eco-consciousness has set poetic as well as environmental agendas: how far do anthologies such as *Wild Reckoning*, edited by John Burnside and Maurice Riordan (Calouste

Gulbenkian Foundation, 2004) combine pastoral tradition with new urgency regarding the feared demise of the natural world it relies on? Does this constitute a development of pastoral tradition or a departure from its original principles, a rejection of its ideology? Do we need a new pastoral? Or should we learn to reread traditional pastoral with a new cultural awareness?

- Terry Gifford suggests (1999, p. 71) that the pastoral's idea of retreat became an acute necessity in the aftermath of the horrors of the First World War, seen in enthusiasm for Edward Marsh's anthologies of *Georgian Poetry* (1912–1922), also current with the revival of interest in A. E. Housman's melancholic volume, *A Shropshire Lad* (1896). Are pastorals comforting gestures, merely a distraction for a society in turmoil, or might they help to redress the ills that caused such misery?

References

Gifford, T. (1999), *Pastoral: The New Critical Idiom* (London: Routledge).

Pope, A. (1963), 'A Discourse of Pastoral (1709)', in *The Poems of Alexander Pope: A one-volume edition of the Twickenham text with selected annotations*, ed. J. Butt (London and New York: Routledge), pp. 119–23.

Light verse

Humorous verse that sticks rigidly to poetic patterns, often regardless of content.

Light verse, as its names suggests, is difficult to pin down: what constitutes light verse, which poets are to be thought of as 'light', and whether 'lightness' ever forms a tradition is a matter of opinion rather than rule. For some lightness is defined by tone; whether it is speaking of love or of war light verse does so with playfulness, wit, irony and dispassion (Abrams, p. 102). For others, lightness comes from a lack of elevation on the part of the poet: W. H. Auden suggested that it occurs 'when the things in which the poet is interested [...] are much the same as those of his audience' (does this statement clarify the case at all?). Apparently, this will mean that 'his language will be straightforward and close to ordinary speech' (p. viii). Yet, wit and irony can be employed with great seriousness; 'ordinary speech' occurs in the most resonant and moving of poems. What is noticeable and arguably consistent about light verse, however, is its relationship with form. Despite its (self-perpetuated) reputation for artlessness – the verse is light in as much as it is not weighed down by declared significance – light verse is notable for sticking to patterns, of **rhyme**, rhythm, **refrain** or

stanza, no matter how bathetic this may become with a crass rhyme or unlikely emphasis. Indeed this bathos is acknowledged and exploited in the best cases. For this reason, light verse requires great skill to produce, but requires little skill (because it delivers familiarity) to enjoy. It is also, perhaps, why light verse is especially associated with well-recognized verse forms and has evolved rigid ones of its own, which appear only rarely outside the 'light' tradition. Forms that feature in light verse include:

- **Limerick**
- **Villanelle**
- **Epigram**
- **Ballad**.

Although noted for simple style and intent, light verse cannot be easily dismissed. Like the aged man in Carroll's 'You are old, father William', it often has more bite than is assumed, and its experience with poetic graft can bring it a wisdom belied by its tone:

> 'You are old,' said the youth, 'and your jaws are too weak
> For anything tougher than suet;
> Yet you finished the goose, with the bones and the beak—
> Pray, how did you manage to do it?'
>
> 'In my youth,' said his father, 'I took to the law,
> And argued each case with my wife;
> And the muscular strength, which it gave to my jaw,
> Has lasted the rest of my life.'
>
> Lewis Carroll (1865), 'You are old, father William', Chapter 5, *Alice's Adventures in Wonderland*, ll. 17–24.

Part of the delight of light verse's often-brilliant technical execution comes from how it applies this skill to so-called humble subjects: bawdy stories, obscene jokes, the doings of the ordinary man and woman, the language of the street and tavern. By treating such subjects 'lightly', it implicitly pokes fun at the poet who uses their art solemnly. In this respect, light verse can veer towards parody or burlesque. Yet although light verse may employ everyday language, or be humorously pragmatic in the face of emotional turmoil, it is not always as sharply contemptuous or harshly satirical as parody. Where parody and burlesque undermine particular cultural forms, light verse demonstrates a more generalized sense of the absurd (or 'impropriety' as A. A. Milne called it (quoted by Amis, p. vi)) by puncturing pretension with a pointed rhyme or an obscene **pun**. Light verse strives to 'raise a smile' (in Kingsley Amis' definition, p. xiii) rather than provoke caustic or hollow laughter; as such it tends to display warmth and a degree of empathy towards its subject and its audience. With its typical 'impropriety', however, it makes fun of the grandeur and mythmaking that surround 'serious' subjects, such as love (see Samuel Wesley's likening of Cupid to a maggot: 'On a Maggot', 1685). The 'despairing lover' of William Walsh's poem, for example, soon finds that the mere prospect of death on the cliffs is enough to cure him, so he returns to a cosy hearth rather than fulfilling his destiny as heroic lover:

> Distracted with care
> For Phyllis the fair,
> Since nothing could move her,
> Poor Damon, her lover,
> Resolves in despair
> No longer to languish,
> Nor bear so much anguish;
> But, mad with his love,
> To a precipice goes,
> Where a leap from above
> Would soon finish his woes.
>
> When in rage he came there,
> Beholding how steep
> The sides did appear,
> And the bottom how deep;
> His torments projecting,
> And sadly reflecting,
> That a lover forsaken
> A new love may get,
> But a neck, when once broken,
> Can never be set;
> And that he could die
> Whenever he would;
> But that he could live
> But as long as he could:
> How grievous soever
> The torment might grow,
> He scorn'd to endeavour
> To finish it so.
> But bold, unconcern'd,
> At thoughts of the pain,
> He calmly return'd
> To his cottage again.
>
> William Walsh (1797), 'The Despairing Lover'.

This poem's sprightly movement (it uses **dimeter, amphibrachs** and **anapaests** – see Chapter 3) uses the 'jogging rhythms' that Amis associates with light verse, which counter the predicted disaster. We can enjoy the lover's torment and smile at his reasoning because we feel reassured that just as the rhymes will be delivered with unwavering regularity, so will the lover be returned safely to us at its end. Light verse's close relationship with sound and rhythm control therefore produces a feeling of security for the reader. However, this is not necessarily a mark of conservatism. Rather, light verse's playfulness can feel like a deliberate confusion of programmatic behaviour, naturalized ideology and social acceptability. It is often a celebration of the underdog (even if he is lampooned he is still the protagonist) and a champion of the overlooked or socially dangerous. Some of its greatest practitioners (Byron, or the Earl of Rochester, for example) were, after all, notorious for their breaking of numerous social codes. It may be fanciful, therefore, to read 'Simple English' as political or social commentary, but such fancifulness is part of light tradition itself. Certainly at its end the reader is left as befuddled as its would-be gloved gent, no longer able to say with certainty what is right or wrong, or indeed right or left. So the sketch alludes to the pitfalls hidden within the encoded – and far from simple – rules of society:

> Ofttimes when I put on my gloves,
>   I wonder if I'm sane.
> For when I put the right one on,
>   The right seems to remain
> To be put on—that is, 'tis left;
>   Yet if the left I don,
> The other one is left, and then
>   I have the right one on.
> But still I have the left on right;
>   The right one, though, is left
> To go right on the left right hand
>   All right, if I am deft.

> Ray Rose Clarke (1917), 'Simple English'.

As Clarke's example hints at, the business of society, rather than the individual, is a regular source of fascination to the light versifier, constituting a subcategory of light verse in itself.

> **Vers de société:** Entertaining verse written for and about society.

Vers de société is written primarily to entertain one's society; that is, the similarly educated friends and acquaintances of a particular poet. Hence its object is to please its own times, rather than posterity. Simplicity, accessibility and familiarity may be associated with the style, but, in English, *vers de société* is associated with the graces and mores of so-called polite society in particular, making it both a description of and entertainment for the educated classes. Concerned as it is with gatherings of chattering classes, it is generally urban in setting and often plays at priding itself on technical brilliance, seeing this as a reflection of its society's elegance. *Vers de société* is thus associated with polished and deft handling of poetic form, often arranged into graceful **couplets** or complex **ottava rima**. Perhaps inevitably, the tone of *vers de société* is often arch, establishing a critical distance between its position as observer and the coded behaviour it describes. As Abrams notes, in this tradition love is a game of witty flirtation; friendship is self-serving entertainment; conversation is self-conscious performance (p. 102). London itself may be fraught with (mock) danger, no place for the uninitiated:

> Others you'll see, when all the town's afloat,
> Wrapt in th'embraces of a kersey coat,
> Or double-button'd frieze; their guarded feet
> Defie the muddy dangers of the street,
> While you, with hat unloop'd, the fury dread
> Of spouts high-streaming, and with cautious tread
> Shun ev'ry dashing pool; or idly stop,
> To seek the kind protection of a shop.
>
> John Gay (1716), 'Trivia, or the Art of Walking the Streets of London',
> ll. 191–8.

Swift's birthday verses for Esther Johnson ('Stella') deliver a template-example of society verse, addressed to a society hostess. And yet they demonstrate a genuine affection for her lasting charm, which will outlive the gaudy and short-lived attractions of younger socialites, to whom the final warning is addressed:

> But let me warn thee to believe
> A truth for which thy soul should grieve;
> That, should you live to see the day
> When Stella's locks must all be gray,
> When age must print a furrowed trace
> On every feature of her face;
> Though you and all your senseless tribe
> Could art or time or nature bribe

To make you look like beauty's queen
And hold forever at fifteen,
No bloom of youth can ever blind
The cracks and wrinkles of your mind;
All men of sense will pass your door
And crowed to Stella's at fourscore.

Jonathan Swift (1727), 'Stella's Birthday, 1721', ll. 43–56.

Vers de société thus shifts between the warm and celebratory (it is written for a poet's social circle) and the cool and analytical. In the nineteenth century the style grew in popularity with the publication of various anthologies and with the adoption of elaborate French-derived verse forms (such as the **ballade**, **rondeau** and **villanelle**) that invigorated the *vers de société* tradition. While those such as Oscar Wilde emphasized the continental influence of such forms, Amy Levy used examples such as 'Ballade of an Omnibus' (1889) to play with ideas of belonging and liberty in an urban setting. Murray Lachlan Young's 'Simply Everyone's Taking Cocaine' (1997) revives the practice for less moving purposes, providing self-conscious entertainment for an 'urbane' pre-millennial society.

> **Nonsense verse:** Verse that defies logic through wordplay, syntactic scrambling or situational absurdity.

Developing the notion that light verse unpicks the fabric of society by reweaving it into 'improper' colours and shapes, nonsense verse brings this to an absurd conclusion. Geoffrey Grigson speaks of the 'special kind of liberated "mirth"' (1979, p. 13) seen in the nonsense poem, which surprises and amuses the reader by garbling syntax, accepting the strange as familiar, or losing sight altogether of recognized meaning, usually in pursuit of patterned sound. Despite this nonsense premise, the verse itself often intones an absurd solemnity by aping the verbal patterning of earnest expression, such as the celebrated opening of a story – 'Twas brillig, and the slithy toves | Did gyre and gimble in the wabe;' (Lewis Carroll (1871), 'Jabberwocky', l. 1–2) – or the incantation of formal prayer – 'Give us thisbe our daily tit' (John Lennon (1965), 'The Faulty Bagnose', l. 31). The appearance of nonsense within the frame of familiarity is not only amusing but also opens up alternative perspectives, or alternative versions of 'truth' and experience, hence the liberation that Grigson describes. Yet, the frisson of freedom is often more effective when it plays against strict control: Grigson identifies this combination in the strength and popularity of nonsense verse in the nineteenth century, when formal verse was more common than in the twentieth century (he suggests that Edward Lear, celebrated nonsense poet, 'needed Tennyson to play against' (p. 14)). Other 'explanations' of nonsense verse use psychoanalytic readings of repression, linking nonsense verse with the Surrealist art movement. However, the popularity of strange creatures and strange lands may also discomfortingly suggest that

Victorian or Edwardian nonsense verse implies cultural confusion at a time of intense colonial expansion, registering a bewildered response to encounters (or quasi-encounters) with other versions of civilization and exotic landscapes:

> And it's O for the jungles of Boorabul.
> For the jingling jungles to jangle in,
> With a moony maze of mellado mull,
> And a protoplasm for next of kin.
> O, sweet is the note of the shagreen shard
> And mellow the mew of the mastodon,
> When the soboliferous Somminard
> Is scenting the shadows at set of sun.
> And it's O for the timorous tamarind
> In the murky meadows of Mariboo,
> For the suave sirocco of Sazerkind,
> And the pimpernell pellets of Pangipoo.
>
> James C. Bayles (1910), 'In the Gloaming', ll. 13–24.

As this example demonstrates nonsense verse indulges particularly in wordplay and soundplay, making ingenious use of **alliteration, rhyme, assonance** and many versions of **schemes** such as **chiasmus** or **zeugma**. However, in addition to overt babble, nonsense may also deny logic or feasibility and present something that makes grammatical sense but semantic nonsense. This is seen in the premise of Edward Lear's 'The Jumblies' (1871) – going to sea in a sieve – or in the unlikely bovine gymnastics of nursery rhyme ('the cow jumped over the moon'). While persistent nonsense can be wearying, its presence serves as welcome provocation to arbiters of taste: nonsense verse, after all, inspires vigilance in terms of how we make sense of our world and the experiences we have within it.

> **Doggerel:** 'Trivial' verse that demonstrates rough and irregular rhythm and rhyme, usually attributed to the poet's lack of skill.

Now mainly used as a term of abuse, doggerel is used to describe verse that has pretensions to seriousness and sincerity, but which falls on its face due to a lack of skill on the part of the poet. The term was famously used by Chaucer, whose 'Tale of Sir Thopas' (from *The Canterbury Tales*), ironically told by the character 'Geoffrey Chaucer', is written with clunky artlessness, provoking the Host to interrupt with the cutting remark, 'This may wel be rym dogerel' (l. 925):

> Yet listeth, lordes, to my tale
> Murier than the nightyngale,
>   For now I wol yow rowne
> How sir Thopas, with sydes smale,
> Prikyng over hill and dale,
>   Is comen again to towne.

Geoffrey Chaucer [c. 1396–1400], 'Sir Thopas', from *The Canterbury Tales*, ll. 833–8.

While doggerel does refer to unsuccessful poetry, this is not always unintentional. Poets who are sometimes considered 'doggerelists' (although it is a moot point where the line is drawn between doggerel and light verse), such as Ogden Nash or Pam Ayres, present their verse with wry humour, in witty acknowledgement of its own playfulness, humbleness or gestures at artistry. As in the comic piano-playing of comedian Les Dawson, it often takes great skill to appear to have none.

Read more

- Wendy Cope seems overtly to produce 'light verse', but her poems are frequently in complex and wry engagement with 'received' tradition. How might light verse engage critically with orthodox writing and culture?
- So called 'serious' poets – particularly of the twentieth century, such as T. S. Eliot, W. H. Auden and Philip Larkin – often experimented with 'lighter' verse. Such poets sometimes adopt a persona for such poems – see Eliot's *Old Possum's Book of Practical Cats* (1939), for example. Why might a poet add this layer of distance in this mode?

References

Abrams, M. H. (1996), *A Glossary of Literary Terms*, 6th edn (Fort Worth: Harcourt Brace College Publishers).

Amis, K. (ed.) (1978), *The New Oxford Book of Light Verse* (Oxford: Oxford University Press).

Auden, W. H. (ed.) (1938), *The Oxford Book of Light Verse* (Oxford: Oxford University Press).

Grigson, G. (ed.) (1979), *The Faber Book of Nonsense Verse* (London: Faber and Faber).

PART II: THE POETRY TOOLKIT

Part II Overview

Forms

Chapter Outline

> ## Form
>
> The shape or configuration of a poem.

You might think that 'form' sounds dull and negative: to be 'true to form' is to be predictable; to 'keep to form' is to obey rules and repress what is excitingly disruptive. Yet this assumes that rules are only ever repressive, when in fact they can be liberating, or at least a challenge. This section moves on from the broad traditions outlined in Chapter 1 to think about how the physical shape that a poem occupies on the page, its length, rhyme scheme, style and logic, not only serve an immediate purpose, but may also indicate longstanding traditions. When a poet arranges poems into established and recognized shapes they intimate that part of their 'meaning' derives from comparison with other examples of the same formal arrangement. Perhaps surprisingly, the patterns poems fall into are also matters of fashion and taste; the sonnet may be cherished as a succinct piece of artistry in one period and dismissed as arcane and stilted in another. What a poet does with the recognized form can then be used to place it within its historical context. Yet, such forms also shape the effect they have on readers today: poems that are long, or short, or rhyming, or rigid, or flowing each approach their readers in different ways. Some assume that we recognize the form as a longstanding one with a rich heritage; some present an old form in entirely new and striking circumstances.

Recognizing a poem's formal traditions can be a useful way into examples that might otherwise be confusing or off-putting. Often their shape or configuration will indicate larger ideas of logic or philosophy, and it helps to understand that background when trying to work out how a poem 'works'. The forms considered here range from the variable, the fixed, the visual, the hybrid and the 'formless'. Since form is often linked closely to features such as **metre**, **rhyme** and **stanza** you might wish to follow up many of the terms used in these discussions in the following chapter, on **prosody**. In the main the chapter will consider formal traditions and conventions without such technical detail, although in some cases it is a good idea to familiarize yourself with the basics of metre in particular.

2.1 Variable forms

These poems generally use established conventions, which are intrinsic to how they are read and understood, and yet the rules may be followed loosely, employing variations to length, or content, or features such as rhythm and rhyme. They each imply formal traditions that shape a reader's understanding of the poem, whether in terms of technicalities such as shape and length or in terms of expressive style, or traditional subject matter, or the methods they use to understand or express an idea.

> ## Ode
>
> A formal and serious **lyric** addressed to a person, object or abstract concept.

Odes derive from Classical culture, and therefore when written in English imply a certain scholarly and formal tone. They often use formulaic and elaborate expression to address a particular subject, which can appear as a flamboyant celebration of that subject and also as an exaggerated striking of a poetic pose on the part of the speaker. These poems were originally used in sung performance and that relationship with oral culture and vocal expression often remains in explicit indicators of speech such as exclamation marks. In terms of subject matter the ode tends to fall into two categories, named for their Classical heritage: the Pindaric (dealing with public matters) and Horatian (dealing with matters of contemplation and quieter thought). They also differ in terms of formal arrangement. Although the ode is a formulaic and serious form of poem that suggests fixed rather than free expression, it importantly shaped attitudes in lyric poetry's relationship with meditation and contemplation, public and private expression, and speech and address. However, its determination to be serious and solemn has also made the ode ripe for parody. Features of the ode:

- addressed to a specific person, object or concept
- elevated, formal, elaborate or self-consciously 'poetic' language
- **apostrophe** and explicit indicators of speech such as exclamation marks, the vocative 'Oh!' and rhetorical question marks
- references to Classical culture
- relatively long length with the poem divided into stanzas or formal divisions of either fixed or irregular shape
- may relate to either Pindaric (or irregular) or Horatian traditions.

Pindaric odes

This style of ode is named after the Greek poet Pindar who wrote several for winners at the Olympic Games, an occasion for exaltation and solemn praise of passionate endeavour. This public tone of proclamation remains in English versions, which are often written for occasions of public significance (see Tennyson's elegiac 'Ode on the Death of the Duke of Wellington', 1852). Pindar designed his odes to be sung by a chorus, formally structuring them with this method in mind. The strict Pindaric ode therefore features three parts:

- *strophe*: section chanted as the chorus moved in one direction across a stage
- *antistrophe*: section chanted as the chorus turned and moved in the other direction across the stage

- *epode*: section chanted while the chorus remained still.

These three movements are then repeated in this sequence across the poem. In English attempts at this formal arrangement the strophes and antistrophes share the same stanza pattern and a second pattern is devised for the epodes. However, following Abraham Cowley's 1656 interpretations of Pindar's odes, in which he abandoned this formal arrangement, this structure has largely disappeared in favour of varied stanza and line lengths. These odes are now often known as *irregular odes*, although they often retain the formal and public tone of the Pindaric. Wordsworth notably chose this mode for his 'Intimations of Immortality', a poem that explores Platonic ideas of the soul's relationship with the body, the child as a figure of potential ('Mighty Prophet! Seer blest!' l. 114), and the process of ageing as a metaphysical as well as a physical shift. Coleridge responded to some of its concerns in his own irregular 'Dejection: An Ode' (1817). Wordsworth's concern with the outer manifestations of inner feeling seems to fit with the irregular/ Pindaric ode's premise of lyrical expression in a public setting. He recollects how, as a child, he projected ideas onto the outside world around him:

> There was a time when meadow, grove, and stream,
> The earth, and every common sight,
>   To me did seem
>   Apparelled in celestial light,
> The glory and the freshness of a dream.
> It is not now as it has been of youre;
>   Turn wheresoe'er I may
>   By night or day
> The things which I have seen I now can see no more.
>
>   The rainbow comes and goes
>   And lovely is the rose,
>   The moon doth with delight
> Look round her when the heavens are bare;
>   Waters on a starry night
>   Are beautiful and fair;
>   The sunshine is a glorious birth;
>   But yet I know, where'er I go,
> That there hath passed away a glory from the earth.

> William Wordsworth (1807), 'Ode: Intimations of Immortality from Recollections of Early Childhood', ll. 1–19.

Horatian odes

The Horatian ode is an altogether quieter and more meditative form that intimates restraint and even modesty. They are named after the Roman poet Horace's songs (*Carmina*) and are notably *homostrophic*, which means that they employ a single stanza form that is repeated throughout the poem. Marvell's ode on Oliver Cromwell is a notable example because it responds to a public occasion, and so may be expected to adopt a Pindaric mode, but it adopts the reserved tones of one who makes a rather politic assessment of a tyrannical reformer:

> 'Tis madness to resist or blame
> The force of angry heaven's flame;
>   And if we would speak true,
>   Much to the man is due,
>
> Who from his private gardens, where
> He lived reservèd and austere
>   (As if his highest plot
>   To plant the bergamot),
>
> Could by industrious valor climb
> To ruin the great work of Time,
>   And cast the kingdom old
>   Into another mould;
>
> Andrew Marvell (1681), 'An Horatian Ode: Upon Cromwell's Return from Ireland', ll. 25–36.

As seen here, the Horatian ode often features simpler, more colloquial language than the Pindaric and, in other examples, suggests an occasion of private rather than public significance. However, they are still carefully constructed with a sense of order and progression in their regulated stanzas. Of significance is the Horatian ode's developing mode of contemplation, rather than the enthusiastic Pindaric ode of proclamation, as seen in Collins' memorial for his friend James Thomson (poet, 1700–1748):

> But thou, lorn stream, whose sullen tide
>   No sedge-crowned sisters now attend,
> Now waft me from the green hill's side,
>   Whose cold turf hides the buried friend!
>
> And see, the fairy valleys fade,
>   Dun night has veiled the solemn view!
>   Yet once again, dear parted shade,
>   Meek nature's child, again adieu!
>
> The genial meads, assigned to bless
>   Thy life, shall mourn thy early doom,
> Their hinds and shepherd girls shall dress
>   With simple hands thy rural tomb.
>
> William Collins (1749), 'Ode on the Death of Mr Thomson', ll. 29–40.

The late eighteenth century saw a profusion of odes and Collins' own experiments with the form (especially 'Ode on the Poetical Character' (1746), which has been recognized as a precursor to Romanticism) interestingly reach forward to the more overtly recognized period of great ode writing with the Romantic poets. Here the method of combining the Pindaric and Horatian modes (as indicated by the discussion of Wordsworth above) especially developed. Shelley's 'Ode to the West Wind' (1820) uses the regular stanza shape of the Horatian mode but is a poem of arrestingly Pindaric enthusiasm. Keats' 'Ode to Autumn' (1820) is often described as Horatian (it has regular stanzas and conducts its sensuous evocation through surprisingly simple diction), but some of his other celebrated odes from the same period (such as 'Ode on a Grecian Urn' or 'Ode to Psyche', which is written in an irregular mode) reach into the enthusiastic register of the Pindaric ode even though it is tracing an experience of intense and private meditation. Sometimes these 'hybrid' odes are known as *meditation odes* that feature:

- a detailed setting scene
- an extended meditation
- a final moment of revelation or insight.

The ode and parody

The ode's overtly serious tone and formal diction does tend to tempt others to puncture pomposity and so the 'mock ode' is a form often used for parody, seen in **light verse** or **doggerel** treatments. Odes on animals are a popular means of dismantling grandeur: see James Hogg's 'Ode to a Highland Bee' (1829), which teases at the mode generally and at Wordsworth's use of it particularly: 'Blest be thy heart, sweet Highland bee, | That thou pass'd by, and changed not me;' (ll. 25–6). An early instance is Wesley's ode to a pig:

> Harmonious *Hog* draw near, and from thy *beauteous Snowt*
>   Whilst we attend with Ear,
>   Like thine prick't up devou't;
>   To taste thy *Sugry voice*, which here, and there,
> With wanton Curls, vibrates around the circling Air,
>   Harmonious *Hog!* warble some *Anthem* out!
> As sweet as those which quiv'ring *Monks* in days of Y'ore,
>   With us did roar;
>
> Samuel Wesley (1685), 'A Pindaric on the Grunting of a Hog', ll. 18–25.

Read more

- Other noted Pindaric odes include Thomas Gray's 'The Bard' (1757) and Ben Jonson's 'A Pindaric Ode' (1640) that has the strophic movements labelled 'turn', 'counterturn' and 'stand'. Irregular odes include John Dryden's 'To the Pious Memory of the Accomplished Young Lady Mrs Anne Killigrew' (1686); Matthew Arnold's 'Rugby Chapel' (1867), which nevertheless has a meditative tone, and Richard Lovelace's 'The Snail' (1659).

- Twentieth-century experiments with the form include W. H. Auden's 'Ode to Terminus', which is Horatian in style and meditates on linguistic registers, the ordering of expression, modern technology, science and the posture of the poet; implicitly, therefore, it meditates on the ode form itself. Hart Crane's 'To Brooklyn Bridge' (1930) is also Horatian in style, arranged into quatrains. It shifts impressively between registers and melds together the Classical, the religious and the contemporary in its address of 'Thee [the bridge], across the harbor, silver paced' (l. 13).

Epigram

A short, sometimes witty poem that expresses a pointed or ingenious thought.

The epigram is the epitome of quick-wittedness. Tiny on the page, it makes grand effects, usually by puncturing endless long-windedness with a jab at the heart of the matter. Epigrams are not simply short poems; they are poems that summarize a complex notion in a phrase or two. They often hinge around two parts: a proposition may be presented and then swiftly answered, or an idea could be introduced before being overturned. This often translates into poems that have two **stanzas** or even just two lines. Frequently the shift in perspective is emphasized by the use of **rhyme** or **scheme** that create a pattern of sound and sense that wittily changes as wisdom dawns. Indeed, these features define the epigram. They may be close to *aphorisms* (pithy statements), but they differ because their poetic arrangement draws visual attention to the parallelisms or contradictions in epigrammatic thought and the revelations they make hinge on poetic devices (such as rhyme, **pun** or **metaphor**). Although they are brief, epigrams therefore exemplify the idea that figurative language makes us see the world from new perspectives. Indeed, the epigram's quickness leaves the reader to reflect on the poem's genius in afterthought, making the epigram a doorway onto larger vistas of meditation:

> What is an Epigram? a dwarfish whole,
> Its body brevity, and wit its soul.
>
> Samuel Taylor Coleridge (1802), 'Epigram'.

Unsurprisingly, given their bantering tone and incisive use of figurative language, epigrams are often found in **light verse** and particularly *vers de société* where they make wry reference to figures and events of significance to a particular social group. Indeed, epigrams can be incomprehensible without considerable commentary, as their arch style addresses an audience 'in the know' and relies more on suggestion than explanation. Epigrams often set such current myths in stone, as seen in Byron's epigram on John Keats. Referring to the hostile periodical reviews that Keats' poems received, the epigram not only savages the reviewers as would-be murderers, but also adds to the mythologizing of Keats as 'Defenceless' (Percy Bysshe Shelley (1821), *Adonais*, l. 239):

> Who kill'd John Keats?
>   'I,' says the Quarterly,
> So savage and Tartarly;
>   'Twas one of my feats.'
>
> Who shot the arrow?
>   'The poet-priest Milman
> (So ready to kill man)
>   Or Southey, or Barrow.'
>
> George Gordon (Lord Byron) (1821), 'John Keats'.

The epigram's savagery is not limited to public figures. It may even turn and bite at its reader, as Pope does here, apparently mocking not only the reader's empty-headedness but also, by implication, anyone who looks to epigrams for enlightenment. Here we are being teased: are epigrams clever or not? (Your pate is the crown of your head.)

> You beat your pate, and fancy wit will come:
> Knock as you please, there's nobody at home.
>
> Alexander Pope (1732), 'Epigram'.

Sometimes epigrams feel quick to mock and less eager to remedy, but in the best examples the classic stance of the epigram-writer – heckler from the stalls – is put to purpose by shining a light on inconsistency, hypocrisy or even immorality, suggesting that epigrams are the touchstone of liberal society. They may savagely criticize those in authority, as in Byron's attack on Castlereagh (whose actions were implicated in the massacre at St Peter's Fields in 1819):

> So Castlereagh has cut his throat! —The worst
> Of this is, —that his own was not the first.
>
> George Gordon (Lord Byron) (1821).

Epigrams may otherwise make a more meditative, wryly humorous comment on an oddly upturned society drifting away from freedom:

Where, where but here have Pride and Truth,
That long to give themselves for wage,
To shake their wicked sides at youth
Restraining reckless middle-age?

William Butler Yeats (1912), 'On Hearing that the Students of our New University have joined the Agitation against Immoral Literature'.

Epigrams needn't always be savage or indeed humorous. Their philosophy – that long-windedness can be punctured with sharp observation – creates a ratio (small to big) that can be turned to more solemn purpose, as when complex meditations resonate from the minute particulars of a phrase:

The Child is Father of the Man;
And I could wish my days to be
Bound each to each by natural piety.

William Wordsworth (1807), Epigram to *Ode: Intimations of Immortality from Recollections of Early Childhood*.

This example relates to the broader definition of 'epigram', which can mean 'a poem for inscription'. More precisely, inscribed poems are *epigraphs*, which derives directly from the Greek *epigraphein*, meaning to write on, or inscribe. Of course all poems may be inscribed (that is, written down), but the epigraph is designed to be written on an object other than a page, usually a building or a monument, but also, as in Wordsworth's example, metaphorically onto the body of a book (an epigraph is a short poem printed at the beginning of a book or a longer poem). If it is written for a grave or tomb it is called an **epitaph**. Technically an epigraph may be inscribed anywhere, as in Pope's example which holds together the two branches of epigram (wit and inscription):

I am his Highness' dog at Kew;
Pray tell me, sir, whose dog are you?

Alexander Pope (1738), 'Epigram engraved on the collar of a dog which I gave to His Royal Highness [Frederick, Prince of Wales, Father of George III]'.

Read more

- See Ogden Nash's **light verse** for many examples of witty and sometimes **nonsense** epigrams that play with the form's reputation for insight.

Epitaph

A poem inscribed on a tomb or grave.

The epitaph sits across two traditions: on the one hand it is linked to the short poem tradition of succinct summary, under the umbrella of the **epigram**. On the other, because it is written in the aftermath of death, it is linked to **elegy**. In the traditional epitaph these two impulses can be difficult to reconcile: the poet must be brief and yet not dismissive. However, as in the case of a resonant epigram, the epitaph may speak more movingly of life and loss than does a lengthy formal elegy. Traditionally the epitaph's shortness was necessary as the poem needed to fit onto the surface of a grave or tomb. This restriction is only evoked in some cases ('epitaph' sometimes operates as a synonym for elegy, and may be of any length). However, the epitaph should at least imply that it is written for a grave, and this location is often expressly acknowledged, making for poems that are disarmingly frank about the material remains of the dead: there is no escaping the fact that the poem's existence points simultaneously to the existence of a corpse (many will state, 'Here lies a woman' or 'Here rests a man'). This raises the question of mortal remains and often an epitaph will meditate on the relative lastingness of body, grave and verse:

> Here lies a most beautiful lady:
> Light of step and heart was she;
> I think she was the most beautiful lady
> That ever was in the West Country.
> But beauty vanishes; beauty passes;
> However rare—rare it be;
> And when I crumble, who will remember
> This lady of the West Country?
>
> Walter de la Mare (1914), 'An Epitaph'.

Browne responds to the epitaph's premise – that it must be joined to another art object (a monument) – by developing this into a **conceit** in which monuments and statues are indicators of deep grief. Indeed, such is the epitaph's power that it not only appears on marble, but it will prompt grievers to mirror it by becoming marble monuments to grief themselves (Niobe is a figure from Classical myth who turned to stone and wept endlessly for her dead children):

> Underneth this Marble Hearse;
> Lyes the subject of all verse,
> *Sidneys* sister; *Pembrookes* mother,

> Death, ere thou hast kill'd another,
> Faire, and learn'd, and good as shee,
> Time shall throw a dart at thee.
>
> Marble Pyles let no man rayse
> To her name; for after days;
> Some kinde woman borne as she
> Reading this; (Like Niobe,)
> Shall turne Marble, and become
> Both her mourner and her Tombe.

William Browne (1623), 'On the Countesse Dowager of Pembroke'.

Evidently the epitaph is an especially public form of grief-poem since strangers and loved-ones will view it; as such it can have a social purpose. Scodel writes very interestingly about the epitaph tradition as one in which notions of high and low, worthy and unworthy, major and minor, central and marginal are reordered by the guiding principle of remembrance. As has been seen so far, the epitaph may mark the death of a 'lady of the West Country' or a dowager countess since death does not discriminate and graves are the most common site for public recognition. Most movingly, as in Wordsworth's epitaph on a child, or in Ben Jonson's epitaph for his son, this democratizing drive is seen in poems for those whose lives had little chance to be recognized. The surface of the grave might well be the first and last canvas for the public acknowledgement of a child's life, and their epitaph is handed the responsibility not only of marking a loss, but also of finally establishing its significance:

> Farewell, thou child of my right hand, and joy;
>   My sinne was too much hope of thee, lov'd boy,
> Seven yeeres tho'wert lent to me, and I thee pay,
>   Exacted by thy fate, on the just day.
> O, could I loose all father, now. For why
>   Will man lament the state he should envie?
> To have so soone scap'd worlds, and fleshes rage,
>   And, if no other miserie, yet age?
> Rest in soft peace, and, ask'd say here doth lye
>   BEN. JONSON his best piece of *poetrie*.
> For whose sake, hence-forth, all his vowes be such,
>   As what he loves may never like too much.

Ben Jonson (1616), 'On my First Sonne'.

In the capitalized letters of the child's (and the father's) name we see the boy's headstone, his name carved neatly in stone, emerging with the poem before us. This occurs just as the poet admits that the child no longer materially exists, but has been translated into his father's 'best piece of poetrie'. The epitaph – a complex interface between the fleshly and the untouchable, the material and the immaterial, the remembered and the decayed – is given painful realization as the child who hardly lived is made enduringly present, but as text not flesh.

Read more

- See Edgar Lee Master's *Spoon River Anthology* (1915) (mentioned in **dramatic monologue**), which is a series of epitaph poems for a community.
- William Cowper wrote many epitaphs for birds and animals as well as for his contemporaries: 'Epitaph on a Hare' (1794); 'Epitaphium alterum' (1800); 'Epitaph on a redbreast' (1815); 'Epitaph on Fop' (1803); 'Epitaph on Mrs Higgins' (1803); 'Epitaph on Mr Chester' (1803).
- See Wordsworth's 'Essays on Epitaphs' [1812] (1876), in *The Prose Works of William Wordsworth*, W. J. B. Owen and Jane Worthington Smyser (eds) (1974), three volumes (Oxford: Clarendon Press).

Reference

Scodel, J. (1991), *The English Poetic Epitaph: Commemoration and Conflict from Jonson to Wordsworth* (Ithaca: Cornell University Press).

Dramatic monologue

A poem written as a speech by a speaker who is not the poet; it encourages the reader to question the speaker's authority or intention.

Dramatic monologues are often rather disconcerting poems to read. Although they are written in the first person, which suggests unmasked expression, the reader gradually realizes that a version of events is being presented and it is up to them to ascertain which other versions are being suppressed. As their name suggests, they allude to theatrical practices and we are encouraged to recognize the performance and stylization (often to the point of self-delusion on the part of the speaker) involved in any seemingly natural speech. A 'monologue' is an uninterrupted speech on the stage, and essentially what we find in a dramatic monologue is a speech delivered by a figure who is clearly not the poet themselves. Of course, many poems are written in voices different from the poet's. Yet, rather than becoming absorbed into the alternative world of a speaker, as one might in other treatments, the reader of a dramatic monologue is guided into establishing a critical distance on what the speaker is telling us. At the very least, the poem forces us to realize that there is a difference between how speakers present themselves and how they actually behave. The point in each of these realizations is that the poem is presented as an irony: what appears to be true is rarely the case. Dramatic monologues may use any arrangement of **metre**, **rhyme** or **line length** (although these tend to be regular poems rather than **free verse**), but the following aspects characterize the form:

- the direct speech of a character (not the poet) uttered at a crucial moment
- representation of the natural rhythms of speech (using colloquialisms, exclamations, pauses, dashes and ellipses) within a formal poetic frame
- a listener who is addressed within the poem, but their presence is only evident to the reader from clues and gestures given by the speaker
- an opening in mid-speech, creating immediacy, directness and the sense that the reader is overhearing a conversation.

The term 'dramatic monologue' did not gain currency until the late nineteenth century, but they emerged in the late 1830s in experiments by Robert Browning (published as 'Madhouse Cells' in 1836) and Tennyson (see 'Ulysses', 1842). Debate continues, however, regarding the form's genesis; as Alan Sinfield suggests, late Romantic experiments with performance and ironic self-presentation, often by female poets in the 1820s, seem precursors to or even early examples of the form. The cultural conditions surrounding the emergence of the dramatic monologue are complex, but they relate to a sense that poetry's place within culture was being questioned or even coming under threat and that the dramatic monologue, with its multiple ironies and shocking content, registered different responses to this development.

The dramatic monologue and sensational shock

As Joseph Bristow discusses, the early Victorian period saw poetry decline in popularity among the reading classes in favour of the growing attractions of the novel. The 'Newgate novel' – a brand of fiction subversively set within the criminal underworld – appeared in the 1830s and later developed into the 'Sensation novel' of the 1860s. Both pandered to readers' fascination with immoral behaviour, violence and retribution and stimulated readers' feelings to shock, suspense, intrigue and fear. In one tradition, the dramatic monologue reflects this cultural backdrop.[1]

Poems such as Browning's 'Porphyria's Lover' (1836), 'My Last Duchess' (1842), 'Soliloquy of the Spanish Cloister' (1842) and 'The Laboratory' (1844) are compelling, dramatic and tense presentations of speakers caught in states of delusional passion, irreligious resentment, murderous intent or even aftermath. They feature exclamation ('The colour's too grim!', 'Laboratory', l. 25), curses ('Zounds!'), and stutterings of rage ('Gr-r-r—there go, my heart's abhorrence!', 'Spanish', l. 1), and employ the language of the street more than the elevated diction of recognized poetry. Most overtly, they deliver the fantasy of watching the workings of the criminal mind. The deranged thought processes of the speakers are demonstrated in the twists and turns of their rhetoric, their flitting from subject to subject, and often in the alarmingly swift leap from a foreboding expectation of disaster to realization that execution has occurred and cannot be stopped. Readers who might have expected to enter into a poetic experience disconcertingly find themselves becoming forced witnesses to crime. Furthermore, the speakers who present their criminal desires or activities do so without recognizing their moral implications and the poem operates as though there are no consequences: as the speaker in 'Porphyria's Lover' boasts, 'And yet God has not said a word!' (l. 60). The onus is put on the reader to create a moral framework for the poem: the dramatic monologue does not provide such a safety net itself.

Unlike the popular fiction that arguably prompts some of the dramatic monologue's content (which was still establishing itself as a tradition) these poems forced readers to encounter the criminally insane within the framework of culturally 'civilized' poetry. Such a clash speaks to the anxieties that underlie a society's regulation of culture and standards of normality. Deranged characters presenting themselves as though they are sane can be more alarming than those who rave uncontrollably, because this is an assault on the patterns of behaviour that society cherishes as a protection against criminality. Such poems challenge us to be disconcerted by the civilizing effect of poetry (what madness does it mask?); they force us to think about how precarious the veneer of civilization can be; how apt it is to be destroyed from within. This is seen in Browning's 'My Last Duchess'. Readers of this poem must pick up clues (rather as a detective in the contemporaneously emerging crime novel might) to piece together a shocking story of marriage. The reader realizes that the Duke, who presents himself as grand, sophisticated, flexible and gentlemanly is in fact deranged by jealousy and seems to have ordered murders on the grounds of injured pride. However, such derangement is contained with the civilizing bounds of **pentameter rhyming couplets**, against which the Duke's chattering exerts an insidious pressure, almost breaking their formal pattern with a simmering violence that hints at his abuse of the wife who humiliated him with her generous smiles for other men:

> [...] O Sir, she smiled, no doubt,
> Whene'er I passed her; but who passed without
> Much the same smile? This grew; I gave commands;
> Then all smiles stopped together. There she stands
> As if alive. [...]
>
> Robert Browning (1842), 'My Last Duchess', ll. 43–7.

A decade or so later, Elizabeth Barrett Browning, in her dramatic monologue, 'The Runaway Slave' (1850), used the shock of witnessing a mother recount how she murdered her own child to imply the barbarity of slavery. Swinburne, meanwhile, used his *Poems* (1866) to present the fevered speech of the sexually voracious woman. 'Anactoria', 'spoken' by the early-Greek lyric poetess Sappho, does not distinguish between sexual desire and violent desire as she vocalizes her passion for Anactoria through descriptions of sadistic wishes:

> Ah that my mouth for Muse's milk were fed
> On the sweet blood thy sweet small wounds had bled!
> That with my tongue I felt them, and could taste
> The faint flakes from thy bosom to the waist!
> That I could drink thy veins as wine, and eat
> Thy breasts like honey! that from face to feet
> Thy body were abolished and consumed,
> And in my flesh thy very flesh entombed!

> Algernon Charles Swinburne (1866), 'Anactoria', ll. 107–14.

Swinburne's technical command of the rhythm of these lines sees him maintain five beats per line, but regularly alter their pace: like 'My Last Duchess' this is an image of the uncontrolled becoming restrained, but always with the threat of anarchy. Significantly, the poem is littered with terms that relate to poetry and harmony – 'feet', 'paces', 'pauses', 'lyre', 'music', 'notes', and so on – which add up to the implication that the violence taking place *in* the poem may also be said to be happening *to* the poem (see Chapter 3 of Prins (1999) for more discussion of this idea). Hence the dramatic monologue is importantly differentiated from other forms of writing and identifies as poetry, but exerts an almost-terrifying violence upon what we understand and accept as poetry.

The dramatic monologue, delusion and disillusion

As mentioned, many of the speakers in dramatic monologues are severely deluded, either in terms of their perspective on the world or in terms of their ability to recognize their own behavioural patterns. Nevertheless, they appear to achieve a strong sense of self through the process of relating their experiences to an audience. In the case of the Duke in 'My Last Duchess', this presentation is wildly divergent from the 'reality' we infer, but in any case the poem intrigues us by showing identity and even expression as a process of performance. In the less overtly shocking tradition of dramatic monologue, it is this very process of identification that forms the subject of the poem.

An early example is Tennyson's 'Ulysses'. In this poem we hear Ulysses (Odysseus) as an older man, now returned to Ithaca (following the trials and tribulations of his journey home – see Homer's *The Odyssey*), but unable to settle to a life of restful kingship after a life of travelling intrigue. Over the course of the poem he decides to leave his kingdom to be administered by his son Telemachus while he returns to a life of travel dictated by the will 'To strive, to seek, to find, and not to yield' (l. 70). Prior to this decision, Ulysses crystallizes his predicament in the line, 'I am become a name:' (l. 11). To 'become a name', the poem suggests, is to have an existence that reaches beyond one's immediate circumstances; as Ulysses claims, 'I am a part of all that I have met;' (l. 18). It is this name – and all it entails – that Ulysses cannot bear to leave behind. This translation from man to myth is the secondary story of this poem: as well as telling of an older man resisting the move towards retirement and decline, the poem also commentates on the transformation of an individual into a 'name', a myth. This involves Ulysses promoting himself as a man of thrusting energy and overlooking the fact that he is, arguably, deserting his duty.

We read this as a lyrical expression of feeling on the part of Ulysses, but we are also directed to treat that expression as an object of analysis and critique. Overarching this dynamic between lyricism and analysis is the fact that the poem too has a claim on the name that this man has 'become': 'Ulysses' is the name of the speaker and of the poem. Doubling up in this way, and drawing explicit attention to that in line 11, means that Tennyson's poem concludes the movement between man and myth (or speech and poem) that the dramatic monologue describes. This reflective quality, where dramatic monologues simultaneously perform and analyse actions, defines the form and, for influential critics such as Isobel Armstrong, Victorian poetry itself, making the dramatic monologue the most overt example of a widespread proliferation of 'double poems'.

This tradition of simultaneous analysis and expression persists in poems such as Browning's 'The Bishop Orders His Tomb', in which a pompous and self-aggrandizing prelate lies on his deathbed making lavish demands for an ostentatious monument to be built in his memory:

> Did I say basalt for my slab, sons? Black—
> 'T was ever antique-black I meant! How else
> Shall ye contrast my frieze to come beneath?
> The bas-relief in bronze ye promised me,
> Those Pans and Nymphs ye wot of, and perchance
> Some tripod, thyrsus, with a vase or so,
> The Saviour at his sermon on the mount,
> Saint Praxed in a glory, and one Pan
> Ready to twitch the Nymph's last garment off [.]
>
> Robert Browning (1845), 'The Bishop Orders His Tomb at St Praxed's Church', ll. 53–61.

The only 'monument' to the bishop that materializes, however, is the poem that grows up around him and across the page, making his a monument not to wealth and grandeur but one to irony and lasciviousness. We are directed to listen askance to the bishop's utterance (mirroring, indeed, those who gather around his bedside) and recognize the absurdly distorted self-aggrandizement that the bishop carries out. In other treatments that scepticism is gradually drawn more and more intimately in the central workings of the poem itself. In 'Andrea del

Sarto' (1855) Browning uses the story of a once-great but now-disappointed artist to meditate on artistic and moral failure. He admits, 'And I'm the weak-eyed bat no sun should tempt | Out of the grange whose four walls make his world' ('Andrea del Sarto', ll. 169–70). In such glimpses the speaker momentarily adopts the stance of the dramatic monologue's reader – not so much performing his identity but analysing it.

In such treatments the dramatic monologue is no longer aligned with speakers' confident presentation of false versions of themselves, but instead becomes the form that peers most intensely at the construction of selfhood. As we watch a speaker construct and deconstruct himself almost obsessively, we are effectively observing a magnified version of the impulse to fashion and adopt a voice for poetic expression. In this way, the dramatic monologue is a risky form that uses a poem to articulate a crisis in poetic power, as may be seen in T. S. Eliot's (1917) 'The Love Song of J. Alfred Prufrock'. The speaker here is arguably also a 'weak-eyed bat' who squirms in the glare of expectation that, as the protagonist in a poem, he step up to the plate. Yet Prufrock's poem is an exercise in prevarication and delay, its protagonist only ever the 'Footman' in a scene, a figure who, rather than 'becoming a name' in the monologue tradition, admits 'I have seen the moment of my greatness flicker' (l. 84). The dramatic monologue, arguably, has swallowed its own tail: so acutely does it anticipate how it will be read that the speaker cannot actually take control of how it is written.

The implications of dramatic monologue

As has been seen, the dramatic monologue repeatedly puts poetry at risk – of condemnation through shocking content, of incomprehension from a reading public unused to finding rough and ready speech in poetry, and of internal collapse driven by its own obsessively sceptical and reflective nature. However, it is a remarkably persistent form that seems to thrive on the risks it takes; Randal Jarrell hints that the dramatic monologue's inherent scepticism sat more comfortably with twentieth-century sensibility than did other more direct forms of poetic expression: 'the dramatic monologue, which once had depended for its effect upon being a departure from the norm of poetry, now became in one form or another the norm' (p. 12). However, despite its shuffling, indeed paralysed manifestation in 'Prufrock', the dramatic monologue also carries with it considerable political potential.

The form's view of identity as performance thinks about the place of performance in all identity, including direct lyrical expression. Such ideas have particular resonance for those who ask how gender, racial or sexual ideology forces individual identity to become a performance, making all lyrical expression a dramatic monologue. Further, writers took the dramatic monologue's interest in encounters between speakers and listeners to examine the power dynamics in such meetings. For example, the question of prostitution as either a moral or a social problem, in which either men or women take control of authority, was played out in a series of nineteenth-century dramatic monologues by Dante Gabriel Rossetti ('Jenny', 1870), Amy Levy ('Magdalen', 1889) and Augusta Webster ('A Castaway', 1870). The latter example in particular explores the effects of giving voice to the usually silenced and invites us to apply the scrutiny we direct at the speaker of a dramatic monologue to the larger social groups they represent. So, the dramatic monologue's holding together of action and analysis gives it dramatic potential, but also sustained critical potential: it replaces the idea that poetry is an escape from society with the insistence that poetry is one of the sharpest tools that may be employed to probe society's inner workings.

Read more

- How might the dramatic monologue, despite its apparent distance and theatricality, become a confessional form? Tennyson suggested that 'Ulysses' expressed more of his feelings of loss than did his long elegy, *In Memoriam A. H. H.* (1850). How might using a persona allow emotions and actions to be addressed more unflinchingly than a lyric?
- Where do we draw the line between lyric and dramatic monologue? Consider Sylvia Plath's 'Lady Lazarus' (1965), for example: might this be a dramatic monologue? Or is it a **personification** of despair? Why might it be useful to distinguish between the two?
- Twentieth-century examples of dramatic monologues often engage directly or indirectly with their Victorian predecessors, but in what spirit? Consider Richard Howard's *Untitled Subjects: Poems* (1969) – often compared with Browning – or Ezra Pound's experiments (see *A Lume Spento*, 1908) and Peter McDonald's *Adam's Dream* (1996): are these Victorian dramatic monologues relocated to other times and places, or rewritings of them? How modern is the dramatic monologue?
- Consider Edgar Lee Master's *Spoon River Anthology* (1915). This is a series of **epitaph** poems that appear to be dramatic monologues spoken from beyond the grave. Is this a vision of society in decline, or the consolidation of a community remembered?

References

Armstrong, I. (1993), *Victorian Poetry: Poetry, Politics, Poetics* (London: Routledge).

Bristow, J. (2000), *The Cambridge Companion to Victorian Poetry* (Cambridge: Cambridge University Press).

Jarrell, R. (1953), *Poetry and the Age* (New York: Vintage Books).

Prins, Y. (1999), *Victorian Sappho* (Virginia: University of Virginia Press).

Sinfield, A. (1977), *Dramatic Monologue: Critical Idiom* (London: Methuen).

Note

1. Thanks to Tom Martin for drawing my attention to the significance of this point.

> ## Blank verse
> Lines of unrhymed **iambic pentameter**.

Since the sixteenth century blank verse has been associated with drama and with serious, often meditative poetry. Henry Howard, Earl of Surrey devised it for his translations of Virgil's *Aeneid* (c. 1540), but it soon became the preferred mode for drama written for the Elizabethan and Jacobean stage. This dramatic use persisted even into the twentieth century, and blank verse was used for modern **epic** by writers such as Milton, Wordsworth and Barrett Browning. Romantic poets such as Charlotte Smith, Shelley and Coleridge used it for contemplative **lyrics** and, despite this air of cultural orthodoxy, blank verse's lack of rhyme sees it appear within or alongside **free verse** experiments. American Modernist writers such as Harold Hart Crane and Wallace Stevens wrote in blank verse and parts of T. S. Eliot's 'The Waste Land' (1922) and *The Four Quartets* (1944), among others of his writings, feature blank verse passages.

As is evident from just this list, blank verse is versatile and serves skilled practitioners in vast range of purposes. The underlying characteristic of blank verse, however, is arguably regularity and restraint. Its fixed number and type of **feet** (five per line, each stressed 'de-dum') risks tedium and monotony when produced on a grand scale (and much blank verse is produced on precisely this scale). Yet when a poet manages this underlying pulse of order with verve and innovation blank verse is wonderfully regulated yet dramatic, harmonious and engaging.

To clarify the terms used to discuss variation in blank verse, check Chapter 3 on **prosody**, but to begin with this example of dramatic blank verse (a speech of fatherly grief) the syllables that could receive emphasis or **stress** when spoken aloud are bolded:

> *Hieronimo:* Ay, **now** I **know** thee, **now** thou **nam'st** thy **son**;
> Thou **art** the **live**ly **im**age **of** my **grief**;
> With**in** thy **face**, my **sor**rows I may **see**.
> Thy **eyes** are **gummed** with **tears**, thy **cheeks** are **wan**,
> Thy **fore**head **troub**led, and thy **mutt**'ring **lips**
> **Mur**mur **sad** words ab**rupt**ly **bro**ken **off**;
> By **force** of **wind**y **sighs** thy **spir**it **breathes**,
> And **all** this **sor**row **ris**eth **for** thy **son**;
> And **self**same **sor**row **feel** I for **my** son.
> Come **in**, old **man**, thou **shalt** to **Is**abel.
> **Lean** on my **arm**; I **thee**, thou **me** shalt **stay**,
> And **thou**, and **I**, and **she**, will **sing** a **song**,

> Three **parts** in **one**, but **all** of **dis**cords **framed**.—
> Talk **not** of **cords**, but **let** us **now** be **gone**,
> For **with** a **cord** Horatio was **slain**.

Thomas Kyd (1592), *The Spanish Tragedy*, III: 13, ll. 161–75.

In this passage of Kyd's revenge tragedy, the grieving father projects his own distress onto the face of an 'Old Man'. The passage moves between the external signs of grief (gummed eyes, pale cheeks, muttering speech) and the emotional experience that lies behind them, slipping between the colloquial and conversational and the reflective and abstract: this demonstrates how blank verse can hold several registers together at once. Thus Kyd changes the blank verse according to the spoken rhythms enacted: 'Murmur sad words abruptly broken off' appropriately introduces reversed **feet** (**trochees** (dum-de) rather than **iambs** (de-dum)) to put a stress on '**mur**mur' and '**sad** words'. The same effect is achieved in line 169, which ends on two trochees as Hieronimo's grief mirrors the old man's face ('thy **son**' in line 168 is reversed and answered by '**my** son' in 169). Line 1's opening trochee puts a stress on 'Lean', but from there the weight is taken on the 'arm' and the iambic regularity returns, providing a stable prop for Hieronimo's speech just as his arm does for the old man. Line 172's commas divide the line into perfect iambic feet 'And **thou**, and **I**, and **she**', as is half acknowledged by 'sing a song', suggesting a comforting harmony (which is what blank verse can deliver) that will salve fevered pain. This rhythmic variation – which keeps the blank verse alive to subtle shifts in human emotion – is matched also by the moves between **end-stopped** lines ('Within thy face, my sorrows I may see.') that suggest achieved significance and **enjambment** where meaning, like the words themselves, is a little more elusive ('thy mutt'ring lips | Murmur sad words').

This is the advantage of blank verse: it holds lines together with regularity and a sometimes consoling, sometimes thundering, sometimes merely entertaining consistency, but it also accommodates the variations of human speech. Of course, the most famous blank versifier is Shakespeare and he, following other contemporary playwrights, developed 'codes' in which blank verse not only followed patterns of speech, but also could indicate meaning, style, significance and culture to the audience. For example, in *King Lear* Edmund (the bastard son of the Duke of Gloucester) speaks in prose when he is conversing with (and deceiving) his brother; when Edgar leaves, Edmund shifts into blank verse to indicate a moment of self-reflection, meditation and contemplation. When the audience hears Edmund's internal monologue, they hear it in blank verse:

> *Edmund*: I advise you to the best. Go armed. I am no honest man if there be any good meaning towards you. I have told you what I have seen and heard but faintly, nothing like the image and horror of it. Pray you, away.

> *Edgar:* Shall I hear from you anon?
> *Edmund:* I do serve you in this business. [*Exit* Edgar]
> A credulous father, and brother noble,
> Whose nature is so far from doing harms
> That he suspects none; on whose foolish honesty
> My practices ride easy. I see the business.
> Let me, if not by birth, have lands by wit.
> All with me's meet that I can fashion fit.

William Shakespeare, *King Lear* (quarto text, 1608) I: 2, ll. 164–71.

The cultural indicators of blank verse are seen across Shakespeare's plays: for example, Ophelia (see *Hamlet*, 1623) is abused by Hamlet in prose, laments his disordered behaviour in blank verse, speaks in garbled prose (and song) when she is herself deranged later in the play, and is elegized by Gertrude in blank verse again, so forming one 'code' in which blank verse is used for meditative, solemn or reflective passages. In comedies such as *Twelfth Night* characters move between employing blank verse in conversation with those they address equally (on subjects such as love, philosophy and melancholy), and falling into prose when addressing employed fools or other members of the household on matters of everyday business, bawdiness or jesting.

Given this manner of cultural conditioning it is unsurprising that writers such as Milton (in *Paradise Lost*, 1667) and Wordsworth (in *The Prelude*, [c. 1805]) employed blank verse for solemn and high-minded purpose (Wordsworth's autobiographical piece may even be thought of as a sustained soliloquy) and that Romantic poets used blank verse for contemplative lyrics, such as Coleridge's 'Frost at Midnight' (1798), which creep upon the poet and the reader ('The frost performs its secret ministry | Unhelped by any wind', ll. 1–2), gathering in strength with the rolling blank verse. Other poets such as Shelley and Wordsworth (in 'Tintern Abbey', 1798) used blank verse to follow the shifting-yet-modulated effects of the natural world on the contemplative poet:

> The everlasting universe of things
> Flows through the mind, and rolls its rapid waves,
> Now dark, now glittering, now reflecting gloom,
> Now lending splendour, where from secret spring
> The source of human thought its tribute brings
> Of waters, with a sound but half its own,

Percy Bysshe Shelley (1817), 'Mont Blanc', ll. 1–6.

Charlotte Smith, meanwhile, converged these natural effects by using blank verse to draw together her experience of her local landscape as beautiful, sublime and lyrical with an eye for historical and scientific-botanical accuracy:

> An early worshipper at Nature's shrine,
> I loved her rudest scenes – warrens and heaths,
> And yellow commons, and birch-shaded hollows,
> And hedgerows, bordering unfrequented lanes
> Bowered with wild roses, and the clasping woodbine
> Where purple tassels of the tangling vetch
> With bittersweet and bryony inweave,
> And the dew fills the silver bindweed's cups –

Charlotte Smith (1807), *Beachy Head*, ll. 117–20.

In poems such as these, which stretch on at great length, passages of blank verse may be divided into thematic movements as they would in prose; these are known as *verse paragraphs* (they are indented as a prose paragraph may be, as seen in the Smith example here). This is the closest thing to a **stanza** that is found in blank verse.

In the nineteenth century blank verse appears in forms that collapse distinctions between lyric and drama, such as in **dramatic monologues** by Tennyson and Browning, and in the hybrid between verse and prose that is Barrett Browning's *Aurora Leigh* (1856), suggesting the fluidity and adaptability of blank verse. The unrhymed iambic pentameter has persisted in a good deal of writing since the nineteenth century, testifying perhaps to its adaptability and to the desire to engage with its cultural associations.

Read more

- See the plays by Elizabethan Jacobean dramatists such as Marlowe, Thomas Middleton, John Ford and Jonson for various treatments of blank verse: some are very fluid and experimental with their use of the line; others stick more rigidly to the **metre**.
- See W. B. Yeats (1903), *The Old Age of Queen Maeve*. How does Yeats use blank verse to weave different traditions together? How does the blank verse relate to the **ballad** tradition and to the lyric tradition, which are also evoked in this poem?
- Poetry written as free verse often includes fragments or even sustained passages of blank verse. Why might free verse tolerate this form of metrical poetry but reject others?
- See twentieth-century drama, such as *The Murder in the Cathedral* (1935) by T. S. Eliot. How does this balance tradition with innovation and endorsement with subversion?

2.2 Fixed forms

These forms stipulate precisely the length of the poem, its use of rhyme, often its use of metre, and sometimes its use of language. These are often thought of as elaborate, intricately arranged pieces of poetry, and a poet might choose them in order to set particularly pressurizing, and so potentially strengthening, restrictions on their expression.

Sonnet

A 14-line poem of rhyming **iambic pentameter**.

The sonnet, either alone or in sequence, has a long and illustrious heritage in Western tradition: it was importantly shaped by Italian writers, but embraced enthusiastically in English practice. Sonnets are noted for strict formal patterning and poets often make much of their tight, enclosed shape. Etymologically 'sonnet' derives from 'son', a diminutive of song, from the Latin *sonus*, 'sound'. It is linked especially with love poetry and many influential sequences, such as Sidney's, use the customs of **courtly love**. However, the sonnet has also been put to political purpose, used for religious praise, and served to express melancholia and despair. Further, the sonnet as love poetry is by no means restricted to heterosexual courtly custom: sonnets often build their **conceits** from mapping various human bonds (erotic, familial, spousal, fraternal) onto a form that evokes the distant and prescribed formulations of convention. The material structure of the form itself propels these and other contradictions. Despite only containing 14 lines, sonnets feature a 'turn' or 'volta' that divides the sonnet into two. This introduces a vital dynamic of change, which challenges the poet not only to express an emotion or proposal succinctly, but also to explore it or 'answer' its proposition. Sonnets consequently raise the stakes for poets: they must use the pressure of restricted space to heighten emotion, maintain momentum, and reach conclusion. The results stand as some of the most affecting displays of poetic flair. English sonnets fall into two main categories (the **rhyme schemes** are marked vertically). (See over).

Note that this layout is sometimes used on the page, but more commonly a sonnet is printed as a continuous block of 14 lines, so you need to examine the rhyme scheme to identify the type. A Petrarchan sonnet divides its 14 lines into an octave (eight) and a sestet (six); the Shakespearean sonnet has three quatrains (four lines each) and a couplet (two).

The volta

The volta, or turn, of a sonnet is its moment of shift. This might be emotional or logical, and may suggest progression, or antithesis. Whichever way, it is vital to the sonnet's sense of structural integrity. As demonstrated overleaf, the volta actually creates a sense of imbalance as its position makes the sonnet 'top-heavy'. The difficulty the sonneteer faces is to right this imbalance by making the shorter section paradoxically carry the weight of answering or summarizing

The Poetry Toolkit

Petrarchan or Italian sonnet

Octave (8-lined group)	a
	b
	b
	a
	a
	b
	b
	a

Volta

Sestet (6-lined group)	c or c
	d d
	c e
	d c
	c d
	d e

Shakespearean or English sonnet

Quatrain (4-lined group)	a
	b
	a
	b

Quatrain	c
	d
	c
	d

Quatrain	e
	f
	e
	f

Volta

Couplet (2-lined group)	g
	g

the multiple implications suggested in the opening sections. Particularly in the Shakespearean sonnet this difficulty is heightened by the need to create development rather than repetition. You might think of the three quatrains in terms of a screw that tightens with each turn until the final pitch of tension is reached in the volta and the sonnet's 'argument' is answered in the space of a couplet. The Petrarchan sonnet's action works a little like a barred door: the octet represents the impenetrability of a lock, the volta the fitting of a key and the sestet its unlocking and release. Gerard Manley Hopkins suggested that it is this imbalanced ratio between parts that actually identifies a sonnet, rather than the number of lines used (p. 155). He tested this with several groups of sonnets that extend the formal shape to its limits, breaking apart the sonnet's rhythm, rhyme and line lengths with thrilling and emotional results (see his 'St Beuno' sonnets [c. 1877] and the so-called 'Terrible' sonnets, or 'Sonnets of Desolation' [c. 1885–1886]). Shakespeare's 'Sonnet 20' shifts between the two conventional structures:

> A woman's face with nature's own hand painted,
> Hast thou, the master mistress of my passion;
> A woman's gentle heart, but not acquainted
> With shifting change, as is false women's fashion:
> An eye more bright than theirs, less false in rolling,
> Gilding the object whereupon it gazeth;
> A man in hue all hues in his controlling,

Which steals men's eyes and women's souls amazeth.
And for a woman wert thou first created;
Till Nature, as she wrought thee, fell a-doting,
And by addition me of thee defeated,
By adding one thing to my purpose nothing.
But since she prick'd thee out for women's pleasure,
Mine be thy love and thy love's use their treasure.

William Shakespeare (1609), 'Sonnet 20'.

Often considered to address a male muse, this sonnet's quatrains play with ideas of gender by comparing the young man's beauty with first a woman's face (quatrain 1), then a women's eyes (quatrain 2) and then, imagining 'Mother Nature' to have created him as she would a woman, the sonnet introduces a comparison with women's bodies (quatrain 3). However, the speaker is forced to recognize that while his beloved may offer an ideal combination of female loveliness with male steadiness (women are associated with falsity, shift and fashion; men with control and sustained gaze), Nature's decision to add male genitalia to this beautiful creature ('By adding one thing to my purpose nothing') breaks this androgyny and settles the case in favour of the speaker's rivals, women. Taking the sonnet volta's cue to effect a change here, he must make the best of a bad situation and respond to the quatrains' 'problem' by using the couplet to claim the young man's love for himself while women have his body ('their treasure', relating to the 'prick' of line 13, suggesting his seed, which could impregnate their womb). So the couplet cleverly concedes victory to heterosexuality while acknowledging love between men, even elevating it to a plane of purity in opposition to the bawdiness associated with male–female relations. The sonnet makes skilful use of the English late volta by taking the fact that couplets (being two lines) tend to produce pairings and running with it, introducing a **chiasmus** in line 14 (a crossover between two notions) that sums up the whole sonnet's delight in the two-faceted 'master-mistress'. Yet the Italian influence remains even here: the octave sets out male beauty to be gazed upon, but the 'And' of line 9 shifts perspective – at the Petrararchan volta position – and the sestet must face the implications of such wonderful androgyny. Experimentation and combinations of convention are strong traditions in sonneteering, and even sequenced sonnets often vary their rhyme scheme or line length across their course.

The sonnet in sequence: varieties of love

Shakespeare's sonnet is one of a sequence (of 154); in creating such a sequence Shakespeare followed Italian writers such as Dante (*Vita Nuova*) and Petrarch (*Canzone*) and English writers Philip Sidney (*Astrophil and Stella*, 1591) and Edmund Spenser (*Amoretti*, 1595). Using courtly love convention, a sequence will traditionally chart the course of an infatuation on the part of the sonneteer for a 'lady'. His love is often dogged by her neglect of him, providing an opportunity for the sonneteer to devise ever more inventive literary formulations of his nevertheless constant love. This is matched by innovative descriptions of the lady's beauty, meaning that moments of despair are offset by the bliss of glimpsed success. The sonneteer's challenge is to combine these short-lived emotional highs and lows (suited to the tightness of the sonnet form) with a sustained and interlinked narrative that demonstrates the beloved's enduring appeal: we might liken the sonnet sequence to a necklace of individual beads strung together to form an attractive whole. However, these sequences' celebration of a 'lady' has been criticized (sometimes over-simply) for their implied silencing of the woman into a muse position, in which she inspires but does not speak, as, for example, when Sidney's Stella is likened to a book for male readers:

> Who will in fairest book of Nature know
>   How Virtue may best lodged in beauty be,
>   Let him but learn of *Love* to read in thee,
> Stella, those fair lines which true goodness show.

> Philip Sidney (1591), '71', from *Astrophil and Stella*, ll. 1–4.

As such, the sonnet tradition itself has been associated with male framing of women, emphasized by the restrictive shape of the form itself. Christina Rossetti described the women of sonnet tradition as 'donna innominate' (nameless ladies) and criticized the tradition for hiding women's 'tender' feelings under male literary flourish. She responded by writing an intricate sequence of sonnets in the female voice (*Monna innominata*, 1880):

> I dream of you to wake: would that I might
>   Dream of you and not wake but slumber on;
>   Nor find with dreams the dear companion gone,
> As Summer ended Summer birds take flight.
> In happy dreams I hold you full in sight,
>   I blush again who waking look so wan;
>   Brighter than sunniest day that ever shone,
> In happy dreams your smile makes day of night.
> Thus only in a dream we are at one,
>   Thus only in a dream we give and take
>   The faith that maketh rich who take or give;
>   If thus to sleep is sweeter than to wake,
>   To die were surely sweeter than to live,
> Tho' there be nothing new beneath the sun.

> Christina Rossetti (1880), '3' of *Monna Innominata*.

Note Rossetti's use of the Petrarchan sonnet form: here the octave sets out a dream vision in which the female exerts the gaze and implies erotic feeling in a blush. She also employs **Petrarchan conceits**, comparing the beloved's smile to the breaking day. However this sonnet hints at the disturbing sides to such conventional loving by aligning the female-spoken sonnet with dream and mirage and by pursuing, in the sestet, the logic that says that if dreaming brings the beloved nearer then extending sleep to death must be desired.

Women had used the sonnet innovatively before this: Charlotte Smith's experimental collection *Elegiac Sonnets* (1784–1786) explore the effects of genre on sonnet shape and expression creating a series of melancholic poems that compare Smith's material circumstances with various traditions of literary emotionalism. These concerns echo some of those of Mary Wroth's extraordinary sequence, *Pamphilia to Amphilanthus* (1621), which demonstrate a poignant wariness of love, often characterized as captivity, despite all attempts to evade it. Her answering sestets, such as the one which ends 'But O my hurt makes my lost heart confess | I love, and must: So farewell liberty.' ('16' of the sequence, ll. 13–14), signify more the closing of a trap than the unlocking of a problem. This notion of being trapped (by love, and by the tight sonnet form) prefigures Elizabeth Barrett Browning's opening to her sequence, *Sonnets from the Portuguese* (1850), in which love masters her by drawing her 'backward by the hair' ('I' of the sequence, l. 11). Written in anticipation of her marriage to Robert Browning, this sequence is remarkable for replacing the usually distant and unrequited love of sonnet tradition with the closeness of near-conjugal bonds. George Meredith's response to marriage, however, was altogether more jaded: his sequence, *Modern Love* (1862) uses distorted sonnets (each has 16 lines) to chart the bitter decline and distortion of marital relations.

Sonnet tradition, of course, is not restricted to heterosexual love. Shakespeare's sonnets, as suggested, address a male muse in loving terms and are an important influence on gay literature, along with other sonnet sequences, such as Michelangelo Buoranotti's. As John Holmes has explored, the gender ambiguity and sensuality of Dante Gabriel Rossetti's sequence, *The House of Life* (1870) also inspired other male writers, such as J. A. Symonds (*Animi Figura*, 1882) to express repressed desire for other men. More recently, Marilyn Hacker's sequence, *Love, Death, and the Changing of the Seasons* (1986) charts a lesbian love affair, and Edmund Miller's (non-sequential) collection, *The Go-Go Boy Sonnets* (2004) celebrates icons of the New York gay club scene.

Exploring other loving bonds, Augusta Webster created a touching sequence of Petrarchan sonnets exploring a mother's love for her daughter (*Mother and Daughter: An Uncompleted Sonnet Sequence*, 1895), which domesticates imagery from love sonnets only to use it to face a mother's deepest fear: 'But looking on the dawn that is her face | To know she too is Death's seems misbelief;' ('XV' of the sequence, l. 9). This parental sonneteering has been revived more recently by Don Paterson in 'Waking with Russell' and 'The Thread' (2004).

The religious sonnet

Linking to the love tradition sonnets are often used to express the love of faithful (or tested) religious devotion. Hopkins' sonnets, mentioned above, daringly combine divine love or faith with earthly and erotic love: this is seen in the language employed, but also in the very decision to use a sonnet (a material form associated with earthly love) to address faith (an abstract notion that looks beyond the material). This follows the examples of Petrarch and Dante, whose sonnet sequences also chart the fraught and passionate transformation of earthly female beauty into a divine symbol of purity. John Donne's 'Holy Sonnets' (1633) radicalize this movement by using sexual metaphor in a theological setting while Wilfred Owen arrestingly merges the spiritual with the earthly in 'Maundy Thursday', a delicate sonnet that uses repeated kisses to intimate the intersection of the abstract with the material at the centre of the Christian Eucharist: '(And kissing, kissed the emblem of a creed.)' (l. 5). More recently, Louis MacNeice's 'Sunday Morning' (1935) evokes the muffling of significance on a secular Sunday, a day likened to 'A small eternity, a sonnet self-contained in rhyme' (l. 10). R. S. Thomas' informal sonnets explore the unconventional spaces that become (or seek to become) hallowed by divine presence: 'The Moor' (1966) and 'The Empty Church' (1978) engage especially with the volta, using its moment of pause and transformation as a **metaphor** for the unseen working of prayer.

The political sonnet

Although associated with the private intensity of love, faith, eroticism or care, the sonnet has also had a considerable public role. John Milton used it (in both Shakespearean and Petrarchan forms, although he subtly alters their fixity with devices such as **enjambment**) to voice his Protestant politics, as in his controversial endorsement of Oliver Cromwell ('To the Lord General Cromwell', 1694). The massacre of the Waldenses sect in 1655 provoked Milton's wrath, voiced in a sonnet that uses the sestet's quick succession of rhymes to chart the rising emotion evoked by news of 'martyred blood and ashes sow[n] | O'er all th' Italian fields' ('On the Late Massacre in Piedmont' (1673), ll. 10–11). Such imagery was angrily revived in Shelley's 'England in 1819', written in response to the brutally suppressed public rally in St Peter's Field, near Manchester:

> An old, mad, blind, despised, and dying King;
> Princes, the dregs of their dull race, who flow
> Through public scorn—mud from a muddy spring;
> Rulers who neither see nor feel nor know,
> But leechlike to their fainting country cling
> Till they drop, blind in blood, without a blow.
> A people starved and stabbed in th'untilled field;
> An army, whom liberticide and prey
> Makes as a two-edged sword to all who wield;

Golden and sanguine laws which tempt and slay;
Religion Christless, Godless—a book sealed;
A senate, Time's worst statute, unrepealed—
Are graves from which a glorious Phantom may
Burst, to illumine our tempestuous day.

Percy Bysshe Shelley (1839), 'England in 1819'.

This bitter attack, levelled in particular at a monarchy seen to suck the blood of its people, uses the sonnet to display the disarray it condemns. The first six lines are held together by alternate rhymes, the next four repeat the pattern but alter the sound, and the final four reiterate the hammering of Shelley's anger in tight couplets. So a sestet (usually the 'bottom' part of a sonnet) teeters here at the top, just as does the monarchy itself. Below it is the bubbling mass of the people – initially partially controlled (although only by bloodshed) by the army of the quatrain in lines 7–10. Ultimately, in Shelley's rallying cry, such control will be rejected for an alternative new dawn, imaged here in the final couplets, which line up to create the circumstances for change, heralded in the unlocking imagery of lines 13–14. The Chartists continued this redirection of sonnet passion to political purpose in their rhetorical battles for parliamentary reform in the middle decades of the nineteenth century. As Mike Sanders notes, the Chartist newspaper *The Northern Star* was inundated with sonnet contributions to its poetry column, raising under-explored questions regarding the class associations of sonneteering.

Read more

- John Clare – poet and rural labourer – wrote sonnets throughout his life, often using innovative variations on the standard forms. Looking at poems such as his animal sonnets (to a marten, fox and, in mini sequence, a badger, c. 1832–1837), or his later sonnets ('Poets love nature'; 'I Am'; 'True love lives in absence'; 'Wood Anenome' 'The Crow', c. 1842–1863) consider how Clare explores his and his community's relationship to literary culture, using the sonnet as a dynamic interface.
- Consider how Wendy Cope's 'Strugnell's Sonnets' (in *Making Cocoa for Kingsley Amis*, 1986) effectively answer – both in form and in content – sonnets by Shakespeare or Sidney that have been cherished by English tradition. What is the effect of Cope's irreverent but skilful reinterpretation?
- Sonnets don't only appear in sequence or standing alone: look out for Shakespeare's use of sonnets in *Romeo and Juliet* (1597), for example. What is the effect of introducing the sonnet tradition into a play such as this? How do these sonnets interact with the dramatic movement of the play?
- See Don Paterson's introduction to his excellent short anthology of sonnets: Don Paterson (ed.) (1999), *101 Sonnets from Shakespeare to Heaney* (London: Faber and Faber).

References

Holmes, J. (2005), *Dante Gabriel Rossetti and the Late-Victorian Sonnet Sequence: Sexuality, Belief, and the Self* (Basingstoke: Ashgate).

Phillips, C. (ed.) (1990), *Gerard Manley Hopkins: Selected Letters* (Oxford: Clarendon Press).

Sanders, M. (2006), '"A Jackass Load of Poetry": *The Northern Star*'s Poetry Column 1838–1852', *Victorian Periodicals Review* 39, 46–66.

Haiku

In English, a very short poem (usually no more than 20 syllables) that represents a moment of perception.

The haiku (the plural is also haiku) is a Japanese verse form. It was originally the starting verse (*hokku*) of a longer collaborative and linked poem (*renga*), but Masaoka Shiki (1867–1902) acknowledged the tradition of treating these as poems in their own right when he renamed them haiku. They are striking for their brevity, which lends itself to creating a sense of momentary perception. Indeed, the haiku strives for objectivity of perception rather than a strongly subjective moment of expression. For this reason, Imagist poets such as Ezra Pound (1885–1972) embraced haiku in the early decades of the twentieth century. Since then many poets have attempted to restrict themselves to 17 syllables (the traditional number), and therefore name their productions haiku. However, there is a great deal to haiku beyond counting syllables. This discussion will restrict itself to the English haiku tradition, which is necessarily an approximation rather than a replication of its Japanese inspiration. Features of the traditional haiku in English include:

- 17 syllables arranged across three lines, traditionally in the formation 5 – 7 – 5, but this often varies
- the present tense
- a moment in everyday life
- a *Kigo* (season word): a word that refers to a season (in the natural world)
- a *Kireji* (cutting word): in English this is a pause appearing at the end of the first or second line
- an image in each of the three lines.

Despite its apparent simplicity, the haiku is a complex and often unfamiliar form for English readers who may be disarmed by its cool objectivity and lack of elaboration. This feels odd within a tradition (poetry) where you expect to find expression, opinion or the promotion of values and ideas. Yet it is precisely this neutrality that attracted those, such as Pound, who were disenchanted by the designs of nineteenth-century English poetry. The fixed requirements of haiku serve effectively to slough off all material that is surplus to the representation of an exact impression, including the poet's feelings about that impression. Rather, the haiku strives to present the impression itself, allowing the reader to experience whatever feelings it produces. In practice this restrictiveness is difficult to sustain and, for all its impression of neutrality, the haiku, like all forms, imposes on the experience it describes, even if merely by suggesting that impressions are momentary and objective. Subjectivity is also perhaps difficult to exclude completely; although at what point observation becomes coloured by emotion is a matter of perspective. In any case, the haiku's reticence stimulates the reader's imagination to emotional response and their quiet reluctance to direct the reader can be deeply moving.

Haru no yo ya	A spring night!
komorido yukashi	A pious prayer confined
dō no sumi.	In a corner of the temple.
Imo no ha ya	Taro leaves!
tsuki matsu sato no	Waiting for the harvest moon,
yaki-batake	The hamlet of burnt field.

Matsuo Basho (1990), Haiku 94 [1688] and Haiku 65 [1687], trans. Toshiharu Oseko.

In practice the features of haiku are debatable: the number of syllables often vary between 11 and 20 and their arrangement also differs. In any case, the use of syllables is only an English equivalent for the Japanese use of *on* (a word corresponding to a sound) and *onji* (a sound symbol). The use of figurative language (**metaphor, simile**, and so on) is sometimes criticized as for some this imposes English wordplay on a Japanese form; in practice this is also difficult to avoid. *Kireji* (cutting), often seen in English haiku as a dash, colon, semicolon or ellipsis (or, in the above examples, exclamation marks) can introduce a sense of progression or movement in an otherwise very fleeting form: the moment of cutting divides the haiku into two parts which are imaginatively held slightly part, but which augment each other. Finally there is the question of content, and how far this is prescribed. Central here is the issue of *kigo*. This reference to the seasons may be literal, as in one of the haiku that make up L. A. Davidson's *The Shape of the Tree* (written 'individually over a span of time'):

an August wind
scattering on hot pavement
brown sycamore leaves

L. A. Davidson (1982), from *The Shape of the Tree: New York New York*.

Or it may be more suggestive, as in a later Davidson haiku from *bird song*:

> the moonflower
> even as it trembles
> no longer a bud

L. A. Davidson (2003), from *bird song: more and more*.

Here the *kigo* is arguably 'moonflower' (which appears seasonally) or 'bud' (suggesting springtime). However, as the moonflower is known for blooming in the evening, the time-span of this *kigo* is both a moment in a year and a moment in a day. This capture of an instant within two cycles then makes an especially effective haiku that exploits the form's ability to contain several impulses within a restricted space. Further, 'trembles' sits quivering at the centre of this moment of held stillness, indicating both its precariousness and the art of the poet who stops and holds such moments even as they pass. *bird song* was very beautifully produced in an edition featuring woodcut illustration by A. C. Kulik, arguably producing *haiga* (the combination of haiku and art).

The necessity of *kigo* has been debated by those who suggest it separates haiku from urban experience. Yet, as Davidson's example demonstrates, seasonality can be felt in various settings and the objective ambition of the haiku is to represent an impression rather than hinge on associations. Nevertheless, as Lee Gurga explores, while appearing to be incidental, the requirement to include a reference to the natural world in flux can allude to a broader philosophy: it commands that the poet is attentive to his or her immediate environment at a particular moment in time, simultaneously understood as a moment within a natural process of decay and renewal and as a moment in the literary tradition that then absorbs it. Gurga goes so far as naming this attentiveness as a defining feature of haiku, and a means by which other 17-syllable poems can be excluded from the tradition. This reading of haiku is influenced by the translator Reginald H. Blyth, who associated the haiku with Zen philosophy. Not all practitioners abide by this connection between a verse form and a philosophical perspective, however, and this has led to great variety of practice, and to enthusiasm for associated forms such as *senryu* (which replaces seasonality with a reference to human nature). The haiku's sense of revelation has also been used for comedy, with many humorous haiku hinging on a **pun** (a common figure in Japanese).

Read more

- Consider Ezra Pound's 'In a Station of the Metro' (1916), often used as an exemplary haiku in English. How far does it subscribe to the tradition? How does it engage with Pound's notion of an 'Image', which he said was 'a vortex or cluster of fused ideas and is endowed with energy'? ('Affirmations',

The New Age, 28 January 1915, included in *Ezra Pound: Selected Prose, 1909–1965*, ed. William Cookson (1973) (London: Faber and Faber).)

- Haiku, especially in the wake of Blyth's translations, was popular with the Beat Generation poets, such as Allan Ginsberg and Jack Kerouac. Kerouac recorded an album, *Blues and Haikus* (1959), which alternated between his recitation of haiku and music from jazz musicians Al Corn and Zoot Sims.
- Contemporary haiku are published through many periodical publications, such as *Blithe Spirit: The Journal of the British Haiku Society*, that of the Haiku Society of America, or in anthologies, such as those annually produced by Red Moon Press. Recently the academic study of haiku has been boosted by the acquisition of 'The L. A. Davidson Haiku Collection' by the Rare Book and Manuscript Library at Columbia University (New York), which includes correspondence and haiku-related materials dating from 1960 to 2007. It will be complemented by 'The William J. Higginson Haiku Collection' at the same library. These investments testify to increasing recognition of the dynamic culture of experimentation and reflection in the modern haiku tradition.

References

Blyth, R. H. (1964), *A History of Haiku in Two Volumes* (Tokyo: The Hokuseido Press).

Gurga, L. (2000), 'Toward and Aesthetic for English-Language Haiku', *Modern Haiku* 31 (Fall).

Limerick

A five-line nonsense poem that relies on a tight **rhyme scheme** and rhythm.

Apparently named after a quirky custom at nineteenth-century parties in which nonsense verses were devised, recited and then answered with the phrase, 'Will you come up to Limerick?', limericks are usually humorous (often bawdy) short poems that follow a regular rhythm and rhyme that is familiar to both children and adults. The pleasure of limericks comes as much from anticipating how their author (the term feels rather grand given that limericks are often quipped rather than studied) will fit a subject to such a familiar sound and shape. Some limericks in fact rely so entirely on this recognition among their audience that they swerve away from crude terms altogether, creating an air of witty repartee, knowing that listeners will be filling in the blanks for themselves. The traditional limerick is structured as follows:

- five lines of robust metre (**iambs** and **anapaests** usually) arranged into **tetrameters** (lines 1, 2, 5) and **dimeters** (lines 3, 4)
- two rhymes arranged into the scheme *a-a-b-b-a*

- the final line either repeats the first one entirely, or uses the same word for its rhyme.

The early champion of the limerick was Lear, whose examples stay most strictly to the above arrangement. As seen here, the repetition of line 1's rhyming word in line 5 creates a tight, enclosed and folding-back shape that reiterates the nonsense it describes; it refuses to provide direction, to move forward from a proposition, or to derive anything other than childish delight from itself:

> There was an Old Man with a beard,
> Who said, 'It is just as I feard!—
> Two Owls and a Hen,
> Four Larks and a Wren,
> Have all built their nests in my beard!'
>
> Edward Lear (1845), 'There was an Old Man with a beard'.

This strict convention has loosened over time, however, and practitioners often escalate the limerick's already nonsense jingle-like tone with completely illogical whimsy. This playfulness associates the form with childishness and nursery rhymes. However, there is also a coarser strain in limerick practice associated with erotic or lewd writing, such as in the obscure and 'specialist' periodical, *The Pearl: A Journal of Facetiae and Voluptuous Reading* which circulated between 1879 and 1881. Gershon Legman's (1969) scholarly consideration of this aspect of limerick tradition, *The Limerick*, suggests that this combination of the infantile with the erotic is linked to the form's distortion of regular speech patterns, which point to a subversion of morals. This implies a transgressive tradition that wittily or disconcertingly violates taboos: perhaps the limerick has a more pointed and acerbic purpose than its surface frothiness implies.

Read more

- See Kenneth Patchen's *Hurrah for Anything* (1957), a volume of 'open-form limericks', suggesting that 'limerick' names a spirit of joyfulness as much as a strict verse form.

References

Legman, G. (1969), *The Limerick* (New York: Bell Publishing Company).

Villanelle

An elaborate 19-line poem, derived from French practice, featuring two **rhymes** and two **refrains**.

Villanelles tend to wear their cleverness openly: their tight scheme of sound and phrase repetition suggests an air of self-conscious ingenuity or even affectation. The term has a mixed heritage: it derives from the Latin *villa*, a country house or farm, associating the form with country singing and perhaps accounting for its use of refrain (early examples were arranged to be sung by up to three voices). The French poet Jean Passeret then fixed the present poetic form (described below) in the late sixteenth century. Until the nineteenth century the villanelle appeared generally only in Continental languages; however, a group of writers associated with Andrew Lang (1844–1912) brought the form to England in the latter quarter of the nineteenth century through translations and their own efforts with fixed French forms. These tended to be examples of **light verse** (in Lang's classification, *vers de société*) that emphasized their elaborate and self-consciously literary nature through references to Classical culture. However, in the twentieth century – of all the fixed French forms, the villanelle appears to have persisted most convincingly – the villanelle's refrain and returning rhymes were used to intimate more complex conditions of melancholy and wistfulness, or else passion and earnestness, as in Dylan Thomas' famous example ('Do Not Go Gentle into that Good Night', 1951). The villanelle's 19 lines are arranged as follows:

- five **tercets** (three lines each) and a **quatrain** (four lines)
- line 3 and line 6 are repeated as refrains in lines 9, 15, 19 and line 12 and 14 respectively
- only two **rhymes** are used throughout in the arrangement, a-b-A a-b-*A* a-b-A a-b-*A* a-b-A a-b-*A*A.

Among late-nineteenth-century practitioners, the form's tight rhyme scheme and line repetitions encouraged refined artistry that concentrated more on artifice and performance than uncontrolled emotion. These late-nineteenth-century villanelles are perhaps the most literal (or laboured) examples of an Aestheticist philosophy of 'art for art's sake' (see W. Davenport Adam's anthology *Latter-Day Lyrics* published in 1878). Such writers set an arch style for the villanelle, directed at a small group of like-minded socialites. In the twentieth century this changed into more democratically humorous verse by poets such as Wendy Cope, or conversely into bleakly melancholic writing, as seen in Sylvia Plath's villanelles. See Cope's 'Lissadell' (2005) for a change of tone, however, as it uses the villanelle's echoes to meditate movingly on the passage of time, remembrance, decay and rhythms of comfort or reassurance in its echo of Yeats'

Tercet	a
	b
	Refrain 1 A

Tercet	a
	b
	Refrain 2 A

Tercet	a
	b
	Refrain 1 A

Tercet	a
	b
	Refrain 2 A

Tercet	a
	b
	Refrain 1 A

Quatrain	a
	b
	Refrain 2 A
	Refrain 1 A

'In Memory of Eva Gore Booth and Con Markiewicz' (1927); the refrain works around the phrase 'And life was good and all was well' (l. 3). Phil Brown's 'Barfly' uses the villanelle's repetitions to intimate the circling confusion and rising paranoia of the bar-room drunk. The rhymes (some perfect, some eye rhymes) and gradually altering refrains suggest the hazy, spinning vision that traps the drinker; yet this is seen through the wry observational stance of the bartender poet, whose command of the elaborate verse form stands in direct contrast to the confused drunk at its centre. Here lies a complex dynamic between control and lack of control, authority and lack of authority that sustains the poem's self-reflexive drive. The poem alludes ironically to the villanelle's association with polite society in its anecdotal treatment of the strangers who populate this social scene, but amusingly (and disconcertingly) maps together the poet and muse, either of whom may be said to have been abandoned by friends, left to negotiate this tense social interaction:

> Mix me a stiff one mate, pour me a tall one,
> I've got a lot to forget tonight,
> and it seems like my friends have all gone

Off to wherever the hell that whore's gone,
luring them in wallet-first through the night,
mix me a stiff one mate, pour me a tall one.

Propping the bar up alone like a moron,
sympathy stares on peripheral sight,
and it seems like my friends have all gone.

Sinking in whiskey-dipped thoughts on the futon,
a red-eyed old man shakes infirm to my right,
mix me a stiff one mate, pour me a tall one.

Don't be a dick mate, I haven't ignored one
snidey stare, like you've got the right,
just 'cos it looks like my friends have all gone.

Yeah that's right mate, fuckin' come on!
Up to you mate, fuck off or fight.
Get me a drink mate, make it a big one,
looks like all the lads have gone.

Phil Brown (2007), 'Barfly'.

Read more

- Other twentieth-century examples of villanelles – in various moods – include: Thomas Hardy's 'The Caged Thrush Free and Home Again' (1901); Sylvia Plath's 'Admonitions', 'Doomsday', 'To Eva descending the Stair' and 'Mad Girl's Love Song'; and W. H. Auden's 'Villanelle'.

Fixed French forms

Elaborate verse arrangements derived from mediaeval French tradition.

The villanelle is just one of a series of so-called 'fixed' French forms of poetry that have also been used in English practice since the nineteenth century. They use complex arrangements of **rhyme** and **refrain** as well as word repetition, which tests the poet's ingenuity to produce something dynamic within certain strictures. In practice these repetitions can feel overwrought and game-like, as though a poet is riddling with sound rather than meaning. In some examples the repetition of sound and phrase can induce a heady or intoxicating indulgent effect, or (as in Hardy's triolet, below) head-spinning dizziness that matches their subject. Other examples (see McCrae's rondeau, below) display a poignant combination of wistfulness and defiance. Andrew Lang headed up the fashion for fixed French forms with his volume, *Ballads in Blue China* (1880). In his introduction to the 1911 edition he remembers how the volume originally featured a white vellum wrapper and included an etched design of a blue Chinese illustration copied from a porcelain jar. The impression is that the poems may be likened to fragile pieces of art, displays of structure as much as content. Poets who have embraced French forms include Algernon Charles Swinburne, Dylan Thomas and several late-nineteenth-century women poets such as Charlotte Perkins Gilman and Amy Levy (see below). Many French forms exist, but those which have received significant English treatment are noted here:

- envoy
- ballade
- rondeau
- triolet
- sestina.

These forms rely on rhymes and repetitions but many also feature an *envoy*, which is a short **stanza** that appears at the end of a longer poem and acts as a 'send-off', often repeating in miniature something of the poem's scheme or concern.

In the descriptions below rhyme schemes are given in small case. However, where a rhyme coincides with a refrain line it is capitalized. Line lengths tend not to be stipulated in these French forms.

Triolet: eight lines rhymed and refrained, *A-B-a-A-a-b-A-B*.

Refrain 1 A	Around the house the flakes fly faster,
Refrain 2 B	And all the berries now are gone
a	From holly and cotonea-aster
Refrain 1 A	Around the house. The flakes fly! – faster
a	Shutting indoors that crumb-outcaster
b	We used to see upon the lawn
Refrain 1 A	Around the house. The flakes fly faster,
Refrain 2 B	And all the berries now are gone!

Thomas Hardy (1901), 'Birds at Winter Nightfall'.

Note how Hardy introduces development and change by shifting the punctuation of each refrain across this whirling-yet-tight arrangement that speeds up as it progresses.

Rondeau: 15 lines in three stanzas, using three rhymes and one refrain:

A-a-b-b-a
a-a-b-C
a-a-b-b-a-C

The term 'rondeau' was sometimes used for any French form, but this arrangement has become typical. Note that the ninth and fifteenth lines are labelled as refrains, but they pick up the first half of the very first line of the poem:

First half of line sets refrain A	In Flanders fields the poppies blow
a	Between the crosses, row on row
b	That mark our place; and in the sky
b	The larks, still bravely singing, fly
a	Scarce heard amid the guns below.

a	We are the Dead. Short days ago
a	We lived, felt dawn, saw sunset glow,
b	Loved and were loved, and now we lie
Refrain (first half of line 1) C	In Flanders fields.

a	Take up our quarrel with the foe:
a	To you from failing hand we throw
b	The torch, be yours to hold it high.
b	If ye break faith with us who die
a	We shall not sleep, though poppies grow
Refrain C	In Flanders fields.

John McCrae (1919), 'In Flanders Fields'.

Here the refrains' half remembrance of the first line suggests a wistful nostalgia, but then, as the 'Dead' throw a 'torch'-like baton to the reader the final echoes are determined to enact a stronger remembrance. The short central stanza acts like an intake of breath that takes the reader below the ground before the final stanza's stirring cry.

Ballade: 28 lines in three stanzas (each rhymed *a-b-a-b-b-c-b-C*) plus a four-line envoy (rhymed *b-c-b-C*).

a	Some men to carriages aspire;
b	On some the costly hansoms wait;
a	Some seek a fly, on job or hire;
b	Some mount the trotting steed, elate.
b	I envy not the rich and great,
c	A wandering minstrel, poor and free,
b	I am contented with my fate—
Refrain C	An omnibus suffices me.

a	In winter days of rain and mire
b	I find within a corner strait;
a	The 'busmen know me and my lyre
b	From Brompton to the Bull-and-Gate.
b	When summer comes, I mount in state
c	The topmost summit, whence I see
b	Croesus look up, compassionate—
Refrain C	An omnibus suffices me.

a	I mark, untroubled by desire,
b	Lucullus' phæton and its freight.
a	The scene whereof I cannot tire,
b	The human tale of love and hate,
b	The city pageant, early and late
c	Unfolds itself, rolls by, to be
b	A pleasure deep and delicate.
Refrain C	An omnibus suffices me.

b	Princess, your splendour you require,
c	I, my simplicity; agree
b	Neither to rate lower nor higher.
Refrain C	An omnibus suffices me.

Amy Levy (1889), 'Ballade of an Omnibus'.

Sestina: six stanzas of six lines each plus a three-line envoy. An elaborate arrangement of repeated end-words is established across the poem.

The sestina relies on word endings rather than rhymes to fix its arrangement. It is notoriously difficult to describe. To begin, the first stanza features six lines. The final word in each of those lines (six words in total) will be used as the final words of all of the other lines in the poem, in a fixed arrangement. In the envoy those six words will be distributed at mid- and end-line positions.

So, the first thing to note about a sestina is the repetition of words rather than rhyme sounds. This might prove extremely restrictive. However to introduce variation some of these words will be **puns**, so they may appear several times but they can mean different things on each occasion.

In terms of the arrangement of these final words a formulation known as 'retrogradation cruciata' (retrograde cross) is used. If the end words in the first stanza are labelled A-B-C-D-E-F we can see how those appear across the poem. Essentially with each new stanza the final three words (here D-E-F) are picked up, flipped over, and put back down among the remaining three words (A-B-C). This creates F-A-E-B-D-C for stanza 2. This is easiest to see illustratively:

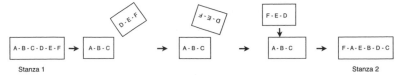

Stanza 1   Stanza 2

The final envoy then 'zips' the final six together into two columns so that the B word shares a line with E; D with C; and F with A:

B / E
D / C
F / A

This example, taken from Rossetti's translations of poems by Dante Alighieri (1265–1321), typifies the form's somewhat dreamy, mesmeric quality. It suggests that significance is intertwined and almost hidden away within the repeated spirals of the form. Just as the speaker is apparently under the charm of this lady so is the reader under the confusing spell of repeated words. Other poets who have used sestinas include Philip Sidney (featured in the 'Fourth Eclogue' of *The Old Arcadia* (1593), opening 'Farewell O sun', for example) and Algernon Charles Swinburne (in 'Sestina' (1872), which unusually alters the retrogradation cruciata in order to employ rhyme).

End-word A (shade)	To the dim light and the large circle of shade
End-word B (hills)	I have clomb, and to the whitening of the hills
End-word C (grass)	There where we see no colour in the grass.
End-word D (green)	Natheless my longing loses not its green,
End-word E (stone)	It has so taken root in the hard stone
End-word F (lady)	Which talks and hears as though it were a lady.

End-word F	Utterly frozen is this youthful lady
End-word A	Even as the snow that lies within the shade;
End-word E	For she is no more moved than is a stone
End-word B	By the sweet season which makes warm the hills
End-word D	And alters them afresh from white to green,
End-word C	Covering their sides again with flowers and grass.

End-word C	When on her hair she sets a crown of grass
End-word F	The thought has no more room for other lady;
End-word D	Because she weaves the yellow with the green
End-word A	So well that Love sits down there in the shade—
End-word B	Love who has shut me in among low hills
End-word E	Faster than between walls of granite-stone

E	She is more bright than is a precious stone;
C	The wound she gives may not be heal'd with grass:
B	I therefore have fled far o'er plains and hills
F	For refuge from so dangerous a lady;
A	But from her sunshine nothing can give shade,—
D	Not any hill, nor wall, nor summer-green.

D	A while ago, I saw her dress'd in green,—
E	So fair, she might have waken'd in a stone
A	This love which I do feel even for her shade;
C	And therefore, as one woos a graceful lady,
F	I wooed her in a field that was all grass
B	Girdled about with very lofty hills.

B	Yet shall the streams turn back and climb the hills
D	Before Love's flame in this damp wood and green
F	Burn, as it burns within a youthful lady,
E	For my sake, who would sleep away in stone
C	My life, or feed like beasts upon the grass,
A	Only to see her garments cast a shade.

Mid-word B; end-word E	How dark soe'er the hills throw out their shade,
Mid-word D; end-word C	Under her summer-green the beautiful lady
Mid-word F; end-word A	Covers it, like a stone cover'd in grass.

Dante Gabriel Rossetti (1861), 'Of the Lady Pietra degli Scrovigni'.

2.3 Visual forms

These poems are specifically arranged according to how they appear on the page, meaning that they are 'properly' read rather than recited.

> ### Concrete (or pattern) poems
>
> Poems arranged so that the shape they occupy on the page reflects their content.

The term 'concrete' derives from 'concrescree', 'to grow together', and in these poems content and form do appear to grow simultaneously. A poem about rain, for example (Apollinaire's *Il Pleut*, 1913), looks like a shower of rain. However, growing suggests a process that takes place over time; concrete poems disrupt this idea because we necessarily encounter them in their entirety at one moment

– when we see their shape formed on the page. Herbert's example illustrates their method:

The Altar

A broken ALTAR, Lord, thy servant rears,
Made of a heart, and cemented with tears:
    Whose parts are as thy hand did frame;
    No workman's tool hath touched the same.
            A HEART alone
            Is such a stone,
            As nothing but
            Thy pow'r doth cut.
            Wherefore each part
            Of my hard heart
            Meets in this frame,
            To praise thy name:
    That if I chance to hold my peace,
    These stones to praise thee may not cease.
O let thy blessed SACRIFICE be mine,
And sanctify this ALTAR to be thine..

George Herbert (1633), 'The Altar'.

The shape that the poem occupies on the page reproduces 'The Altar' of its title. Why is this unusual? Although readers tend always to take some notice of a poem's shape on the page, its subject or meaning is usually understood as the reader progresses through its lines. In concrete poetry this premise is shifted because it embodies meaning through shape rather than in sequence, so at least part of the poem's significance is apparent immediately, even before it is 'read'. A chosen shape, rather than rhythm, **rhyme** or **tradition** dictates line length in these poems, leading us to think hard about what makes these poems at all.

Herbert engages particularly impressively with the idea of 'concrete poetry': the 'top' of the altar uses a series of **metaphors** that imply construction ('cemented', 'frame', 'workman's tool'), so drawing attention to its 'concrete' nature. Holding up this top layer is a column labelled 'Heart', implying the strength and centrality of the heart as the organ that embodies a relationship with the Lord (and here it is hard like stone and fitted to a frame, again implying the poem itself). At the bottom of the altar is a desire that sacrifice (undertaken by Christ to save man) is transferred to the poet who created this shaped poem. The explanation for this is, 'That, if I chance to hold my peace, | These stones to praise thee may not cease' (ll. 13–14). To 'hold one's peace' is to remain silent, so the implication is that if the poet dies, and falls silent, this altar poem will remain to bear witness to his love for Christ: with this sacrifice the 'stones' (for which stand words) in this silent concrete poem can ring out the Lord's praises.

The logic of this final movement reveals the complex relationship with speaking and voice that concrete poetry implies. Although it would appear to be a very modern form of poetry, dependent on the advances of print culture, John Hollander, who has himself written several concrete poems, links this writing to an older Renaissance notion that characterized poetry as a speaking picture. This importantly suggests an art object placed before the viewer rather than (as poetry often implies) a piece of writing that suggests a speech, and from which we need to work out 'who' is speaking. Indeed, once spoken aloud concrete poems lose their concrete, and so their poetic, quality. We may say then that concrete poems characterize poetry as a written rather than an oral mode – we don't need to establish who is speaking to unravel a poem's meaning because that is created through its relationship with the page rather than its relationship with a speaking body. Herbert's anticipation of holding his peace (staying silent) intimates this subtle shift in emphasis.

Hollander has taken this disruptive heritage further by inscribing a concrete poem into concrete itself. This radically demands that we consider how and where a poem is encountered as intrinsic to its meaning. In common discussion we often speak of having read a poem without necessarily distinguishing whether that was in an authored book, an anthology, in a newspaper or on a computer screen. This implies that at some level we consider the poem to stand alone, regardless of its immediate circumstances. Hollander's concrete 'concrete poem' challenges this idea by demanding that it is either encountered directly in its concrete form, or otherwise only seen in photographs or understood through hearsay; this is an extension of concrete poetry's tendency to reframe our view of poetry and poetic method by escaping the oral status of poetry (and so 'the speaker' as we term voice in a poem) completely, even opening up possibilities for multilingual experimentation.

Indeed, French writers Stéphane Mallarmé (with *Un Coup de Dés*, published 1914) and Guillaume Apollinaire (*Calligrammes: Poems of War and Peace 1913–1916*, published 1918) importantly influenced the twentieth-century vogue for pattern poetry. This began a worldwide interest in technological experimentation in the literary and visual arts, resulting in many concrete poems and even the notion of a 'worldwide' language. The poet Kenneth Goldsmith has founded an excellent website for archiving avant garde experimentation that features many examples and academic discussions of concrete poetry: www.ubu.com.

Read more

- See John Hollander, *Types of Shape* (1969) and *Rhyme's Reason: A Guide to English Verse* (New Haven: Yale University Press, 1981), which features a photograph of his concrete poem in concrete (p. 32).
- See the work of poet Ian Hamilton Findlay for further experimentation with materials and settings: his poems in neon, for example, were gathered together for a retrospective exhibition (entitled, 'The Sonnet is a Sewing Machine for the Monostich') at the Victoria Miro Gallery in London in 2007.

Acrostics

Poems in which the first letter of each line, when read vertically, spells a word relevant to the poem's subject.

Acrostic poems play with hidden messages and meanings, buried within a poem's more obvious subject matter. A significant word or often the name of a person is spelled out through prominent letters throughout the poem, most frequently the first of every line. They are related to the *abecedarian* poetic form, found in ancient Semitic and Hebrew religious poetry: see Psalm 119 in the Old Testament (in the King James ordering), which is divided into sections according to the Hebrew alphabet. Chaucer also experimented with the form, as did Dr Seuss who wrote abecedarians for children. This developed into the acrostic that is familiar today. Ben Jonson created an acrostic poem as an **epitaph** for Margaret Ratcliffe:

> **M**arble, weepe, for thou do'st cover
> **A** dead beautie under-neath thee,
> **R**ich as nature could bequeath thee;
> **G**rant then, no rude hand remove her.
> **A**ll the gazers on the skies
> **R**ead not in faire heavens storie,
> **E**xpresser truth, or truer glorie,
> **T**han they might in her bright eyes.
>
> **R**are as wonder was her wit;
> **A**nd like *Nectar* ever flowing:
> **T**ill time, strong by her bestowing,
> **C**onquer'd hath both life and it.
> **L**ife whose griefe was out of fashion,
> **I**n these times few so have ru'd
> **F**ate in a brother. To conclude,
> **F**or wit, feature, and true passion,
> **E**arth, thou hast not such another.

Ben Jonson (1616), 'On Margaret Ratcliffe'.

As Heather Dubrow has noted, the acrostic spelling of the subject's name down the opening letters of each line makes this poem a 'vertical monument' (p. 47), so imagining Ratcliffe's grave even when seen 'out of context' on a printed page.

Carroll used an acrostic to hide the name of his muse (Alice Pleasance Liddell) at the end of his novel; perhaps the children's 'eager eye' is intended to spot the arrangement that is hidden from the adult 'waking' ones?

A boat, beneath a sunny sky
Lingering onward dreamily
In an evening of July—

Children three that nestle near,
Eager eye and willing ear,
Pleased a simple tale to hear—

Long has paled that sunny sky:
Echoes fade and memories die:
Autumn frosts have slain July.

Still she haunts me, phantomise,
Alice moving under skies
Never seen by waking eyes.

Children yet, the tale to hear,
Eager eye and willing ear,
Lovingly shall nestle near.

In a Wonderland they lie,
Dreaming as the days go by,
Dreaming as the summers die:

Ever drifting down the stream—
Lingering in the golden gleam—
Life, what is it but a dream?

Lewis Carroll (1871), *Through the Looking-Glass and What Alice Found There*, Chapter XII.

Read more

- Acrostics were popular in the sixteenth and seventeenth centuries for celebratory poems (see John Davies' *Hymnes of Astraea* (1599), which praise Elizabeth I).
- The acrostic in William Blake's 'London' (1794) on the other hand is noted for its searing rather than praiseworthy commentary, installed visually in the poet's structure.
- More recently Anna Rabinowitz has produced a book-length acrostic poem based on her family's experiences related to the Holocaust: *Darkling: a poem* (2001).

Reference

Dubrow, H. (1990), *A Happier Eden: The Politics of Marriage in the Stuart Epithalamium* (Ithaca: Cornell University Press).

2.4 Hybrid forms

These are rather slippery forms that could appear in the chapter on tradition, since they are much less fixed than the formal shapes seen elsewhere in this chapter. However, they are considered here in terms of the very specific traditions they combine together. Of course, as soon as a form is described as hybrid it begins to defy classification – that is part of their appeal – so these are more open to debate than other forms.

> ## Verse drama
>
> A dramatic narrative written in verse that, by accident or design, is read rather than performed.

The verse drama is linked to other dramatic or narrative forms of poetry, such as **blank verse** drama and the **dramatic monologue**, but it is useful to consider the form as distinct from these two so as to see its ambition to constitute a new brand of writing with its own cultural purpose. Note that on the one hand dramas have been written in verse since Classical civilization (often because cultures verse differently from prose) and on the other that the term 'verse drama' sometimes refers simply to plays that are read rather than performed: it is a term with many applications. Many aspects of drama's relationship with verse are more properly investigated by theatre historians, but this discussion will briefly consider the nineteenth-century verse drama as a poetic form that reached into the realms of drama for certain aesthetic reasons. The notion of a verse drama implies several questions: What different cultural purposes do poetry and drama serve? Why would a poet wish to produce a drama that cannot be staged? (What stops it from being staged?) What is the difference for the audience between reading and watching a drama? The verse drama explores these questions through form and content.

Verse dramas are sometimes known as 'closet dramas' and are linked to 'monodrama' (drama for one speaker). Closet drama is written specifically for reading (sometimes in a group reading) rather than performance; the verse drama (which arguably developed more as a Victorian form) shifts slightly from this premise as they were sometimes intended for the stage, but their generally limited commercial success effectively made them 'closet dramas' or even restricted them to silent individual reading. However, commercial success, or even suitability for the stage is not always a subtle indicator of aesthetic success according to the verse drama's own terms. Although they vary in subject matter the form's recurring themes are not entirely natural bedfellows with the visual spectacle of the theatrical stage: they examine abstract psychological character, variations in emotional texture, debates of theoretical political or philosophical concerns, and meditations on action that took place in the past rather than in the present of the drama itself. Verse dramas might include:

- many soliloquies (speeches addressed to oneself, suggesting reflection and meditation)
- 'unstageable' settings such as vast geographical spaces
- shocking content
- allusions to previous dramatists, such as Shakespeare or Greek tragedians.

In Robert Browning's view the purpose of bringing these two forms together is to make 'action in character rather than character in action' (p. 9). In practice this often means that changes in psychology or clashes between psychological (or personality) types constitute the 'events' of the play. The 'verse' of verse drama is then most closely linked to **lyric** (as the poetic form associated most closely with feeling, psychological conditions and meditation) and the verse drama implicitly pressurizes the lyric into becoming a semi-public form by moving these meditations from a private space to one that takes place before an audience. In the case of Browning's *Strafford* (1837), which sits towards the 'drama' end of the verse drama scale, this results in a piece that relates the struggle between Crown and Parliament immediately preceding the English Civil War, but through the prism of a power struggle between two personalities, making their psychological journeys the 'action' of the play.

Byron's *Manfred* on the other hand dispenses with the particulars of historical setting altogether, and places the 'action' in a visually impressive and spectacular scene. This strips away all sense of contingency, allowing Manfred's personal and psychological status to command the stage alone. In this setting very little action takes place beyond the death of Manfred (in the final lines); the subject of the piece is Manfred's struggle to come to terms with a vague past 'sinfulness' (which, it is hinted, involved incestual love) and establish a stable and constant sense of self (which suggests the achieved identity of tragic heroes but importantly involves the premise of lyric). A combination of drama with poetry, therefore, is a dynamic vehicle for a protagonist caught between action and self-disgust:

> [*An eagle passes*] Aye,
> Thou winged and cloud-cleaving minister,
> Whose happy flight is highest into heaven,
> Well mays't thou swoop so near me – I should be
> Thy prey, and gorge thine eaglets. Thou are gone
> Where the eye cannot follow thee, but thine
> Yet pierces downward, onward, or above
> With a pervading vision. Beautiful!

How beautiful is all this visible world,
How glorious in its action and itself!
But we who name ourselves its sovereigns, we
Half-dust, half-deity, alike unfit
To sink or soar, with our mixed essence make
A conflict of its elements, and breathe
The breath of degradation and of pride [.]

George Gordon (Lord Byron) (1817), *Manfred*, Act I, Scene 2, ll. 29–43.

As this scene demonstrates, the verse drama is arguably unstageable not only in terms of abstraction but also because of material setting. The extraordinary mountains and ravines in *Manfred* would push the scenery department to its limits (not to mention the problem of having an eagle on hand to fly across the stage), but Byron in fact delighted in the perversity of writing a drama that could not be staged (although he may have been irritated to know that it was, in Covent Garden in 1834, ten years after Byron's death). What is important about evoking such extreme settings is that the verse drama appeals to the imagination rather than visual perception: it suggests a poetic rather than a dramatic experience, which takes place while reading rather than watching.

Yet the verse drama also implies 'unstageability' as a political as well as an aesthetic concern. As hinted by the incest in *Manfred*, the form duelled with the censor in its treatment of extreme experiences. Shelley's *Cenci* (1820) was not staged until later in the nineteenth century (and only then in private, by the Shelley Society) because of its shocking content (it features familial rape and violence). Although as the century progressed the verse drama often veered away from the material stage (and so the theatre censors) it continued to include shock as an artistic principle. Verse drama was popular with the Spasmodic 'school' of poets, whose versions (as Richard Cronin points out) featured unorthodox content, such as murder, sexual licentiousness and religious and political subversion, perhaps registering in these overt shock tactics their own formal deviancy (see Philip Bailey's *Festus*, 1839, or Sydney Dobell's *Balder* (1853)). Poetry's ability to investigate these discomforting areas of experience may constitute one of verse drama's claims to aesthetic significance.

Women writers used the verse drama to interrogate cultural and social obligations that informed female lives (both within and outside the plays). Augusta Webster's *Disguises* (1879) features a woman who is (as Adrienne Scullion points out) both shrewd monarch and 'a passionate and sexual figure' (p. 198) – a dual identity which fits the form. George Eliot's *Armgart* (1871) adds further formal instability by focusing on the fortunes of an opera singer (verse dramas were sometimes adapted into opera). Finally the two women (Edith Cooper and Katharine Bradley) who wrote together as 'Michael Field' doubled an already doubled form by producing two-form verse dramas under a two-authored pen (examples include *Callirrhoe* and *Fair Rosamund*, 1884).

Read more

- Early examples of the closet drama include John Milton's *Samson Agonistes* (1671) – an unusual instance of a Puritan gesturing towards the morally ambiguous arena of the stage – and those by writers such as Anne Finch, Margaret Cavendish and Elizabeth Cary (see Marta Straznicky (2004), *Privacy, Playreading, and Women's Closet Drama, 1550–1700* (Cambridge: Cambridge University Press)). These examples often set themselves against the theatre for political and moral reasons.

- Other Romantic and Victorian examples include Joanna Baillie's *De Montfort* (1798), Coleridge's *Remorse* (1813), Henry Taylor's *Philip van Artevelde*, Algernon Charles Swinburne's *Atalanta in Calydon* (1865) and Tennyson's 'monodrama' *Maud* (1855).

- The twentieth century has seen few verse dramatists in English, although Gordon Bottomley (1874–1948) wrote several during the first half of the century.

References

Browning, R. (1969–), 'Preface to *Strafford*', in *The Complete Works of Robert Browning* (Athens: Ohio University Press), ii: 9.

Cronin, R. (2002), 'The Spasmodics', in R. Cronin, A. Chapman and A. H. Harrison (eds), *A Companion to Victorian Poetry* (Oxford: Blackwell), pp. 291–304.

Scullion, A. (2002), 'Verse Drama', in *A Companion to Victorian Poetry*, as above, pp. 187–203.

Verse novel

A narrative that encompasses the scope of a novel, but is written in verse.

Verse novels emerged in the nineteenth century, alongside the rise of the novel proper. Essentially they are long poems that tell a story (as does a novel), are often divided into sections (as with a novel's chapters), feature a broad scope of characters (as does a novel) and feature topics considered 'novelistic', such as the development of an individual, or social commentary, or a journey. Yet they are written in formal verse, often employing regular **metre** and even **rhyme**. Although verse novels bear some resemblance to **epic** poems, and they share characteristics with any poem that tells a story, including **romances** and **ballads**, they differ because they concentrate specifically on questions of form: as well as relating a story they also comment on the novel as a form and poetry as a tradition. They are also different from **prose poetry** because they are written in metre, which means that they relate to the novel not as a form of writing (i.e. prose), but as a concept and a set of cultural traditions.

Elizabeth Barrett Browning's *Aurora Leigh* (1856), while often identified as an epic poem, is also overtly designed as a verse novel, and Barrett Browning intended this hybrid as she wrote. It tells the story of Aurora Leigh's development as a female poet, and debates gender politics, art and the cult of domesticity that influenced women's lives. Her story is written against a background of social commentary, often prompted by the fortunes of Marian Erle (which reach into the world of prostitution, sexual violence and single motherhood) and the status and nature of marriage (through Aurora's relationship with her cousin Romney). In this respect the poem directly addresses questions that were exercising contemporary novelists (the poem actually lifts plot features from Charlotte Brontë's *Jane Eyre*, 1847). Dino Felluga suggests that by writing in a hybrid form Barrett Browning critiques not only the social conditions prevalent in Victorian society, but also the novel as a form intimately connected to bourgeois (the main audience for novels) ideology.

This identifies the verse novel as a form for political and social critique. Since it yokes together two forms of writing verse novels arguably do not invest fully in either (which is not to suggest that they are 'failed novels' or 'failed poems'). It does mean that they are self-reflective: they draw attention to themselves as cultural products (of various value) at the same time as they relate their story. Arguably, 'pure' forms such as the novel or poem proper proceed as though their status is already settled (although, of course, many do comment on their own structure as well as on their content). The verse novel on the other hand poses form as a question. Further, their two identities mean they are underpinned by duality rather than singularity, which suggests multiple rather than single truths. Felluga argues that this is a central facet of the verse novel's purpose, and that it accounts for their emergence in the nineteenth century, because their inherent relativity reflects the century's concern with questions of religious and scientific truth and the rise of Marxist concepts of ideology: 'the verse novel, through its juxtaposition of opposing generic conventions and expectations, helped to foreground the contingency of all values and the ideological nature of all formal choices' (p. 184).

Other verse novels that emerged in that century include Pushkin's *Eugene Onegin* (1833) and Clough's *Amours de Voyage*, which was serialized in the Boston periodical, *Atlantic Monthly* during 1858. Barrett Browning's verse novel is written in **blank verse** (as was Milton's epic *Paradise Lost*) and Clough's in his own version of **hexameter** (a Classical **quantitative metre** used by Virgil). So these already hybrid forms introduce another layer of complexity by introducing the epic and, in Clough's case, the novel of letters popular towards the end of the eighteenth century. Clough's version of the hexameter is very colloquial, in line with the realist novel, as seen in this overtly iconoclastic passage:

> Rome disappoints me much; I hardly as yet understand, but
> *Rubbishy* seems the word that most exactly would suit it.
> All the foolish destructions, and all the sillier savings,
> All the incongruous things of past incompatible ages,
> Seem to be treasured up here to make fools of present and future.

Arthur Hugh Clough (1858), 'I: Claude to Eustace', *Amours de Voyage*, ll. 19–23.

This determination to fuse forms together, demanding that each comments on the others, continues in the modern verse novel (the form is still relatively popular today). Ben Borek's *Donjong Heights* (2007) uses **tetrameter rhyming couplets**, so echoing eighteenth-century *vers de société*, to relate a story set in a tower block in south London (with shout-outs to Samuel Johnson (1709–1784), who suggested that if you are tired of London you are tired of life). It opens by setting a cinematic scene (the reader adopts the gaze of the camera) before settling on a protagonist with a love of French novels and who dresses, like his verse, 'Both tasteful, smart and casual' (Chapter 1).

Many verse novels are structured around different perspectives with sections handed over to different speakers, evoking the multi-voiced nineteenth-century novel. Yet it also includes forms and genres among its cast of characters, each vying for attention and creating between them a cultural as well as a social and political commentary.

Read more

Other nineteenth-century experiments include Browning's *The Ring and the Book* (1868–1869) and, in some considerations, Tennyson's *The Idylls of the King* (1859–1874). In recent years several verse novels have appeared (note that with the exception of Vikram Seth these suggested examples are written by writers who identify primarily as poets):

- Les Murray (2000), *Fredy Neptune*
- Anne Carson (2001), *The Beauty of the Husband*
- Vikram Seth (1987), *The Golden Gate*
- Craig Raine (1994), *History: the Home Movie* (another multi-genred version of the hybrid verse novel).

Reference

Felluga, D. (2002), 'Verse Novel', in R. Cronin, A. Chapman and A. H. Harrison (eds), *A Companion to Victorian Poetry* (Oxford: Blackwell), pp. 171–87.

2.5 'Formless' forms

Finally we come to poetry that overtly rejects all rules and formal arrangement, but which arguably still implies a certain degree of tradition, hence its contradictory name. Since the key to these forms is their rejection of regular metre these discussions should ideally be seen in context with metrical verse, dealt with in Chapter 3, on **prosody**. However, they have strong identifying features of their own, and can be considered in terms of their cultural significance as well as their technical method.

Free verse

Poetry arranged according to content and rhetoric and not by rules of **metre** or **rhyme**.

Free verse (or *vers libre* as it is sometimes known) is often defined more by what it's not than by what it is. Considered baldly, 'free verse' liberates itself from all bonds: it does not use rules of form, metre, rhyme, or indeed any aspect of **prosody**. Such defiance is attractive if you associate rules with repression and, for many early free-versifiers, this attitude was necessary if art was to be rescued from lazy and servile patterns. However, T. S. Eliot punctured such optimism by pointing out that 'there is no freedom in art' (1917, p. 32). The history of free verse is therefore unusual since it includes a debate of whether it actually exists and, if it does, what defines it as verse and what defines it as free. Those who question its existence ('Vers libre does not exist', Eliot (1917), p. 31) are perhaps too quick to respond to the 'free' part and too quick to overlook the 'verse' part. Verse is defined by metrical patterns; to bring this into play with 'free' doesn't suggest a complete absence of principle or arrangement, but the presence of something dynamic: a pulsing tension. Free verse perhaps does not exist if it is taken to be complete freedom (where is there ever complete freedom?), but it seems reasonable to hazard some points that suggest a poem is written in 'free verse':

- Lines lengths vary (sometimes wildly) across the poem.
- Line breaks occur according to the content under consideration rather than in any fixed pattern.
- Where patterns do occur they use rhetorical **schemes** rather than metre or rhyme.
- The poetry is conscious of its arrangement on the page: the space around a poem is as important as the text itself.
- Rhythm and some sound patterning (usually **assonance, consonance**

and **alliteration**) provide coherence within individual lines, but are not replicated throughout the poem.

- Accordingly, rhyme is absent.
- The 'natural' stress patterns of speech are maintained as much as possible.

At this point it is worth acknowledging that formal verse often demonstrates some of the above features (**blank verse** is unrhymed; many poems feature lines of different lengths; schemes are often more important than rhymes; all print poetry is conscious at some level of its appearance on the page, and so on). The key is that free verse rejects any *pattern* in such occurrences, and it demands that most rather than just one of the above conditions are met.

As discussed in the section on **stress** (Chapter 3), all speaking has rhythm and technically all utterances could be described prosodically. This is not rejected in free verse. Unlike **accentual-syllabic** (or formal) verse, however, free verse preserves as far as possible the 'normal' or usual pattern of stress found in everyday speech. This is because free verse does reject metre: it might feature stresses and emphases in a line, and derive impressive effects from them, but it does not packet them up into regular units and then insist that they provide the template for all lines. So, words are not split oddly or given unusual emphasis in order to fit with an imposed pattern. Free verse is able to feature this sort of gentle, simple arrangement without forcing onto it a metrical straitjacket:

> the word in its mouth like a plum that has almost ripened,
> the sound it will make when it speaks
> like falling rain;
>
> John Burnside (2005), 'Annunciation with Zero Point Field', l. 37–9.

These lines are not overtly metrical: they are not arranged into regular line lengths; they do not rhyme; the longer line in particular almost reaches into prose. Yet, there is a rhythm here: the lines follow a generally rising metre in a series of **iambs** and **anapaests** ('[the word] [in its **mouth**] [like a **plum**] [that has **al**-] [most **rip**ened]'). They appear in gradually shortening lines, falling onto the page like the predicted rain. Yet that gradual shortening precisely dismantles regularity: a **pentameter** line (five **feet**) may be suggested, but the next one is split across two lines:

[the sound] [it will make] [when it speaks]
[like fall-] [ing rain;]

The effect is to emphasize 'speaks'. If the line had been arranged, 'the sound it will make when it speaks like falling rain', 'speaks' would have received a secondary stress in comparison with a heavier one on 'fall'. Splitting the line puts emphasis on the action rather than the comparison of the **simile**. We might be tempted to see in this arrangement something of Eliot's ideal: 'the constant suggestion and skilful evasion of iambic pentameter' (p. 33). Yet this pattern is evoked only to be broken for a particular effect, and so it seems reasonable to see this as a tradition of its own: the tradition of loosened pattern and free verse. Metre is one of these lines' images of potential – it is almost present and so almost ripe like the plum; it is almost heard and so may yet speak like falling rain, but it does not: it is immanent rather than established in the poem.

It is difficult to say what does dictate the length of the free verse line or its arrangement on the page, or its number of emphases, or its arrangement of sound; to set rules for this would be to destroy its 'free' character. The poet is free to arrange his or her words according to whichever principles they desire: to create a particular soundscape, to draw attention to particular words, to tear words away from tired phrases, to please the reader, to alarm the reader, to intimate confusion, to create delight. As seen here, this can result in poetry that sprawls across the page in pursuit of image and expression:

> Look, I must do something more
> than merely tell you this. The words
> are just too plain, not plain enough!
>
> You poets know it:
> Words are little gods to you.
>
> I've tried to hunt the word with enough of God in it
>   to do her right.
>
> And when I'm dead, please pin a little scratch of skin
>   of me to Peter's door.
>
> It seems like all my life's been battering it.

> Graham Hartill (2004), 'Brochwel Looks Back on Melangell', ll. 21–8.

This freedom has always carried with it a certain political potential, however: being free does not mean you disregard consequences. This can be seen in Whitman's innovative example:

> Through me many long dumb voices,
> Voices of the interminable generations of slaves,
> Voices of prostitutes and of deformed persons,
> Voices of the diseased and despairing, and of thieves and dwarfs,
> Voices of cycles of preparation and accretion,
> And of the threads that connect the stars – and of wombs, and of the
>   fatherstuff,
> And of the rights of them the others are down upon,
> Of the trivial and flat and foolish and despised,
> Of fog in the air and beetles rolling balls of dung.

> Walt Whitman (1865), '[24]', *Leaves of Grass*, ll. 509–17.

This early example of recognized free verse (nineteenth-century American writing importantly devised and shaped free verse's development; see Annie Finch) was greeted with both warmth and consternation by nineteenth-century audiences; some celebrated, some feared its defiant inclusion and unrestrained expression of passionate bonds between people. The form as well as the content of free verse works in coalition in this writing: the lack of metrical regularity means that all the 'voices' that now speak will do so naturally and without bending to rules instituted by cultures that otherwise reject them. This is a rallying cry that is resolutely spoken in the language and tone of the every day, and it is arranged according to its own terms of inclusion and variety: lines extend to allow more into the fold, lines contract to remember oppression. Nevertheless the writing is undoubtedly patterned and rhythmically robust, although rhythms are established not by regular feet but by repetitions of sounds (individually in **alliteration** and **assonance** and in phrases through **anaphora**). The 'd'-sounds of the fourth line quoted are emphasized not because they fall in with a regular beat – the final 'd' is pushed far to the end – but because the ear/ eye catches hold of repetition.

Such an abundance of choice is perhaps the reason why free verse became so dominant in Anglophone writing after the nineteenth century. This and the fact that it offers a direct route to cultural reconsideration: you can liberate yourself from an oppressive culture by rejecting its established rules and patterns. This is not to say, however, that liberation always brought the democratization that Whitman suggests. Early twentieth-century poets such as the 'Imagists' Ezra Pound and H. D., and later modernists such as W. H. Auden and D. H. Lawrence, rejected metrically regular and elaborate verse (which they felt had dominated Victorian writing) not so much in the spirit of freedom as in the spirit of reinvigoration. To reject the old shapes of verse was to cast away sets of crutches, crutches that had propped up the lazy for too long. Now writers would be forced to fall back on their ingenuity, to reject verbosity and excessive qualifiers, adjectives and subordinate clauses (which they accused poets of using to fill up metrical arrangements rather than to achieve insights). Poets should concentrate on reaching the meat of a thing. This was designed to put more, not less, pressure on the poet and one may argue that the overt rules of metrics and prosody were replaced with more covert but no less discriminating rules of taste and an almost-mystical and undefined notion of ability: Auden suggested, 'I think very few people can manage free verse, […] You need an infallible ear, like D. H. Lawrence, to determine where the lines should end'. And, if it is difficult for the poet, what about for the commentator? Charles Bukowski asserted that, 'as we work toward a purer, looser, more holy warmth of expression and creation, the critics are going to have to work a little harder to find out whether it's water or piss in the holy grail, and even then they might end up wrong' (p. 24).

Alongside such endorsement of free verse other poets such as Robert Bridges and T. S. Eliot expressed little faith in the experiment (or even belief in the category in Eliot's case), finally concluding, in Bridges' case, that free verse could not withstand the pressure of freedom and suffered from the lack of a 'rich state uniform' of metrical prosody. Despite this free verse flourished and dominates poetry still in the twenty-first century, confirming either poetic innovation or the demise of 'high' culture, according to your perspective. The gain is poetry that can be incisive, experimental and engagingly figurative (when there are no metrical rules to fall back on, devices such as **metaphor** and **simile** strengthen to carry the weight of significance). Free verse can invoke real jolts of surprise, recognition or fear and its lack of restraint can be wonderfully insightful, demonstrating how human emotion and experience, like free verse itself, is sharply felt but not always systematically understood. In some cases the inclusion of conversational rhythms and simple phrasing is also a moving and inclusive gesture that draws poet, reader and addressee together onto one plane of communication. On the other hand, free verse can also paradoxically feel excluding: poems are so intensely focused on specific experiences, on images and symbols of obscured significance, or simply on resisting all hints at metrical regularity, that they can feel prickly, dismissive of the reader and entirely self-referential. We are sometimes denied the bodily experience of pulse, metre and feet: features that can be the only way into a poem that presents a world or an emotion or a time so different from one's own.

Read more

- Annie Finch (1993) suggests that free verse is in constant dialogue with metre, in fact, tracing the presence of formality within poets' overt experimentation: *The Ghost of Meter: Culture and Prosody in American Free Verse* (Michigan: University of Michigan Press).
- In terms of examples of free verse, almost all post-nineteenth-century poets writing in English have experimented with non-metrical poetry.

References

Auden, W. H. (1974), 'The Art of Poetry No. 17: In conversation with Michael Newman', *Paris Review* 57, available at www.theparisreview.com.

Bridges, R. (1930), 'Humdrum & Harum-Scarum: A Lecture on Free Verse', in *Collected Essays and Papers of Robert Bridges* (Oxford: Oxford University Press).

Bukowski, C. (2004), 'To John William Corrington' (1 March 1961), in *Selected Letters, 1958–1965* (London: Virgin Books).

Eliot, T. S. (1917), 'Some reflections on *Vers Libre* (1917)', in F. Kermode (ed.) (1975) *Selected Prose of T. S. Eliot* (London: Faber and Faber), pp. 31–6.

Prose poetry

Writing that appears as prose on the page, but is characterized by rhythm and figurative language.

Many of the free verse debates apply also to prose poetry: the double title suggests as much confusion as definition. Prose poetry takes the lack of regularity seen in **free verse** a stage further. In free verse there is still the sense that line length is defined, that each phrase is understood as part of a line that has a fixed beginning and end. In prose poetry this is relinquished altogether: as in prose writing, the lines run on regardless, dictated only by paragraph length and the size of the paper. So why should such writing be considered poetry? What are its organizing principles? This is where the debates regarding natural **stress** and rhythm in expression are raised again: since all utterance may be said to have some rhythmic quality, for it to be verse must it repeat that stress and rhythm regularly? Must it at least define itself into fixed lines? If both are rejected, what differentiates prose poetry from prose proper?

The prose poem formally emerged in the nineteenth century, spearheaded by the French poet Charles Baudelaire's (1869) collection, *Little Poems in Prose*. Building on the character of these writings, together with other examples by the poet Arthur Rimbaud (*Illuminations*, 1886) and elaborate prose writers (such as Walter Pater), M. H. Abrams suggests that prose poetry is 'densely compact, pronouncedly rhythmic and highly sonorous' (p. 172). In the most formal efforts, this is exactly what is attempted, as seen in Wilde's example here:

> When Narcissus died the pool of his pleasure changed from a cup of sweet waters into a cup of salt tears, and the Oreads came weeping through the woodland that they might sing to the pool and give it comfort.
>
> And when they saw that the pool had changed from a cup of sweet waters into a cup of salt tears, they loosened the green tresses of their hair and cried to the pool and said, 'We do not wonder that you should mourn in this manner for Narcissus, so beautiful was he.'
>
> Oscar Wilde (1893), from 'The Disciple'.

The writing is arranged as prose, but it uses repetitions of phrase ('a cup … a cup … a cup'), sound (sweet, tears, Oreads, weeping, green; waters, salt; pool, loosened; wood, comfort, wonder) and image (water, pool, tears) to hint at a genre organized as much by sensual as intellectual principle. Likening itself to a **lyric** poem, this passage of prose may refer to a narrative, but it expresses a mood, emotion or feeling rather than strictly following a series of events.

Although Wilde offers his piece as a 'prose poem', suggesting a formal category, commentators such as Walter de la Mare suggest that 'prose poetry' has existed for as long as writing has, describing it simply as 'fine writing *in excelsis*', which nevertheless must strive to avoid 'purple patches'. Prose poetry is therefore not so much a chosen form as a description of a piece of writing: the most figurative and stylistically exuberant chapters of a novel by Charles Dickens (as de la Mare considers) maybe thought of a 'prose poetry'. Questions of cultural hierarchy clearly hover around the category 'prose poetry' (does describing a piece of prose as 'poetic' mean that one is assigning it a higher cultural value?), suggesting that prose poetry is defined as much by the reader as by the writer. Categorization therefore moves into the realms of taste and preference, areas that cannot be satisfactorily defined. While de la Mare is appalled by examples of 'prose poetry' that he finds in the excesses of women's fashion magazines or wine tasting notes, W. B. Yeats was impressed by the poetic potential of Pater's prose writings in *The Renaissance* (1873), going so far as to break the patterns of prose and turn it into lines of poetry for his collection *The Oxford Book of Modern Verse*:

> She is older than the rocks among which she sits;
> Like the Vampire,
> She has been dead many times,
> And learned the secrets of the grave;
> Ad has been a diver in deep seas,
> And keeps their fallen day about her;
> And trafficked for strange webs with Eastern merchants;
> And, as Leda,
> Was the mother of Helen of Troy,
> And, as St Anne,
> Was the mother of Mary;
> And all this has been to her but as the sound of lyres and
>   flutes,
> And lives
> Only in the delicacy
> With which it has moulded the changing lineaments,
> And tinged the eyelids and the hands.

Walter Pater (1936), 'Mona Lisa', arranged by W. B. Yeats, *The Oxford Book of Modern Verse, 1892–1935*.

Which is the prose, which the poem and which the 'prose poem' is muddied in such a treatment: Yeats implies the existence of prose poetry (he chooses a piece of prose when picking piece for a verse anthology) and yet denies it (he 'turns it into' a **free verse** poem).

However, subsequent developments in poetry and the growth of free verse have seen many arresting and innovative experiments in prose poetry that do identify as these hybrid forms: see works by Amy Lowell, Susan Stewart and Frank O'Hara, for example. Such prose poems sometimes employ subtler senses of rhythm and figurative arrangement: the lushness of expression associated with prose poetry may be toned down radically, producing writing that is meditative and often ascetic or disarming in its reluctance to deliver on expectation. Prose poetry has also been made into longer forms (although these are differentiated from **verse novels**), such as in Smart's account of her love affair with the poet George Barker:

> O the water of love that floods everything over, so that there is nothing the eye sees that is not covered in. There is no angle the world can assume which the love in my eye cannot make into a symbol of love. Even the precise geometry of his hand, when I gaze at it, dissolves me into water and I flow away in a flood of love.
>
> Elizabeth Smart (1945), 'Part Three', *By Grand Central Station I Sat Down and Wept.*

This final example evokes the influence of the King James Version of the Bible in Anglophone tradition. Smart's 'prose poetic' expression of an intense experience of desire is framed by reference to the Song of Solomon of the Old Testament, and here we perhaps see the earliest form of the prose poem:

> My beloved spake, and said unto me, Rise up, my love, my fair one, and come away. For, lo, the winter is past, the rain is over and gone; The flowers appear on the earth; the time of the singing of birds is come, and the voice of the turtle is heard in our land; The fig tree putteth forth her green figs, and the vines with the tender grape give a good smell. Arise my love, my fair one, and come away.
>
> Song of Solomon, 2.10–13.

Prose poetry, then, is either: poetry that rejects the formal restraints of verse, but seeks to maintain its relationship with sound, rhythm, repetition and (you might sense) significance; or prose that leans towards reverie and mystical incantation, that veers away from grammar and sequential arrangement and replaces it with association, echo, repetition and sensual experience. Where the two meet, whether they are contradictory or two sides of the same coin, is perhaps only for the reader to decide. Perhaps you should ask yourself, rather than the writing: do you experience a particular piece poetically, or prosaically?

Read more

- See Edwin Morgan's disorienting 'prose sonnet', written in response to John Cage (1968), 'Opening the Cage: 14 variations on 14 words'.

References

Abrams, M. H. (1996), *A Glossary of Literary Terms*, 6th edn (Fort Worth: Harcourt Brace College Publishers).

de la Mare, W. (1935), *Poetry in Prose: Warton Lecture on English Poetry* (London: British Academy).

Prosody

Prosody

A poet's (or poem's) technical method or arrangement; by extension, the technical study of poetry.

Much of what appeals to us about poetry – its sound, pace, tone, patterns, even shape – can be difficult to describe. As has been suggested throughout this guide, it is poetry's way of expressing something, as much as what it expresses, that constitutes its power and appeal. When we try to break down that effect for analysis we fear we might break the poetic spell: a prose description of a poem can feel disappointingly reductive. However, understanding technical methods and arrangements are also a way of hearing, seeing and feeling them, and to ignore this aspect of a poem is to ignore its vitality and its very way of expressing or interrogating a feeling, attitude or event. It is also true that poems can be unapproachable or elusive and this is when a sensitive use of prosody can be just the thing for revealing what it is about a poem that is remarkable or affecting.

To find our way into a poem's rhythm and pace we can use prosody's systems and vocabulary to help a) identify a poem's rhythmic features, b) enjoy and experience them while reading and c) share that knowledge with others. In linguistics prosody is the study of pronunciation, including accent, intonation and stress: essentially what we are doing when we use prosody, or when we identify a poet's prosody, is identifying accents, intonations and stress, just as you might in conversation. Although the notion of 'systems' and 'vocabularies' might seem themselves reductive, they are nevertheless useful ways of sensing the dynamic effect of pattern-making and pattern-breaking in poetry.

By embracing prosody we can pick out moments where a poem seems especially affecting, surprising or impassioned – it allows us to see where a particular emphasis lies, where a sound chimes with another sound, where a pause breaks up expectation. Or, we can articulate why another poem feels passive (or relaxing) by pointing to its systematic use of formal features. This might be seen in specific instances (such as when a word is given an odd emphasis) or in a poem's global effect, when individual lines come together to form a larger coherent pattern. While these clearly affect our experience of a poem, these patterns may also be revealed as the foundation of a poem's emotional, political or social effect, and also as sources of history and tradition.

Scansion is the process of dividing verse up into coherent units, usually named **feet**, and marking them. How those feet are arranged then indicate the poem's **metre**. You are probably familiar with rhythm as the pattern of emphasis that runs throughout a poem (it's 'beat'); when this is arranged into a formal pattern it is named metre. Both rhythm and metre are temporal (they take place over time). A way of revealing rhythm or metre, and making it available for discussion and debate, is to translate that temporal effect into a visual one by marking a poem's feet, stress and metre on the page. This process of translating sounds into visual patterns is called scansion: to 'scan' a poem is to identify and illustrate its rhythmic or metrical pattern. Sometimes the concept of scanning is also used to judge a poem: it may be said that a poem 'scans well' if it controls the meeting between words, rhythm and meaning elegantly or convincingly; equally a poem does 'not scan' if the words becomes stuck against the rhythm of the line, if their syllables clunk rather than ripple with the rhythm, or if the pauses between words sit awkwardly with the pauses between beats. This is seen in **doggerel** poetry.

One danger of concentrating on the 'rules' of prosody is that this might intimidate readers into believing there is one correct way of reading and describing a poem. Of course some consistency or singularity is implied by the very process of scansion and by the whole project of prosody: if an effect is worth naming, we imply it can be reproduced. However, scanning poetry is not a mystic art but a cultural activity that is dependent on a reader's own speech patterns. The point of scansion and prosody is not so much to 'fix' a reading onto a poem and insist upon it, as to use a system that can reveal a poem's effects and make them available for analysis and communication. Therefore, although two readers may scan a poem differently, technical vocabulary allows them to share their insights and adds weight to each of their assertions.

3.1 Stress

> ## Stress
> The emphasis given to one syllable over another.

The first stage in scanning a poem is to feel for its pattern of stress. The exact reasons for and definitions of stress are a matter of debate in discussions of prosody: does emphasis come from volume, or from the length of time a syllable takes to pronounce, or from the meaning it has within a phrase? All of the above are valid and are properly considered by scholars of linguistics; the study of phonetics and so forth are beyond the scope of this book. For the purposes of introducing prosody, stress is used here simply to mean the emphasis we perceive some syllables in a word to receive in comparison to other syllables. The pleasure of speaking and listening partly comes from sensing how language falls into rhythmic patterns, even without intention on the part of the speaker. This is especially apparent in the English language, which uses stress to denote meaning; indeed, it is difficult to speak more than a couple of words in English without creating stress patterns. In some cases, for example words such as 'suspect', stress is vital to mark the difference between a noun (**sus**pect) or a verb (sus**pect**). Other words are stressed differently with different accents: Birmingham in England is stressed '**Birm**ingham'; Birmingham in Alabama is stressed 'Birming**ham**'. More variation comes in when words are strung together in a sentence as a speaker tends to stress the same word differently according to its meaning within a particular sentence. So, for example the sentence, '**I** en**joyed** the **cake** you **made** for **tea**' has a regular stress pattern derived from the usual way in which those words are pronounced. However, a speaker may very the level of stress each syllable receives:

- Stress 1 may be heaviest if the speaker was the only one who enjoyed the cake.
- Stress 2 may be heaviest if the speaker is remembering the enjoyment.

- Stress 3 may be heaviest if the speaker wants to imply that the cake was enjoyable, but the rest of tea was not.
- Stress 4 may be heaviest if the speaker wants to imply that the made cake (perhaps rather than the bought one) was good.
- Stress 5 may be heaviest if the speaker enjoyed the cake at tea particularly (perhaps the one at lunch was not so good).

Of course, this could go on … the regular stress pattern of 'you made' may be switched if the speaker wants to imply that only the cake made by this person was good, and so on. The point is that sentences have an underlying stress pattern that comes from regular pronunciation, and these are layered over with heavier and lighter effects according to circumstances. The same may be said of poetry. In fact, Walter de la Mare points to the 'felicity' with which 'prose-rhythms are interwoven into the metrical scheme' in good poetry. Some poetic lines are regulated as unobtrusively as prose sentences – the stresses are present, but they serve meaning rather than patterned sound; others are so enchanted by stress patterns that these take over from the sense of the words. Some poems require a good reader to allow stress to shape but not dictate lines that may otherwise be spoiled if a reader chants rather than recites the words. In this example, the alternate stresses are present (bolded here), but the melancholy tone of the poem should persuade the reader to let those stresses simply hold the lines together. A regular heavy stress on alternate syllables, as seen in the capitalized example, would crassly reduce the metaphoric passing back and forth of love to a literal game of hot potato:

> Thy **love** thou **sent**est **oft** to **me**,
> And **still** as **oft** I **thrust** it **back**;
> Thy LOVE thou SENTest OFT to ME,
> And STILL as OFT I THRUST it BACK;
>
> James Russell Lowell (1845), 'A Contrast', ll. 1–2.

It is excellent practice to read poems aloud, and don't be put off if you at first sound more like a mangler of lines than a great orator. The more you do this, the more natural your reading pattern will become. It helps to feel relaxed and to approach the whole line at once. Although it is very useful to be aware of the natural stress pattern of each word, it can be distracting to keep stopping to inspect whether that usual pattern is occurring when the word appears in a poetic line. Rather, try reading the whole line aloud in a fixed pattern.

Take any poem written in regular lines (one from this book, or from an anthology, or from a favourite poet) and keep it with you for this discussion. Try reading the whole of each line aloud in a fixed pattern, such as:

- de-dum, de-dum, de-dum, de-dum, or
- dum-de-de, dum-de-de, dum-de-de, dum.

Try using a pattern subtly, just as a mere pulse in the lines – is this enough to allow you to feel the poem's organization? Perhaps you need to increase the emphasis of the pattern for it to become clear; try emphasizing the stressed syllables a little more heavily. Is it conforming to expectation? Or are you stumbling around, reading against the poem's flow? If this patterned way of reading doesn't seem to be working, try reading the lines as you would prose and keep reading until you start to notice a pattern emerging. Or simply try a new pattern, let the stresses go a little; they needn't fall into an on–off pattern. Maybe two or three unstressed syllables will pass before you reach a stressed one.

Maybe the pattern is now clear, but this heavy marking style is overwhelming your sense of the poem's content. Now that the pattern is apparent wind back a little and let your stresses fall into the more regular weight you give syllables in everyday speech. Enjoy the rhythm you have established, and let the poem carry you along; read the poem several times, sometimes for the rhythm, sometimes for the sense; soon it becomes clear that one cannot be understood without the other. As you go along, dot with a pencil on the page as you hit a stress, marking the syllables as you reach them. This will help you to sense the poem's rhythm and also see how many stresses a poem has in each line. This will help you describe the poem and think about the traditions and expectations that surround it.

Of course the appearance of lines on the page will help when it comes to assessing stress. Lines of a regular length are more likely to fall into regular stress patterns and once you have a feel for the arrangement in one line, you can probably continue and replicate that pattern in the others. Indeed, once you sense that each line has a regular number of stresses – say three to a line – try to hold on to that number. To make each of the lines conform you may notice the odd occurrence where a line is longer, but it still has the same number of stresses as those around it. Sometimes an extra stress seems to be pushing for attention. As will become clear, these are occasions where the line's feet are being substituted. The poem may be adding in or leaving out stresses in a regular way, making an arrangement that moves back and forth between, say, three and four stresses per line.

For the most part the stresses you start to see, hear and feel emerging can be described simply as 'stresses'. However, the degree of stress applied to a syllable can vary. The details of these categories of emphasis and pronunciation are again more properly discussed by scholars of linguistics. However, the categories of weak and strong (or primary and secondary, even tertiary) stress can be useful if you want to point out that some syllables have an extra feeling of stress – as seen in the discussion of the sentence about cake. The difference may be seen here between Southey's **ballad** and Wordsworth's **blank verse**. Part of the ballad's appeal is its sense of conformity and fulfilled expectation: it is generally happy to fall into a very regular beat in which all stresses are roughly equal:

> He **stopped**: it sure**ly was** a **groan**
> That **from** the **hov**el **came**!
> He **stopped** and **list**ened an**xious**ly –
> A**gain** it **sounds** the **same**.

Robert Southey (1799), 'The Sailor who had Served in the Slave-Trade',
ll. 1–4.

Now compare this passage from Wordsworth's autobiographical poem: here the poet remembers a rowing trip on the lake. As he remembers this through verse so the rhythms of the lines converge with the rhythms of the rowing. This creates a rippling effect that maintains the regularity of blank verse, but which gently adds texture to the lines through alternating the strength of the stresses. Across the passage seen here you may feel three different levels of stress – the tertiary, almost non-existent stress is marked in *italics*, the secondary regular stress in **bold** and the primary stresses in **BOLD CAPS**. Within these very regular, unrhymed lines a stress hierarchy serves the sense, with most emphasis falling on syllables that complete **internal rhymes** and tell of the strongest movement's in the boy's oar-strokes:

> I **went** a**lone** in*to* a **shep**herd's **boat**,
> A **skiff** that *to* a **will**ow **tree** was **tied**
> With*in* a **rock**y **cave**, its *u*sual **home**.
> The **MOON** was **up**, the **LAKE** was **SHIN**ing **clear**
> A**mong** the **HOAR**y **moun**tains; **from** the **SHORE**
> I **PUSHED**, and **STRUCK** the **oars**, and **STRUCK** *again*
> In **cad**ence, *and* my **lit**tle **boat** moved **on**
> Just *like* a **man** who **walks** with **state**ly **step**
> Though **bent** on **speed**.

William Wordsworth (1974 [c. 1799]), 'The Two-Part Prelude', Part I.
82–90.

Note that because regional accents are different, and readings of poems may differ, how two readers scan a poem may also be quite different. Even if two people agree on the number of stresses that appear in a line they may disagree about where those stresses appear. In the above example one reader may count the tertiary stresses as still stressed syllables and name the feet accordingly; another may consider that the syllables are so lightly stressed that they are in fact unstressed syllables, and name the feet differently. Indeed, even just one reader may sense that a poem could be scanned in two equally valid ways, and poems may capitalize on this sense of tension or duality in its lines. In Gerard Manley

Hopkins' reading, this is the case of counterpoint, in which two different stress patterns are present simultaneously in a poem.

> **Counterpoint rhythm:** Hopkins' term for a line in which 'two rhythms are in some manner running at once' (2002, p. 107).

The point of scanning a poem is to allow its rhythms to become clear, not to impose a rhythm onto it; scansion will allow these two, or three, different readings to be discussed and considered.

To sum up, try to feel relaxed as you read; try out a pattern on the lines; mark the stresses with a pencil on the page; tap out a rhythm as you read; and finally, enjoy the poem for its sound as much as its sense – become carried away. Try not to stand apart from a poem, but rather feel its rhythm in your voice and body as you read; let it become part of you for the time that you spend reading it. To learn about stressing and scanning poems in more detail have a look at Thomas Carper and Derek Attridge's (2003) *Meter and Meaning: An Introduction to Rhythm in Poetry* (London: Routledge), an excellent and thorough guide to listening to and reading poems.

Note

In some discussions stressed and unstressed syllables are called short and long syllables. Although there are strictly some differences between these ideas it's usually reasonable to see them as synonymous. See the discussion of **quantitative metre** below.

Reference

de la Mare, W. (1935), *Poetry in Prose: Warton Lecture on English Poetry* (London: British Academy).

Hopkins, G. M. (2002), 'Author's Preface', in *Gerard Manley Hopkins: The Major Works*, ed. C. Phillips (Oxford: Oxford University Press), pp. 106–9.

3.2 Metre

> ### Metre
> The regular rhythmic pattern seen and heard in verse.

When stresses fall into a regular arrangement in a poem the pattern it creates is known as its metre. In most English verse, as is discussed below, that pattern is formed from combinations of syllables or stresses, or both. We might liken a poem's metre to a skeleton: it shares general characteristics with other examples of its species, but the skeleton may be prominent in some cases and hidden by flesh in others. Just as we think of some people as 'fine-boned' while others are 'heavy-set', so the same basic metre may be light and sprightly in one poem and heavy and imposing in another. The origin of a poem's metre might also be more or less evident: a poem might draw attention to the Continental influence in **accentual-syllabic** verse through using vocabulary that remembers the Romance languages, such as Italian; others may naturalize that basic metre by employing its structure, but filling it with Anglo Saxon-derived terms. Thinking of older metres, such as **quantitative** or **alliterative** metre, a poet may challenge themselves to revive those methods to gain an older perspective on a theme or idea. Or they may wish to reject more modern metre along with all of its cultural assumptions and impositions. Or maybe they simply want to experiment with new techniques. In whichever spirit a metre is employed, it holds up formal poems, giving them shape and distinction and its effects on the reader are both intellectual (we might study the reasons a metre is chosen, the poet's skill at using it, and the cultural forces it displays) and physical (metre affects the voice we use to recite and the postures we adopt as we read; even our breathing is set in motion by a poem's metre).

There are three main types of English metre:

- *syllabic (or quantitative) metre*: no stresses but a fixed number of syllables per line
- *accentual (or alliterative) metre*: four stresses and any number of syllables per line
- *accentual-syllabic metre*: fixed number of stresses and fixed number of syllables in each line.

Metre dictates the lengths of the lines used in poetry in line with the rough principles laid out above and, as elsewhere in this book, the breaks between lines quoted in discussion are marked '|'. The integrity of each individual line varies, however, according to which of these traditions are followed.

In accentual-syllabic verse patterns tend to emerge both within the line itself and in its relationship with other lines – as seen in **rhyme** or in **stanza** patterns. Syllabic verse tends not to carry specific sound patterns across line breaks (i.e. the repetition of sound only fits with the rest of the line, not to the lines preceding or following them, so rhyme is rare). Different metres also tend to produce different effects of continuation: the lack of stress in syllabic verse can mean that lines sound as though they flow together, almost becoming prose; accentual-syllabic verse is more likely to sound as well as appear as individual lines. However, in terms of distributing the sense and content of a line variations do occur:

- *End-stopped lines*: lines in which the sense of a phrase fits with its line length; lines will often feature punctuation at their ends to emphasize this.

Example: 'Few know the toiling statesman's fear or care, | The insidious rival and the gaping heir' (Samuel Johnson (1749), 'The Vanity of Human Wishes', ll. 47–8).

- *Enjambment*: when the syntax of a phrase carries over across a line break.

  Example: 'O deck her forth with thy fair fingers; pour | Thy soft kisses on her bosom;' (William Blake (1783), 'To Spring', ll. 13–14).

- *Caesura* (from the Greek 'cutting'): a pause or break occurring within a metrical line. In this book caesuras are marked '||'.

  Example: 'Look on her face, || and you'll forget 'em all' (Alexander Pope (1714), *The Rape of the Lock*, Canto 2, l. 18).

Note that a caesura often coincides with a punctuated pause, such as a comma, but this is not always necessary: it may occur as a rhythmic pause.

Finally, a metrical line can be described according to how it ends:

- *masculine lines*: individual examples that end with a stressed syllable
- *feminine lines*: individual examples that end with an unstressed syllable.

Caesuras may be named similarly:

- *feminine caesura*: a pause that follows an unstressed syllable
- *masculine caesura*: a pause that follows a stressed syllable.

Quantitative metre

Written in imitation of Greek and Latin, the lines have no stresses, but the number and length of syllables is counted.

Quantitative metre is difficult to execute in English because it is such a stressed language (see above discussion of **stress**). Indeed, it is difficult even to imagine and to recite as poetry because we are so used to listening out for stresses: when heard quantitative metre sounds close to prose. However, other languages – such as Greek and Latin – are regulated by syllable length (the time it takes to pronounce) rather than syllable stress. In emulation of Greek and Latin poets, some Anglophone poets (particularly in the Elizabethan period and again in the nineteenth century with experimenters such as Longfellow and Tennyson) attempted English versions of this metre. Quantitative metre regulates the number and length of syllables that appear in each line and these are given names deriving from the Greek (monosyllabic for one syllable; disyllabic for two; trisyllabic for three and so on).

It is debatable whether long–short syllables apply to English, but something of their character may be heard in the difference between the length of the first 'e' in 'elephant' (long) and the second one (short). This is because the first 'e' is attached to a consonant, making that the longer syllable: el-e-phant (long–short–long). As a schoolboy one of Tennyson's exercises was to apply this Classical method to the English language and determine the 'weight' of words according to the length of their syllables (this early training perhaps accounts for the metrical quality of much of Tennyson's writing). However, the idea of a 'long' syllable tends to translate into a 'stressed' syllable in English and the **feet** used in **accentual-syllabic** verse are translations of the quantitative long and short syllables into stressed and unstressed syllables. In reading, you should try to resist the rise and fall of English speech, although this is difficult to sustain, and creates something closer to a chant, or to the sound of intoned prayers. The precariousness of English quantitative metre is written into Tennyson's attempt at Catullus' hendecasyllabic line (11 syllables per line):

> All in quantity, careful of my motion,
> Like the skater on ice that hardly bears him [.]
>
> Alfred Tennyson (1863), 'Hendecasyllabics', ll. 5–6.

Ideally in quantitative metre the number and the arrangement of the long and short syllables is regular and the lines fall into sections (long–long; long–short–short; long–short; long–short; long–short) and Classical writers who used this method often created particular arrangements of long and short syllables (such as those seen in **Sapphic stanzas**) that are referred to as 'metres'. When poets use quantitative metres in English (such as the **hexameter**) they tend to take the original patterns and adapt them to English speech by 'translating' them into stressed and unstressed feet patterns, as suggested above. When used in this way, these Classical metres can fit surprisingly well with English speaking rhythms, often sounding more natural than the on–off patterns of the more common **iambic** metre.

Read more

- The **haiku** is a quantitative verse form, taken from the Japanese (another unstressed language).
- Twentieth-century poets such as Marianne Moore (see 'The Fish' or 'No Swan So Fine'), Dylan Thomas (see 'In my Craft or Sullen Art') and Thom Gunn (see the collection *My Sad Captains*, 1961) experimented with quantitative metre: their handling produces an arresting and even poignant release from the familiarity of **accentual-syllabic** verse. However, for the main, quantitative verse does not have a strong tradition in English.

Alliterative metre

A fixed number of stresses in each line (four); the number of syllables varies. Stresses are emphasized by sound repetition.

Alliterative metre is the oldest form used in English verse and is sometimes considered 'native' to England. It works around the occurrence of four stresses. These are often arranged into two pairs, either side of a **caesura**. The number of syllables between these four stresses, however, varies, allowing significant differences in line length across a poem. In strict tradition each of these stresses alliterates; that is, they each share the same sounds (usually the first letters) in order to draw attention to their stresses (see the entry on **alliteration** for more discussion of this technique). In practice this alliteration can be fairly loose. In any case, the rolling rhythm of four often-alliterating stresses can produce an almost mesmerizing effect, perhaps accounting for its use in narrative poems. The Old English **epic** *Beowulf* was written in alliterative verse, and this translation by Leslie Hall attempts to recreate its stresses and syllables (the caesuras are also marked):

> He said he the war-king would seek o'er the ocean,
> The folk-leader noble, since he needed retainers.
> For the perilous project prudent companions
> Chided him little, though loving him dearly;
> He **said** he the **war**-king ‖ would **seek** o'er the **oce**an,
> The **folk**-leader **no**ble, ‖ since he **need**ed re**tain**ers.
> For the **peril**ous **proj**ect ‖ **pru**dent com**pan**ions
> **Chid**ed him **litt**le, ‖ though **lov**ing him **dear**ly;
>
> Leslie Hall (1892), *Beowulf*, IV, ll. 11–14.

Coleridge experimented with this metre in his other-worldly **romance** tale, *Christabel*, and his approach is spirited rather than slavish. His alliteration occurs at the beginnings, ends, and middles of words and the whole effect is framed with rhyme, arguably producing a hybrid metre that has a foot in two cultural camps. Coleridge himself suggested that the freedom afforded by alliterative metre meant that he could alter the length of lines 'in correspondence with some transition in the nature of the imagery, or passion' ('Preface'):

> And Christabel saw the lady's eye,
> And nothing else saw she thereby,
> Save the boss of the shield of Sir Leoline tall,
> Which hung in a murky old niche in the wall.
> 'O softly tread,' said Christabel,
> 'My father seldom sleepeth well.'

And **Christ**-a-bel **saw** the **lad**-y's **eye**,   [9 syllables]
And **noth**-ing **else** saw **she** there-**by**,   [8]
Save the **boss** of the **shield** of Sir **Le**-o-line **tall**,   [12]
Which **hung** in a **murk**-y old **niche** in the **wall**.   [11]
'O **soft**-ly **tread**,' said **Christ**-a-bel,   [8]
'My **fath**-er **sel**-dom **sleep**-eth **well**.'   [8]

Samuel Taylor Coleridge (1816), 'Christabel', ll. 155–60.

Note how the long lines coincide with the looming presence of Sir Leoline. This fluid, flowing approach to alliterative metre is combined with northern-English speech patterns in Armitage's recent translation of the mediaeval **romance**, *Sir Gawain and the Green Knight*. The original was composed around 1400 and while its story is compelling, its use of Old English requires specialist knowledge for it to be enjoyed easily today. Armitage (from Huddersfield) notes in his introduction that he nevertheless detected 'an echo of his own speech rhythms' in the original, which interestingly raises the possibility that the alliterative stress-pattern is native to the north Midlands of England; certainly his translation of the poem into modern English sits convincingly with the alliterative metre, and Armitage also retains the 'bob and wheel' pattern that is sometimes seen in alliterative verse.

A *bob and wheel* is a stanza arrangement that appears to 'hang' below the main body of alliterative metre on the page. The *bob* has one line with one stress; the following *wheel* has four lines, each containing three stresses. Across these five lines a **rhyme scheme** emerges (*a-b-a-b-a*). In terms of content, the 'bob and wheel' tends to summarize the preceding stanza, or ironically comment on it.

This extract from Armitage's translation demonstrates his supple handling of alliterative metre: the main stanza gives us the knight's internal monologue (he is about to become caught up in a dangerous game of flirtation with the wife of his host); the 'bob and wheel' wryly reminds us of the wife's perilous charms:

Yet he said to himself, 'Instead of this stealth
I should ask openly what her actions imply.'
So he stirred and stretched, turned on his side,
lifted his eyelids and, looking alarmed,
signed himself hurriedly with his hand, as if saving
     his life.
   Her chin is pale, her cheeks
   are ruddy red with health;
   her smile is sweet, she speaks
   with lips which love to laugh:

Simon Armitage (2007), *Sir Gawain and the Green Knight*, Fitt III, ll. 1198–206.

Despite its attractive possibilities, alliterative metre became marginalized by the rise of accentual-syllabic verse, now the most familiar metre in English, which took off after the Norman invasion. Some poets in the twentieth century (such as W. H. Auden and C. S. Lewis) continued to experiment with alliterative verse, but for the main part, formal verse became dominated by **accentual-syllabic** verse. In music, however, the tradition is echoed as a kind of alliterative metre is often used in rap music. Rap's sharp ear for the sound and patterns of words makes good use of the heavy stresses and alliteration of this metre, with its poetry often squeezing an amazing number of syllables between each pulse of the beat.

Accentual-syllabic metre

Stresses *and* syllables are counted and fixed into regular patterns.

Accentual-syllabic, as its name suggests, binds stresses and syllables together. This is the most familiar metre for English speakers as it is used in most formal poems. Unlike the other metres discussed so far, it is strictly characterized by repetition rather than variation, because it fixes the number of syllables and the number of stresses, and even their position in a line. However, this is not to say that accentual-syllabic verse is uniform: the following section on feet will demonstrate how variations occur.

Chaucer, who spoke French and read Italian is often credited with introducing this metre to English tradition, or at least is celebrated as an early exponent. He boosted the stature of English verse at a time when French dominated fashionable society and Classical languages dominated 'serious' literature by combing his enthusiasm for the patterns he found in Dante, Petrarch and Boccaccio with the French influence and, vitally, his native English tongue. This produced verse that bears the mark of the strong stresses of Old English but also echoes the lighter touch of short- and long-syllable combinations. The other important development associated with this metre is **rhyme**. We have seen rhyme in **alliterative** metre; however, as lines become more regular in this system, so their patterns become clearer, and the possibility for harmonizing those patterns with sound as well as stress emerges, so evermore elaborate rhyme patterns developed.

In accentual-syllabic metre each line of poetry features a fixed number of stresses, and associated with each stress is a fixed number of syllables. These are arranged into 'packets' of stresses and syllables called **feet**, which dictate where the stress lies within each packet. Each line is identified according to a) the stress pattern seen most commonly in each foot and b) the number of such feet in a line. So, the term **iambic pentameter** tells us that a) the foot used most commonly is the **iamb** (two syllables, one stress: de-dum) and b) that there are five iambs in each line. This is the line that Chaucer used in *The Canterbury Tales*, seen in the description of the hunting passions of the rather worldly monk (the stresses are bolded): 'Gre**houndes** he **hadde** as **swift** as **fowl** in **flight**' ('The General Prologue' [c. 1388–1392], l. 190).

The foot-type/foot-number system can be used to describe all metres in accentual-syllabic verse. However, the parts that make up this system can also arguably be used in discussions of **free verse**, as will be seen. The next section of this chapter will explain the variety of feet and line lengths available in accentual-syllabic verse. The following chapter introduces the mechanics of **rhyme** (which usually emphasizes a metrical pattern, but it may mask it) and Chapter 5 brings these areas together to introduce the system of **stanzas** (arrangements of whole lines into groups).

3.3 Feet

Feet

Units of verse containing an arrangement of stressed and unstressed syllables.

Ah sweet, and sweet again, and seven times sweet,
The paces and the pauses of thy feet!

Algernon Charles Swinburne (1866), 'Anactoria', ll. 117–18.

As Swinburne recognized, and demonstrated beautifully, there is something compelling and even intoxicating about the rhythmic delivery of parcels of verse. Whether hammering down relentlessly or falling soothingly onto your senses, the repeated delivery of stressed- and unstressed-syllable combinations can be both comforting and stimulating. When scanning a poem we seek these rhythmic engagements, which are so vital to a poem's logic and effect.

The notion of long and short syllables packaged together into certain patterns was seen in **quantitative metre**. Although English is a stressed language, that Classical system was brought into English practice to describe the arrangement of stressed and unstressed syllables in verse: this is the origin of the idea of feet in English. So the long syllable of Greek or Latin becomes the stressed syllable of English verse, and the short syllable becomes the unstressed one. The groups those fall into, and the positions of the stresses within them, are then known and characterized as feet. Greek and Latin names are still used to describe the arrangement of these feet, as will be seen below. Not everyone accepts that the foot system is appropriate for English verse, because it is essentially a system imposed onto it and deriving from an alternative tradition. Nevertheless, it is a useful tool for describing and recognizing a poem's rhythmic arrangement and many discussions of poetry use these terms to help explain and describe poetic effects.

So how to identify feet? Once we have read a poem with an ear for its beat, and marked the stresses on the page the feet of the poem begin to emerge. Often you'll notice that the number of unstressed syllables surrounding each stress are regular: you can then bracket these together with each stress and then see the line's feet. These markings show you not only the number of stresses and syllables but also where each stress is placed within each foot. In this book boundaries between feet are marked with '[ ]' (these replicate the pencil lines you might put on a page to visualize the poem's separate feet). To take two lines from Cowper as an example:

Here are the lines unscanned:

> While admiration, feeding at the eye,
> And still unsated, dwelt upon the scene.

Next the stresses are marked in bold (or would be marked by dots with a pencil on the page):

> While **ad**miration, **feed**ing at the **eye**,
> And **still** unsated, **dwelt** up**on** the **scene**.

It is clear that the stresses fall evenly into alternate positions with the unstressed syllables, so next these can be bracketed into groups: 'feet'.

> [While **ad**-] [mi-**ra**-] [tion, **feed**-] [ing at] [the **eye**,]
> [And **still**] [un-**sat**-] [ed, **dwelt**] [up-**on**] [the **scene**.]

William Cowper (1785), *The Task*, Book 1, ll. 157–8.

So we see that the lines have five 'packages' – feet – and this makes them *penta*meters. Each foot is an iamb (described below): the lines can be described as **iambic pentameters**.

However, although this poem appears to be very regular and even conservative by sticking to the iambic pentameter line, we see that commas actually introduce **feminine caesuras** (pauses after an unstressed syllable) into both lines' central foot. So there is something idiosyncratic here, glimpsed within the apparent calm of the poem. Just as the poem is interested in the visual sense (it describes a person gazing at a scene), so these little pauses are revealed when we visualize the feet on the page. The power that the natural scene has on the poet is even suggested by these tiny pauses, since they threaten to break the iambic feet: the scene is so impressive the poet almost forgets his metrical skill. Note also how foot-divisions do not always coincide with word-endings: words can be split between feet as the metre rather than the words carries sway.

In formal verse the number and type of feet per line is uniform (so the line length, the syllable count and the position of the stress in each foot is fixed), and the effect of bringing a series of identical feet together will be considered below. However, even in the most regular verse forms, some alterations occur, in the following ways:

- *substitution*: when one of the usual feet in a line is substituted with one that has a different stress pattern
- *inversion*: a type of substitution where the irregular foot reverses the stress pattern seen in the others
- *outride*: a foot containing extra unstressed syllables
- *catalectic* line: a line in which one (or more) unstressed syllable is missing; usually this is the final syllable, allowing the line to end on a stress
- *hypercatalectic* line: a line that has an extra unstressed syllable
- *acephalous* (from the Greek, 'headless') line: when the unstressed syllable in the first foot is missing.

The overall type of metre employed in a poem may also be described according to the stress pattern seen most commonly in each foot:

- *falling metre*: lines containing feet that end on an unstressed syllable
- *rising metre*: lines containing feet that end on a stressed syllable.

Finally, in order to fit with a poem's overall metre (but sometimes in order to introduce a chatty or informal tone to the poem) individual words may be altered to fit foot patterns. This happens by changing the pronunciation or spelling by dropping or adding syllables; this is known as *metaplasm*, and it occurs in various ways, some of the most common being:

- *Synaeresis*: when two consecutive vowel sounds within a word are contracted into one.
    Example: in the rhyme 'roses are red, violets are blue', violets is pronounced 'vi'lets' to fit with the metre.
- *Synaloepha* (or *elision*): when a word ending with a vowel is followed by word starting with a vowel, and those two sounds are contracted into one.
    Example: 'th'other' for 'the other' in 'On th'other side' (Milton (1667), 'Book IX', *Paradise Lost*, l. 888).
- *Syncope*: when a syllable within a word is cut away by dropping either a consonant between two vowels or a vowel between two consonants.
    Example: 'over' becomes 'o'er' in 'May fan the cool air gently o'er my rest' (Keats (1817), 'Sleep and Poetry', l. 112); later in the same poem 'slumbering' is pronounced 'slumb'ring' in "Tis might half-slumbering on its own right arm' (l. 237).

English verse tends to use only two- or three-syllable feet and some metrical systems insist that an English foot can only contain one stressed syllable: if more than one occurs the foot must split into two different feet. The practice of identifying feet can be a fraught business, reminiscent of the joke about mixing a martini: if ever you are lost alone in the wilderness start mixing a martini, in no time someone will turn up to tell you you're doing it wrong. Don't let this put you off. The more you scan poems for feet the more you can be sure you have found a good combination. This means spending time with a poem, and looking for a pattern that makes the most logical sense of the syllables. If the pattern you devise fits with the natural way you would read the lines, and it accounts for all the syllables in a neat way then this is the 'right' scanning of the poem.

This is a list of the feet discussed in this chapter with the stress patterns illustrated visually (○ for an unstressed syllable; ● for a stressed one). As you can see, they are arranged in order of general agreement:

Generally accepted English feet
- Iamb   2 syllables   ○●
- Trochee   2 syllables   ●○
- Anapaest   3 syllables   ○○●
- Dactyl   3 syllables   ●○○

Contentious English feet
- Spondee   2 syllables   ●●
- Pyrrhic   2 syllables   ○○
- Amphibrach   3 syllables   ○●○

Doubted English feet
- Amphimacer   3 syllables   ●○●

Generally accepted English feet

> ### Iamb
> A two-syllable foot, unstressed followed by stressed.
> Example word: be**hold**

The iamb is the commonest foot in English verse. When thinking of poetry we usually recall iambs; 'De **dum** de **dum** de **dum** de **dum**' in fact has a name: it's an iambic **tetrameter**. The iamb's movement from unstressed to stressed creates a pattern that seems to progress forwards to deliver each emphasis. This forward movement is suited to storytelling and iambic metre is common in simple tale-telling (as in the **ballad**) and in more formal narratives such as dramatic **blank** verse or English **epic**. However, the iamb appears across all types of English poetry and is sometimes even considered the 'natural' pattern of English speech. Although many liken the iamb's pattern to a heartbeat, the iamb should be thought of as 'familiar' rather than 'natural': after all, English verse did not begin with the iamb.

> If music be the food of love, play on,
> [If **mu**] [sic **be**] [the **food**] [of **love**,] [play **on**,]
>
> William Shakespeare (1623), *Twelfth Night, or What You Will*, I: 1, l. 1.

Trochee

A two-syllable foot, stressed followed by unstressed.

Example word: **app**le (or even **tro**chee)

By moving from a stressed to an unstressed syllable trochees create patterns of **falling metre**: a true trochaic line would end on an unstressed syllable. However, they usually cut off that final unstressed syllable, making a **catalectic** line. When they are run together the trochee's stress-to-unstress pattern produces a rocking motion that might be light and sprightly, as in Taylor's nursery rhyme, or they might impart a note of heavy, pounding emphasis, as in Blake's famous use of trochees in 'The Tyger':

> Twinkle, twinkle, little star.
> [**Twin**kle,] [**twin**kle,] [**litt**le] [**star**.]
>
> Jane Taylor (1806), 'The Star', l. 1.

> Tyger! Tyger! burning bright
> [**Tyg**er!] [**Tyg**er!] [**burn**ing] [**bright**]
>
> William Blake (1794), 'The Tyger', l. 1.

Note that both of these examples employ catalectic lines in order to retain a strong stress, so they have masculine endings. Henry Wadsworth Longfellow's 'The Song of Hiawatha' (1855) keeps the strict trochaic line, creating feminine endings ('[**From** his] [**foot**steps] [**flowed** a] [**river**]', l. 8).

A trochee is often substituted in an iambic line (usually as the first foot) to draw emphasis to a particular word, to catch the reader off guard, or to begin by commanding attention with the first syllable.

Anapaest

A three-syllable foot, with a stress on the last.

Example word: Tenne**ssee**

Anapaests' **rising metre** tends to produce a fast-paced rhythm that runs forwards in a speeded-up version of the iamb. This may produce a charging effect, as in Browning's 'How the Brought the Good News from Ghent to Aix' (1845), or an irreverent teasing quality, as in Clough's example (note that like many anapaestic poems most of the lines are **acephalous** – they lack the first syllable):

> I drive through the streets, and I care not a d—mn;
> The people they stare, and they ask who I am;
> And if I should chance to run over a cad,
> I can pay for the damage if ever so bad.
> > How pleasant it is to have money, heigh ho!
> > How pleasant it is to have money.
> [I **drive**] [through the **streets**,] [and I **care**] [not a **d—mn**;]
> [The **peop**-] [le they **stare**,] [and they **ask**] [who I **am**;]
> [And **if**] [I should **chance**] [to run **o**-] [ver a **cad**,]
> [I can **pay**] [for the **dam**-] [age if **ev**-] [er so **bad**.]
> > [How **pleas**-] [ant it **is**] [to have **mon**-] [ey, heigh **ho**!]
> > [How **pleas**-] [ant it **is**] [to have **mon**(ey).]

Arthur Hugh Clough (1850), *Dipsychus*, Scene IV, ll. 148–53.

Although these examples produce a direct sense of forward movement, anapaestic metre can produce a more meandering but still insistent pressure, as in Swinburne's 'Dolores', where the anapaest drive disturbingly presses Dolores to reveal the source of her mesmerizing eroticism: 'Wert thou pure and a maiden, Dolores, | When desire took thee first by the throat?' (Algernon Charles Swinburne (1866), 'Dolores', ll. 43–4).

Anapaests are often used in comic verse, its rolling rhythm being suited to bantering wordplay. Alice Meynell (1893) in fact considered them to have come 'quite suddenly into English poetry and brought coarseness, glibness, volubility, dapper and fatuous effects': she may have been thinking of **limericks**' use of them. Although she admitted that 'a master may use it well' (such as Swinburne, perhaps, although the content of his technically proficient verse was shocking), she claimed that 'as a popular measure it has been disasterous' (p. 6).

Since triple metre is difficult to sustain, and tends to have an overwhelming effect on the tone of poem, anapaests often appear only as a substituted foot within an iambic line, rather than providing the dominant metre, as in the second foot here:

Than we in the East dare look for buds, disclose
[Than **we**] [in the **East**] [dare **look**] [for **buds**,] [dis-**close**]

Gerard Manley Hopkins (1918 [c. 1865]), 'To Oxford', l. 2.

Dactyl

A three-syllable foot, with a stress on the first.

Example word: **scor**pion

In common with its shorter partner, the trochee, when dominating the dactyl's first position stress can slow the pace of a poem, creating a stately or ominous effect, as in Tennyson's bitter telling of the 'blunder' during the Crimean war:

Half a league, half a league,	[**Half** a league] [**half** a league,]
Half a league onward,	[**Half** a league] [**on** ward,]
All in the valley of Death	[**All** in the] [**vall**ey of] [**Death**]
Rode the six hundred.	[**Rode** the six] [**hun**-dred.]

Alfred Tennyson (1854), 'The Charge of the Light Brigade', ll. 1–4.

Dactyls may have a lighter, quicker pace in some treatments, but the initial stresses will often convey a hammering effect on the reader's senses, suiting them to poems of outrage or disillusion, as in Browning's poem written to Wordsworth on becoming Poet Laureate. Addressing a poet known for his iambic metre, Browning seeringly turns his back on his senior by reversing that stress pattern into a **falling metre** (which draws attention, incidentally, to **schemes** such as the **anaphora** used here):

Just for a handful of silver he left us,	[**Just** for a] [**hand**-ful of]
	[**sil**-ver he] [**left** us,]
Just for a riband to stick in his coat –	[**Just** for a] [**rib**-and to]
	[**stick** in his] [**coat** –]

Robert Browning (1845), 'The Lost Leader', ll. 1–2.

However, as with the anapaest, dactylic metre is relatively uncommon in English verse (it is a **quantitative metre**, as seen in Homer's epics), so dactyls appear more usually as substituted feet, as in this example from Emily Dickinson. This is a predominantly trochaic poem, but the dactylic 'Heavenly' suggests the possibility that the tight rhythm may unravel a little, only to have it closed again with 'Hurt'. 'Heavenly' sits like a glimpse of redemption, shimmering but unsustainable:

There's a certain slant of light,
Winter afternoons,
That oppresses, like the heft   [**There's** a] [**cer**-tain] [**slant** of] [**light**,]
Of cathedral tunes.

[…]

Heavenly hurt it gives us.
We can find no scar   [**Heav**-en-ly] [**hurt** it] [**gives** us.]
But internal difference
Where the Meanings are.

Emily Dickinson (1890 [c. 1861]), 'There's a certain Slant of light', ll. 1–8.

Contentious English feet

> ## Spondee
> A two-syllable foot, both stressed.
>
> Example word: **football**

Some insist that spondees cannot exist in English, partly because a foot should only contain one stress, and partly because it is impossible for two successive stresses to be even. Examples are therefore usually compound words, such as the one given here, and many would still suggest that 'football' is truly a trochee (**foot**ball). For these reasons, spondees cannot be sustained for a whole line, but are contextual feet: that is, they gain a double stress only when seen in context with the whole of the metrical line. They tend to add special emphasis, partly by doubling the stress, but also by causing a sudden disruption in a lilting line. The appearance of an equally stressed foot is an arresting feature, causing the reader to slow down, or even to alter their breathing pattern completely. Donne's 'Holy Sonnet' is written predominantly in **iambic** rhythm, but the central spondees (asterisked) perform the battering that the speaker demands while also conveying the tense over-breathing that characterizes his desire:

Batter my heart three personed God; for, you
As yet but knocke, breathe, shine, and seeke to mend;
That I may rise, and stand, o'erthrow mee, and bend
Your force, to break blow, burn and make me new.

[**Batt**er] [my **heart**] [three **per**] [soned **God**;] [for, **you**]
[As **yet**] [but **knocke**,] [***breathe, shine**,] [and **seeke**] [to **mend**;]
[That **I**] [may **rise**,] [and **stand**,] [o'er-**throw** mee] [and **bend**]
[Your **force**,] [to **break**] [***blow, burn**] [and **make**] [me **new**.]

John Donne (1633), 'Holy Sonnet: XIV', ll. 1–4.

See also **Sapphic stanzas**, which specify a spondee in their final lines.

Pyrrhic

A two-syllable foot, both unstressed.

It is not really possible to give an example word for the pyrrhic. This is because there is no stress at all, which can only happen between other stressed feet that offset the pyrrhic's quietness. Therefore, as with the spondee, the pyrrhic is a rare foot in English verse, and it is not possible to have a fully pyrrhic line. However, pyrrhics appear in partnership with spondees, providing the hushed quiet just before that foot's heavy beats. Pyrrhics might denote anticipation, or sometimes a quiet reticence. They can also be a deft way of conveying near-silence in a poem, as they are as close as speaking can come to silence. This example by Elizabeth Barrett Browning simultaneously suggests an awed hush inspired by the strength of a bond between two lovers and provides the quietness that will allow us to hear them 'beat double' more clearly. The rhythm is predominantly **iambic** but line 10 sees two substitutions – a pyrrhic followed by a spondee:

> The widest land
> Doom takes to part us, leaves thy heart in mine
> With pulses that beat double. What I do
> And what I dream include thee,

> [The **wid**] [est **land**]
> [Doom **takes**] [to **part**] [us, **leaves**] [thy **heart**] [in **mine**]
> [With **pul**] [ses that *] [**beat doub-**] [le. **What**] [I **do**]
> [And **what**] [I **dream**] [in**clude**] [thee,

> Elizabeth Barrett Browning (1850), 'VI', *Sonnets from the Portuguese*,
> ll. 8–11.

A similar effect to this is seen in Robert Frost's 'Stopping by Woods on a Snowy Evening' (1923), where the final two syllables of 'promises' form a pyrrhic foot before the final iamb of 'to keep': 'But **I** have **prom**ises to **keep**' (l. 14).

Amphibrach

A three-syllable foot arranged with one stress at the centre.

Example word: ba**na**na

Gerard Manley Hopkins considered the amphibrach to have 'the most bound and canter' of metrical feet; 'it bounds like waves' he suggested. Indeed, it does have a leaping quality and feels like a stool or a step to be hopped over. Since it would be difficult to keep on hopping like this the amphibrach is almost never employed throughout a poem, although a line of them might occur occasionally within a predominantly **rising metre**d poem (see Swinburne's 'Dolores', mentioned above, for example). In Byron's example amphibrach lines alternate with iamb-anapaest ones, creating shifts between sprightly movement and solemn intoning:

They name thee before me,	[They **name** thee] [be**fore** me,]
A knell to mine ear;	[A **knell**] [to mine **ear**;]
A shudder comes o'er me—	[A **shudd**er] [comes **o'er** me—]
Why wert thou so dear?	[Why **wert**] [thou so **dear**?]
They know not I knew thee,	[They **know** not] [I **knew** thee,]
Who knew thee too well:—	[Who **knew**] [thee too **well**:—]
Long, long shall I rue thee,	Long, **long** shall] [I **rue** thee,]
Too deeply to tell.	[Too **deep**-] [ly to **tell.**]

George Gordon (Lord Byron) (1815), 'When we two parted', ll. 17–24.

More commonly the amphibrach appears in single substitutions for two- or three-syllable feet (an example may be seen appropriately in the phrase 'o'er**throw** me' in the poem from Donne above). When the amphibrach appears alone or at the end of a line, as in Longfellow's gentle poem that likens the falling snow to the falling of carefully placed sounds of verse, it can create a softly lilting effect:

This is the poem of the air,
  Slowly in silent syllables recorded;
This is the secret of despair,

[**This** is the] [**po**em] [**of** the] [**air**]
  [**Slow**-ly in] [**si**-lent] [**syll**-a-bles] [re-**cor**-ded;]
[**This** is the] [**sec**-ret] [**of** des-] [**pair**]

Henry Wadsworth Longfellow (1863), 'Snow-Flakes', ll. 13–15.

Doubted English feet

The final possible arrangements of three-syllable feet are controversial because they suggest that two (or three, or no) stresses appear within one foot. Some suggest that they should always be split into more conventional arrangements, especially when the two stresses are next to each other – effectively incorporating the already controversial spondee into the foot. These feet are really more useful in Classical verse (written in Greek or Latin) where the 'stresses' denote long syllables versus short ones. For the record these are listed here, but definitive examples are rare and contested:

- *bacchius*: three-syllable foot, with two final stresses – de-**dum**-**dum**
- *antibacchius*: three-syllable foot, with two initial stresses – **dum**-**dum**-de

- *molossus*: three-syllable foot, all stressed – **dum-dum-dum**
- *tribach*: three-syllable foot, none stressed – de-de-de.

The final arrangement that has received a degree of acknowledgement is the amphimacer.

Amphimacer

A three-syllable foot arranged with a stress at each end.

Example word: **sacrifice**

The amphimacer just about squeezes an unstressed syllable in between two stresses. It is often seen in phrases rather than individual words, such as (rather unpoetically) '**in**come **tax**'. Along with all his other experiments with metre, Tennyson attempted whole lines of amphimacers in 'The Oak':

Live thy Life,	[**Live** thy **Life**,]
Young and old,	[**Young** and **old**,]
Like yon oak,	[**Like** yon **oak**,]
Bright in spring,	[**Bright** in **spring**,]
Living gold;	[**Liv**-ing **gold**;

Alfred Tennyson (1889), 'The Oak', ll. 1–5.

Given that the oak is celebrated for its steadfastness and weathering of storms, perhaps it's appropriate that this poem forms a thickset column of buttressing stresses. However, this is a rare experiment and, like the amphibrach, the amphimacer usually only makes its appearance as substitution.

Note that the lines from Tennyson's 'The Charge of the Light Brigade', considered in the discussion of **dactyls**, could arguably be scanned as amphimacers ('[**Half** a **league**,] [**half** a **league**]'). However, given that the poem goes on in dactylic metre it seems reasonable to leave those as dactyls with a weight only on 'half', as indeed can be heard in the recording of Tennyson's own reading of the poem. A less controversial example may be seen in Coleridge's 'Lesson for a Boy', which features four amphimacers in line 9. This is a good poem to end discussion of feet in English as it attempts a lesson in accent-syllabic verse. In addition to the amphimacers, see how it performs each of the feet it names (Coleridge uses the 'long/short' terminology rather than 'stress/unstress'):

Trochee trips from long to short;
From long to long in solemn sort
Slow Spondee stalks, strong foot! yet ill able
Ever to come up with Dactyl's trisyllable.
Iambics march from short to long.
With a leap and a bound the swift Anapæsts throng.
One syllable long, with one short at each side,
Amphibrachys hastes with a stately stride—
First and last being long, middle short, Amphimacer
Strikes his thundering hoofs like a proud high-bred Racer.

[**First** and **last**] [**be**-ing **long**] [**midd**-le **short**,] [**Amph**-i-**mace**](r)
[Strikes his **thund**-] [er-ing **hoofs**] [like a **proud**] [high-bred **Race**](r)

Samuel Taylor Coleridge (1834), 'Lesson for a Boy', ll. 1–10.

Feet and cultural assumptions

As a final word, we may think of feet simply as a convenient way of dividing verse into units. However, as some of these examples have demonstrated, each of these feet arrangements has cultural associations. The iamb may be considered 'natural', or pleasing to the ear and so suggest ordered, civilized expression; the trochee may be thought disruptive, aggressively haranguing the ear, or else simple and childlike, an immature form that has not yet settled into iambic rhythm. Dactyls may be associated with Classical civilization and particularly when they appear in succession in longer lines create an air of scholarly seriousness. When they are used more playfully or colloquially, as in some of Browning's poems, the dactyl falls in more with other triple-syllable feet, such as anapaests, which, as we've seen, at one time were regarded as 'unpoetic', disruptive, unruly feet that distracted from the serious mode of contemplation that some readers wished to preserve for poetry. Thus we see that feet have culture to bring to a poem as well as a rhythm; Annie Finch's study considers this notion in more detail, and her introduction includes a useful summary of the cultural associations ascribed to metrical feet.

References

Finch, A. (1993), *The Ghost of Meter: Culture and Prosody in American Free Verse* (Michigan: University of Michigan Press).

Hopkins, G. M. (2002), 'Author's Preface', in *Gerard Manley Hopkins: The Major Works*, ed. C. Phillips (Oxford: Oxford University Press), pp. 106–9.

Hopkins, G. M. (1959), *Journals and Papers*, ed. Humphry House (London: Oxford University Press), pp. 274–5.

Meynell, A. (1893), *The Flower of the Mind* (London: Grant Richards).

3.4 Metrical lines

> ## Stich
> A line of poetry.

Having seen how lines of verse fall into feet, we come to naming these lines metrically; that is after their metre. The term 'stich' is used fairly infrequently, in fact; a line of poetry tends to be characterized first by the type of feet it includes and secondly by the number of feet. If the number of feet varies in each line of the poem then the metre is named simply after the type. This chilling example by Southey mainly uses iambic feet, but the line lengths vary:

> [Old **Sa**-] [rah **loved**] [her **help**-] [less **child**]
> [Whom **help**-] [less-**ness**] [made **dear**;]
> And **life** was **happ**iness to **him**
> Who **had** no **hope** nor **fear**.
>
> Robert Southey (1798), 'The Idiot', ll. 5–8.

Here the number of feet shifts between four and three per line and so the poem may be described as showing alternating iambic tetrameter (four feet) and trimeter (three feet). This happens to be known as a **ballad stanza**, but we could also simply say that the poem is 'iambic', since that is the dominant foot-type used.

Examples of common metrical lines, defined by type and number of feet, however, are given here. Looking at these examples, have a go at dividing the lines into the number of feet listed. What type of feet will you need to make the syllables fit? Iambic? Trochaic? Anapaestic? Are any syllables left out or added in unusually?

One-foot line: monometer

Example: 'Each on each', Robert Browning (1855), 'Love Among the Ruins', l. 72.

Two-foot line: dimeter
(seen in mad-song stanzas, Burns stanzas)

Example:

> What should I say
> Since faith is dead
> And truth away
> From you is fled?
> Should I be led
> With doubleness?
> Nay, nay, mistress!

> Thomas Wyatt (1815 [c. 1503–1542]), 'CCXLV: What should I say', ll. 22–8.

Three-foot line: trimeter
(seen in ballad stanzas, rime couée)

Example:

> Rising from unrest,
> The trembling woman pressed
> With feet of weary woe;
> She could no further go.

> William Blake (1794), 'Little Girl Found', ll. 17–20.

Four-foot line: tetrameter
(seen in ballad stanzas, In Memoriam stanzas, mad-song stanzas, rime couée, Burns stanzas)

Example:

> Helen, thy beauty is to me
> Like those Nicean barks of yore,
> That gently, o'er a perfumed sea,
> The weary, wayworn wanderer bore
> To his own native shore.

> Edgar Allan Poe (1845), 'To Helen', ll. 5–9.

Five-foot line: pentameter
(seen in blank verse, sonnets, heroic couplets and quatrains, Venus and Adonis stanza, rime royale, ottava rima, Spenserian stanza)

Example:

> Through weeds and thorns, and matted underwood
> I force my way; now climb, and now descend
> O'er rocks, or bare or mossy, with blind foot
> Crushing the purple whorts;
>
> Samuel Taylor Coleridge (1802), 'The Picture', l. 1–4.

Six-foot line: hexameter
(or Alexandrine in English, usually specified as iambic, and seen in Spenserian stanzas)

Example:

> Bending the ear of the hedgerow with stories of fire and sword
> James Fenton (1983), 'Wind', l. 8.

Example:

> The glory they transfuse with fitting truth to speak.
> Percy Bysshe Shelley (1821), 'Adonais', l. 468.

Seven-foot line: heptameter
(if it is iambic it is called a fourteener, after the number of syllables)

Example:

> His heart is warm, his hand is true, his word is frank and free;
> Eliza Cook (1838), 'The Gallant English Tar', l. 21.

Eight-foot line: octameter
Example:

> Blight and famine, plague and earthquake, roaring deeps and fiery sands,
> Alfred Tennyson (1832, revised 1842), 'The Lotus Eaters', l. 160.

Foot variations in metrical lines

We saw in the Southey example that poems can vary in the number of feet per line; poets may also vary the type of feet in each line. When this happens regularly a looser terminology is sometimes used that refers only to the number of feet: so the poem is 'in hexameter' or 'in tetrameter', depending on the dominant pattern. Here all of Blake's lines are tetrameter, but their feet alternate between iambs and anapaests, so the poem may be described as 'in tetrameter':

> But if at the Church they would give us some Ale,
> And a pleasant fire our souls to regale,
> We'd sing and we'd pray all the livelong day,
> Nor ever once wish from the Church to stray.
>
> [But **if**] [at the **Church**] [they would **give**] [us some **Ale**,]
> [And **a**] [plea-sant **fire**] [our **souls**] [to re-**gale**]
> [We'd **sing**] [and we'd **pray**] [all the **live**-] [long **day**,]
> [Nor **ev**-] [er once **wish**] [from the **Church**] [to **stray**.]
>
> William Blake (1794), 'The Little Vagabond', ll. 5–8.

Finally we come to caesural stress. Caesuras, as seen, are pauses that occur within a metrical line. Sometimes these pauses are counted in the scansion of a line because, although they are not spoken aloud, they carry the weight of emphasis. This can be seen if we look at an Alexandrine that occurs at the end of a series of iambic pentameter lines in Pope's 'Essay on Criticism'. In this passage he is complaining about monotonous and lazy versifying. He ends:

> A needless Alexandrine ends the song
> That, like a wounded snake, drags its slow length along.
>
> Alexander Pope (1711), 'An Essay on Criticism', ll. 355–6.

An Alexandrine in English contains six iambic feet, and its extra length is cleverly demonstrated here as it grows an extra foot after the pentameter lines. However, in line with Pope's criticism of 'bad' versifiers, he introduces some disruptions to the iambic order by putting caesural pauses in unusual positions. The iambic rhythm leads us to expect, 'That **like** a **woun**ded **snake** drags **its** slow **length along**'. However, there are two pauses here which bracket 'like a wounded snake' from the rest of the line, suggesting another scanning pattern running alongside this one. Introducing these pauses might seem at first to show the mangling that Pope regrets. But, this variation might actually save Pope's line from falling into the anticipated monotony of a sing-song rhythm. Accepting that a caesura can count in the scanning, we can rescan the line and see that the commas act as unstressed syllables, suggesting they are filled with intakes of breath:

> [**That**,] [like a **woun**-] [ded **snake**] [, **drags**] [its slow **length**] [a**long**.]

By scanning like this we keep the six feet in the line, but we find that Pope cleverly puts a stress on 'drag' (to emphasize that movement) and also introduces anapaests into the iambic metre ('like a **woun**'; 'its slow **length**'). So, the rising metre of the Alexandrine is maintained, but is given some extension. In fact, these pauses create a stress pattern that sounds more like natural speech, albeit with a weary, sighing tone (as fits the context). The pauses are felt in the counting as we breathe them, holding up the pentameter pace (pentameter being Pope's preferred metre) and the line's usual appearance of robust ('straight') pentameter becomes itself a 'wounded snake': a line with extra kinks in its body.

4 | Rhyme

Chapter Outline

Rhyme

The repetition of identical or similar sounds, usually at the end of poetic lines.

Rhyme can be the most delighting and engaging aspect of verse and is often thought of as the defining feature that separates poetry from prose. Its appeal to the ear keeps us engaged as we listen for matching sounds and the way it brings words together unexpectedly can be surprising and even revolutionary. Yet, the harmonious effect it creates can also feel deadening, predictable, even crass. At worst, what feels comforting and attractive for one reader feels restrictive and prescriptive for another. Rhyme therefore divides as much as it harmonizes. This means that while it seems to be a purely aesthetic question, it can also have political significance.

Harmony (rhyme) has something of a conservative reputation: the proficient, matching quality of rhyme, particularly in such forms as **heroic couplets**, can seem to overvalue rule and regulation, to erase contradiction and smooth away passion and idiosyncrasy. In such a view, to abandon or even just to loosen rhyme is to be revolutionary, as seen in many post-1918 poetic innovations, or Romantic experiments with 'everyday speech' in poetry. A poet may feel that there is no place for rhyme in a world that has lost all sense of harmonious relationship. On the other hand, excessive rhyme can also be revolutionary. Algernon Charles Swinburne, for example, used complex patterns of four, five, six, seven, eight or ten lines of interlocking rhymes in a spirit of experimentation and daring: technical brilliance and sophisticated rhyming patterns denoted scandal and subversion as he allied this rhyming excess with sexual, moral and religious excesses.

The principle behind rhyme is repetition and near-collision: rhymes are the repetition (or the almost-repetition) of a sound that you have just heard. This principle of return or meeting can be used as a healing, soothing or celebratory gesture, as when Elizabeth Jennings rhymes 'caress' with 'gentleness' when she tries to characterize the emotion she feels for a friend. Despite the sense content, the matching sounds suggest a relation between the two words – both tactile and reserved – that is comforting, as though that pairing was somehow meant to be:

> Such love I cannot analyse;
> It does not rest in lips or eyes,
> Neither in kisses nor caress.
> Partly, I know, it's gentleness
>
> Elizabeth Jennings (1972), 'Friendship', ll. 1–4.

However, the same principle can produce unsettling and disturbing effects. For example, in Thomas Hardy's often-uncomfortable **elegies** (*Poems of 1912–13*) for his wife, the repeated sound of rhyming creates a sense of entrapment (see the enclosing gestures at the end of each stanza in 'Lament', for example). Or, it pulls the rug from beneath the elegist's feet, as in 'The Going', where the rhyming of 'you I see' with 'used to be' implies something ideal (that perception is linked to presence, and that 'seeing' implies 'being'), but undercuts it, because this is only an illusion of his wife, just as 'be' is not quite a repetition of 'see':

> Why do you make me leave the house
> And think for a breath it is you I see
> At the end of the alley of bending boughs
> Where so often at dusk you used to be;
>
> Thomas Hardy (1914), 'The Going', ll. 15–18.

Most disturbingly, when Hardy rhymes 'proud' with 'shroud', in 'A Circular', there is a sharp bitterness in the pathos that the rhyme evokes. The poem's principal meaning addresses the poignancy of reading a circular that advertises new fashions (an image of sprightly liveliness) addressed to the wife who has recently died and is now dressed in a shroud. Yet the rhyme placement hints painfully at a link between the woman's pride and her quick and unexpected demise: does the poet almost admit that he associates her death with pride when living? Is this an admission that was hidden (as it is still nearly hidden) in their everyday life?

> And this gay-pictured, spring-time shout
> Of Fashion, hails what lady proud?
> Her who before last year ebbed out
>   Was costumed in a shroud.
>
> Thomas Hardy (1914), 'A Circular', ll. 9–12.

English verse has not always relied on rhyme for its structure and character – see the discussions of **alliterative metre** for more on this. Yet the European influence encouraged an enthusiasm for rhyme that developed into near-dependency: rhyme for many defines poetry. For other readers the presence of such rhyme, however, is anachronistic in English verse, or at least evidence of a continental 'softening' that takes us away from the ruggedness and earthiness of the rhythms of English. Chaucer was an early pioneer of this continental influence, particularly in his development of the elaborate stanza form, **rime royal**, used in *Troilus and Criseyde*. Yet, while Chaucer is often celebrated for his adaptation of continental rhyme schemes, the pursuit of rhyming harmony has been known to arouse suspicion: rhyme's sense of artificiality or of delight in the sound rather than the sense of words can destabilize cherished ideas about the seriousness and moral purpose of poetry. Similarly, a sense of the absurd can emerge when syntax is contorted in order to achieve a rhyme – as seen in Betjeman's wry inversions in 'Distant View of a Provincial Town'. The repetition of rhyme can suggest excess, a piling up of mere flourishes of brilliance that detract from the seriousness some would associate with poetry:

> Beside those spires so spick and span
>   Against an unencumbered sky
> The old Great Western Railway ran
>   When someone different was I.
>
> John Betjeman (1937), 'Distant View of a Provincial Town', ll. 1–4.

However, just because rhyme tends to draw a reader in, to enchant them and please them, does not mean that it can't be incisive and often startlingly thought-provoking. We might say that it is precisely rhyme's mesmerizing effect that holds our attention, and capitalizes on this engagement by forcing us to contrast the enchanting rhymes with the disturbing sense they reveal. For example, see Elizabeth Barrett Browning's 'The Cry of the Children' (1843), in which rhymes reveal the brutality of factory spaces in which the only repeated sounds are those of industry and the crushing of child-workers' spirits. Or see Blake's simple rhymes and complex commentary in *Songs of Innocence* (1789) and *Songs of Experience* (1794).

Indeed, it is often when we are lulled into dismissing a poem's intent (as in so-called **nonsense verse**) that we are in danger of overlooking a poem's critical potential. At its most extreme, rhyming for the apparent sake of it produces a shrewd commentary even as it seems to make light of our love of its repetition and pattern. In Edward Lear's 'The Jumblies' (1871) the journey to sea in a sieve (a nonsense in itself) parodies how poems can chase their own tails in an effort to rhyme. Rather than delivering a solemn truth, the attractive repeated sounds also imply an emptying of meaning, a series of leakages of significance, just as the water leaks from the sieve. It cautions us not to accept easily that similarity or repetition in rhyme suggests some sort of harmonious 'rightness'.

> And when the sieve turned round and round,
> And everyone cried, 'You'll be drowned!'
> They called aloud, 'Our sieve ain't big,
> But we don't care a button; we don't care a fig—
>   In a sieve we'll go to sea!'
>   Far and few, far and few,
>   Are the lands where the Jumblies live.
>   Their heads are green, and their hands are blue;
>   And they went to sea in a sieve.
>
> Edward Lear (1871), 'The Jumblies', ll. 6–14.

Rhyme is one of poetry's features that most obviously reminds us of poetry's relationship with speech. Clearly it is particularly evident in spoken poetry, and rhymes help recital by providing 'hooks' for the ear, making the words strung between them easier to remember. For this reason oral cultures often tell their own histories in rhyming poems, songs and **ballads**. However, there is also the phenomenon of **eye rhymes** in which words which do not necessarily rhyme when spoken but create a visual chime that is 'rhyme-like' on the page, hinting at the culture of rhyme even as they don't quite conform to it. This suggests that there is more at stake in rhyme than pure sound. Rather, the rhyme indicates certain patterns of thinking, reasoning and feeling.

Rhyme appeals simultaneously to the senses – the ear and the eye – and to the mind in memory and in the act of comparison it invites between words. It moves between sound and sense, between thinking and hearing, between similarity and difference, and of course between word and word. It is a process that jolts us out of time – often in a welcome way – because, as the ear (or eye) perceives the 'answer' rhyme, it also remembers the sound's previous appearance, producing an oscillating effect that conjures 'truth' or revelation from between the two different words. The ideas and thought processes inspired can offer radically new ways of understanding the world: as W. K. Wimsatt suggested in an important essay, rhymes impose a 'counter-pattern' on how we express ourselves and so offer alternatives to the 'logical pattern' we are taught to expect. Indeed, rhyme can mirror how we gather experience and knowledge: patterns are spotted, but then frequently reappear in slightly altered ways; as Mark Twain is said to have quipped, 'History doesn't repeat itself, but it does rhyme'.

While we might be keen to identify **rhyme schemes**, it is important to be alert to the precise dynamics at play in each individual instance of rhyme. Therefore discussion of rhyme-scheme is deferred until the end of this chapter. Note that where rhymes are pointed out in examples here they are *italicized*.

Reference

Wimsatt, W. K. (1954), 'One Relation of Rhyme to Reason', in *The Verbal Icon: Studies in the Meaning of Poetry* (Kentucky: University Press of Kentucky), pp. 153–68.

4.1 Perfect rhyme

Perfect rhyme

When the sounds of two words match exactly, usually by repeating the main stressed vowel and any consonants following it.

Perfect rhymes are the most obvious and familiar of rhymes, and the ones we recognize in everyday speech around us as well as in poetry. They are often labelled according to the number of syllables involved in the rhyme:

- *masculine rhyme*: rhymes of one stressed syllable
  Example: reach and speech
- *feminine rhyme*: rhymes of two syllables that end on an unstressed note
  Example: yellow and fellow
- *triple rhyme*: rhymes involving three syllables.
  Example: greenery and scenery

As English verse is often **iambic**, so ending on a stressed syllable, masculine rhymes emphasize the heavy ends of lines. They might create a particularly sombre effect, with each single-syllable rhyme tolling like a bell, as in Donne's defiant address of death:

> Death be not proud, though some have called thee
> Mighty and dreadfull, for, thou are not soe,
> For, those, whom thou think'st, thou dost overthrow,
> Die not, poore death, nor yet canst thou kill mee;
>
> John Donne (1633), 'Holy Sonnet X', ll. 1–4.

Alternatively the short snap of a masculine rhyme might emphasize parallelisms and ingenious construction that is carried lightly, as in Pope's *The Rape of the Lock*:

> The Knave of Diamonds tries his wily arts,
> And wins (oh, shameful chance!) the Queen of Hearts.
>
> Alexander Pope (1714), *The Rape of the Lock*, Canto III, ll. 87–8.

As the number of rhymed syllables grows and the line endings are unstressed the effect tends to lighten, as in Shelley's 'To a Sky-Lark!' Here we sense the bird taking wing as its flying movement is echoed in the chiming of its feminine-rhymed singing:

> Higher still and higher
>   From the earth thou springest
> Like a cloud of fire;
>   The blue deep thou wingest,
> And singing still dost soar, and soaring ever singest.
>
> Percy Bysshe Shelley (1820), 'To a Sky-Lark!', ll. 6–10.

Naturally a poem might move between different types of rhymes, often for specific effects, such as in Moore's 'The time I've lost in wooing':

> The time I've lost in wooing,
> In watching and pursuing
>   The light that lies
>   In woman's eyes,
> Has been my heart's undoing.
>
> Thomas Moore (1834), 'The time I've lost in wooing', ll. 1–5.

Here the double feminine rhymes (wooing/suing/doing) create the light-hearted frolic of the sexual chase, yet at the centre of that pursuit is the pointed (and **punning**) masculine rhyme of 'lies' with 'eyes'. This hints ironically at the so-called 'truth' of femininity, which is not light and gentle, as feminine rhyming suggests, but sharp and deceptive.

More sombrely, in Smith's 'To Night' the masculine rhymes (find/sign'd; art/heart) reflect the poem's content – resignation and collapse – by beating out the poet's 'exhausted heart'. In such a setting the strict, terse quality of the single rhymes in fact suggests the calming effect produced by embracing such control. Yet, in moving forwards, looking to death (where death is a meeting with God) the tone shifts and becomes a little more open: the release from earth to heaven is seen in the move from masculine to feminine rhyme (given/heaven):

> Tho' no repose on thy dark breast I find,
> I still enjoy thee—cheerless as thou art;
>   For in thy quiet gloom the exhausted heart
> Is calm, tho' wretched; hopeless, yet resign'd.
> While to the winds and waves its sorrows given,
> May reach—tho' lost on earth—the ear of Heaven!
>
> Charlotte Smith (1788), 'To Night', ll. 9–14.

Moving to triple rhymes, the very sense of sustained inventiveness needed to keep on creating extended rhymes creates a humorous tension as a poet finds ever more complex ways of meeting the rhyme's demands. Byron's *Don Juan*, for example, repeats this technique throughout the telling of a scandalous tale, often to highlight the artificiality and extravagance that underpins its driving narrative:

> By this time Don Alfonso was arrived,
> With torches, friends, and servants in great number;
> The major part of them had long been wived,
> And therefore paused not to disturb the slumber
> Of any wicked woman, who contrived
> By stealth her husband's temples to encumber:
> Examples of this kind are so *contagious*
> Were one not punish'd, all would be *outrageous*.
>
> George Byron (1819), *Don Juan*, Canto I, Stanza 138, ll. 1097–104.

The technique is even parodied in triple rhyme, later on, with, 'His speech was a fine sample, *on the whole*, | Of rhetoric, which the learn'd call *"rigmarole"'* (Stanza 174, ll. 1391–2).

Internal rhyme

The repetition of sounds within a line of verse.

As we have seen in the examples so far, perfect rhymes are particularly common at line endings (called *end-rhymes*). This placement makes the rhymes most obvious to the eye and ear. However, rhymes can occur within lines as well as at the ends of them. These internal rhymes can create a layering effect of sound, building up a rich texture of repetition that might create a lushness of aural stimulation, or might create a disturbing sense of frenzied sound. Internal rhymes might predict end-rhymes, as in Blake's 'The Garden of Love':

> And Priests in black *gowns* were walking their *rounds*,
> And binding with *briars* my joys and *desires*.
>
> William Blake (1794), 'The Garden of Love', ll. 11–12.

Or they may remain entirely internal, as in Hopkins' 'God's Grandeur':

> Generations have trod, have trod, have trod;
>   And all is *seared* with trade; *bleared*, *smeared* with toil;
>
> Gerard Manley Hopkins (1918 [c. 1877]), 'God's Grandeur', ll. 5–6.

Internal rhymes might even reach across lines, skipping over the line endings altogether, as in Rossetti's *Goblin Market*.

> The *cat-faced* purr'd,
> The *rat-paced* spoke a word
> Of welcome,
>
> Christina Rossetti (1862), *Goblin Market*, ll. 109–11.

Internal rhyme treads a careful line between artificiality (as the sounds are contrived to chime) and naturalness (the position of the rhymes occurs naturally rather than in fixed positions). However, as we will see below, internal rhymes are actually more likely to be **imperfect rhymes**. Perfect rhymes in quick succession can create an overloading effect; the gradual building up of imperfect chimes, on the other hand, can create a more subtle effect of accumulation. Indeed, imperfect rhymes that slip beneath our radar seem suited to an internal position: their obliqueness finds them hiding within lines rather declaring themselves more obviously at line ends. Internal rhyme in combination with imperfect rhyme can be subversive: it is a gesture at harmony and a rejection of its obviousness.

169

4.2 Imperfect rhyme

> ### Imperfect rhyme (or *slant rhyme*)
> Constructions where the rhymes are only partial or slight correspondences of sound because only the vowel *or* the consonant sounds are repeated.

Although imperfect rhymes are common in everyday speech and in poetry they are not always immediately obvious as 'rhymes' per se because they seem almost to miss each other; or they meet each other more precariously. It is strange at first to think of a chimed vowel sound or consonant sound alone as rhyme because we are so used to rhymes involving both: we are familiar with thinking that *cat* and *bat* rhyme, but *feet* and *beam*? Or, *book* and *back*? These seem more 'aslant'. Imperfect rhymes can occur as follows:

- *consonance*: when only the final consonant sounds correspond
  Example: che*ck* and plu*ck*
- *assonance*: when only the internal vowel sounds correspond
  Example: d*ee*p and m*ea*t
- *pararhyme*: when the consonant order is repeated, but the vowels differ.
  Example: *flesh* and *flash*; or, *bid* and *bad*

Wilfred Owen's experimental war poetry demonstrates many imperfect rhymes. His 1918 poem 'Miners', for example, uses all of the above imperfect rhymes:

> The centuries will burn rich loads
>   With which we groaned,
> Whose warmth shall lull their dreamy lids,
>   While songs are crooned.
> But they will not dream of us poor lads,
>   Lost in the ground.
>
> Wilfred Owen (1918), 'Miners', ll. 29–34.

This insistence on imperfect rhyme might suggest how, in the wake of war, life for Owen was bereft of certainty: perfect rhymes became imperfect ones. While originally about a colliery disaster, Owen admitted that the poem became 'mixed up with the War at the end'.[1] Owen's unclear thinking is reflected in imperfect rhymes that even suggest the muffled hearing of a soldier whose senses have been blunted by the sounds of war. Owen's new relationship with sound suggests that as war destroys lives and nations it destroys cultures and traditions; a new method of speaking and expressing is needed to intimate that devastating effect.

So, while Owen hinted at tradition by using patterns and repetitions in his poetry (this is not **free verse**), he skewed that tradition towards the imperfect, the oblique and the almost misheard. The repetitions of sound hold the **stanza** together, almost claustrophobically, but the imperfection of the pararhymes, (loads, lids, lads) assonance (loads, groaned) and consonance (groaned, crooned) means that perfect rhyme – harmony – is buried; like the men it is 'lost in the ground'.

Other examples of imperfect rhyme suggest, at least at first, harmoniousness, as in Poe's 'The Bells'. Early on assonance creates the sound of bell-ringing, implying happiness and pleasure. However, it is revived later in the poem as the repeated screech of terror and fear (adding a foreboding to the line, 'What a world of happiness their harmony foretells!'):

> Hear the mellow wedding bells,
> Golden bells!
> What a world of happiness their harmony foretells!
>
> [...]
> Hear the loud alarum bells–
> Brazen bells!
> What a tale of terror, now, their turbulency tells!
> In the startled ear of night
> How they scream out their affright!
>
> Edgar Allan Poe (1849), 'The Bells', ll. 15–17; 36–40.

T. S. Eliot used assonance to add aural texture to the materiality he gives to an image of smoke in 'The Love Song of J. Alfred Prufrock' (1915): 'The yellow smoke that rubs its muzzle on the windowpanes' (l. 15).

Consonance, of course, emphasizes the endings of words, even when it appears within a line. In a lively celebration of the energy that characterizes 'each mortal thing', Hopkins indulges in extravagant sound repetitions that thrust their energies outwards (like the 'mortal things' themselves) creating a zinging quality at each word's end:

> As kingfishers catch fire, dragonflies draw flame;
>   As tumbled over rim in roundy wells
>   Stones ring; like each tucked string tells, each hung bell's
> Bow swung finds tongue to fling out broad its name;
> Each mortal thing does one thing and the same:
>   Deals out that being indoors each one dwells;
>   Selves—goes its self; myself it speaks and spells,
> Crying What I do is me: for that I came.
>
> Gerard Manley Hopkins (1918 [c. 1877]), 'As Kingfishers catch fire', ll. 1–8.

Paul Muldoon's 'Hard Drive', however, uses consonance to create a sense of entrapment, of being pushed into a corner (the opening line is, 'With my back to the wall'), as the poem wrings out the tension of feeling constantly under threat of discovery:

> With an ear to the grou*nd*
> and my neck on the bloc*k*
> I would tend to my wou*nd*
> in Belleek and Bellanalec*k*.

Paul Muldoon (2002), 'Hard Drive', ll. 5–8.

Muldoon's rhyme here of 'ground' with 'wound' anticipates the rhyme that misses sound altogether (**eye rhymes**).

Note

1. See note to the poem in *Wilfred Owen: War Poems and Others*, ed. Dominic Hibberd (1973) (London: Chattto and Windus), p. 123.

4.3 Sight and sound effects

Alliteration

The repetition of the opening sounds of words.

Example: *R*ed *R*iding Hood

Alliteration was introduced as a tradition in the chapter on **metre**, but instances of alliteration occur in **accentual-syllabic** verse too. The quick repetition of opening word sounds can be difficult to handle: hence the alliteration in tongue-twisters such as '*R*ound the *r*agged *r*ock the *r*agged *r*ascal *r*an'. Similarly alliteration can create urgency in the structure and in the recitation of a poem. The popularity of alliteration in advertising jingles and slogans indicates its rhetorical power: it is attractive and attention-grabbing to have initial sounds repeated, creating a feeling of 'fitness' that makes a phrase more memorable. In less hectoring examples, however, it might have a murmuring, softening effect, as created by the 'm'-sounds in Coleridge's 'Kubla Khan': 'Five *m*iles *m*eandering with a *m*azy *m*otion' (1797, l. 25).

Although alliteration most familiarly occurs in the first letters of words, as was seen in **alliterative metre**, it can also echo in mid-position consonants. In Betjeman's 'Love in a Valley' sounds stutter across each line. As the speaker descends down into the valley alliteration creates the sense of a narrowing range of sounds: the letter 'd' reverberates between the lush valley sides (particularly effectively in 'rhododendrons') before it flattens off into the lighter 'l'-sounds of the tennis court, where shrubbery has been cleared and play may begin:

> Deep down the drive go the cushioned rhododendrons,
>   Deep down, sand deep, drives the heather root,
> Deep the spliced timber barked around the summer house,
>   Light lies the tennis-court, plantain underfoot.
>
> John Betjeman (1937), 'Love in a Valley', ll. 9–12.

When alliteration is concentrated in soft 's'-sounds it is called *sibilance*, as can be heard and seen in another of Betjeman's poems, 'A Bay in Anglesey' (1966), which opens with 'The sleepy sound of a tea-time tide'. This move from soft sibilance to harder alliteration (in the 't'-sounds) continues throughout the soundscape of this poem, evoking the shapes and contours of the natural world as it harmonizes with the sea.

Eye rhyme

Rhymes that only exist to the eye because the spelling rather than the sound chimes.

Example: laughter and daughter

Eye rhymes are, by definition, related to print culture and their success relies partly on a certain sophistication in the relationship between poet and audience – they are a nod to our ability to read and spell and they acknowledge the poem as a printed, material object held in the hand and viewed as well as heard. Their effect can be complex and coded. Indeed, a rhyme that only occurs in silent reading, but which still commands attention, is suited to secret-sharing between poets and readers: this might be a secret joke, a secret bitterness or a secret subversion.

Shakespeare's *Sonnets* (1609) are celebrated for their sense of poetry as a material, lasting object: the poet vows to create a 'monument of gentle verse' for the young man. Shakespeare's use of eye rhymes engages energetically with this idea: for example, in the fourth sonnet of the sequence, Shakespeare eye rhymes 'alone' with 'gone'. This brings out a connection between those two terms (if the young man remains *alone*, i.e. does not father a child, he will eventually be *gone* from the earth).

> For having traffic with thy self alone,
> Thou of thy self thy sweet self dost deceive.
> Then how when nature calls thee to be gone,
> What acceptable audit canst thou leave?
>
> William Shakespeare (1609), 'Sonnet 4', ll. 9–12.

The fact that the poem uses an eye rhyme to say this suggests that the printed poem itself (where the eye rhymes will be seen) can remedy this problem. The poem, rather than a child, will be the young man's legacy. So, while the threat of annihilation hangs over this sonnet, it also celebrates its own ability to create lastingness in the form of printed rhymes. This is most famously seen in the sequence's repeated eye-rhyming of 'prove' (with the poetry itself often providing 'proof') with 'love'.

Eye rhymes might intimate connections and ideas that a poem almost cannot bring itself to declare openly. Tennyson's *In Memoriam A. H. H.*, for example, is noted for a **rhyme scheme** that relies on clear, masculine rhymes. However, Lyric XXVIII daringly eye-rhymes 'Christ' with 'mist'. In that short moment of silenced rhyming we glimpse (ironically) the anxiety that haunts the entire lengthy poem: that the fog of grief has obscured the poet's view of God. As the following stanza acknowledges, it is 'as if a door | Were shut between me and the sound;' (l. 8):

> The time draws near the birth of *Christ*:
>   The moon is hid, the night is still;
>   The Christmas bells from hill to hill
> Answer each other in the *mist*.

> Alfred Tennyson (1850), *In Memoriam A. H. H.*, Lyric XXVIII, ll. 1–4.

Onomatopoeia

When a word's sound replicates or evokes the thing or action it describes.

Example: bang

Although onomatopoeia strictly refers to the property of a particular word, all of the rhyming and repetition encountered in this section can come together to form a global 'onomatopoeic' effect in a poem. Phil Brown's 'Soda Song' plays on this effect:

> The soda-fizz bubbles
> leap and crackle;
> lip-pinching pop jumps
> and tingle tongue gush.
> Sorely guzzled gulps of gas
> and water washing, crashing,
> crushing and throat ringing,
> tonsil wincing mouth grimaced
> grossly, mostly moaning.

> Phil Brown (2007), 'Soda Song', ll. 1–9.

The title's **alliteration** and **assonance** sets in motion the exuberant sound-play that will see this poem translate the everyday experience of drinking a glass of fizzy water into a song of onomatopoeia. This is seen in the specifically onomato-poeic words chosen: 'fizz', 'crackle', 'pop'. But these are emphasized by rhythm: **spondees** ('pop jumps'; 'tongue gush') and **trochees** ('leap and crackle') are partly responsible for the staccato effect that creates the feel of bubbles fizzing and bursting in the closed mouth. The build up of sound effects then uses *synaesthesia* (when the stimulation of one sense leads to experience in a different sense) to evoke touch by stimulating our hearing. Alliteration comes thick and fast: '*t*ingle *t*ongue', '*g*uzzled *g*ulps of *g*as', '*w*ater *w*ashing', '*cr*ashing *cr*ushing', '*m*ostly *m*oaning'. Not satisfied with repeating the opening letters, indeed, the alliteration runs **pararhymes** across the opening syllables ('*tin ton*', '*leap lip*'), competing with the consonance that led the sharp, cracking entry of the soda to the mouth (lea*p*, li*p*, po*p*, jum*p*[s]). These consonant repeats are not alone: they frame the assonance (sod*a* and b*u*bbles, l*i*p and p*i*nch, j*u*mps and t*o*ngue) that holds the energetic movements of the poem together through echo. Otherwise, the jolting stresses and spluttering sounds might bounce off each other with such force that they break the unity of the poem altogether. As the mouth holds onto this volatile soda so the sounds hold onto the shape of the poem and, as the bubbles dissolve and the fluid's movement turns to more of a swirl than a burst, internal **feminine rhymes** take control with their softening, recognizable harmony ('washing, crashing, crushing', 'ringing wincing'). Accordingly, the assonance that had been staccato becomes sustained, leaking across whole lines, slowing the pace so the water can finally be swallowed ('ton*si*l w*i*ncing mouth gr*i*maced', 'gr*o*ssly, m*o*stly m*o*aning'). Sound effects working in coalition can, indeed, replicate the action described: both water fizzing in the mouth and, by virtue of the fact that you must work hard to sustain precision and clarity when reading this poem aloud, the action of controlling words/water in the mouth.

4.4 Rhyme schemes

Rhyme scheme

The ordered pattern of end-rhymes across a poem.

We have seen rhymes, both perfect and imperfect, appear across poetic lines and they even feature in **free verse** or unrhymed **blank verse**, but rhyme is especially associated with patterned line endings. When this occurs these formal arrange-ments are marked or noted in a 'rhyme scheme', which allows us to see a poem's larger pattern of rhymes and to sense various dynamics within the poem itself. Rhyme schemes might be dictated by tradition, or they may be devised by an individual poet.

To identify a rhyme scheme, take a poem and give a letter, in alphabetical order, to each different sound you hear at a line end. So, label the first line-end sound with 'a' and then label any subsequent repeats of that sound also with 'a'. Give the next *different* line-end sound a 'b', together with subsequent occurrences of that sound, and so on. The pattern that emerges can then be described in shorthand as, 'a-b-b-a' or 'a-b-a, b-c-b, c-d-c', or whatever. Line ends that don't rhyme with any of the other sounds in a regular poem are labelled 'x' to indicate 'no rhyme'.

As discussed in the case of the **sonnet**, rhyme schemes can be associated with particular traditions (so the **quatrains** of a Shakespearean sonnet have 'a-b-a-b' rhyme schemes). This is particularly relevant to **stanza** forms, as will be discussed in the next chapter. However, rhyme schemes can be vital to poems not written in stanzas. Here rhyme patterns may be repeated, even if that repetition is not emphasized in clear breaks on the page. For example, Browning's 'Porphyria's Lover', establishes a complex rhyme scheme that creates a wave-like soundscape:

The rain set early in ton*ight,*	[a]
The sullen wind was soon a*wake,*	[b]
It tore the elm-tops down for sp*ite,*	[a]
And did its worst to vex the l*ake:*	[b]
I listened with heart fit to br*eak.*	[b]
When glided in Porphyria; str*aight*	[c]
She shut the cold out and the st*orm,*	[d]
And kneeled and made the cheerless g*rate*	[c]
Blaze up, and all the cottage w*arm;*	[d]
Which done, she rose, and from her f*orm*	[d]
Withdrew the dripping cloak and shawl, …	

Robert Browning (1836), 'Porphyria's Lover', ll. 1–11.

As the rhyme scheme shows, an 'a-b-a-b-b, c-d-c-d-d' pattern appears and propels the poem forward in a swirling motion that makes it difficult to break off at any particular point. Although it helps to run through the alphabet to see the pattern emerge, once this is identified it is simply called 'a-b-a-b-b'. Over the course of the poem, this beautiful rippling effect develops into a sinister endorsement of the shocking events that the poem relates. Our ear becomes so enchanted by this echoing rhyme scheme that we actively listen out for the final repetition that frames each mini-sequence. It is with sickening realization then that we find ourselves seduced into overhearing the death by strangling that Porphyria suffers. From such a position it is difficult for us to adopt a moralized aesthetic stance on this poem: in deeply disturbing ways, we are sensually enchanted by what cognitively appals us (ll. 36–40):

That moment she was mine, mine, *fair*,
  Perfectly pure and good: I *found*
A thing to do, and all her *hair*
  In one long yellow string I *wound*
  Three times her little throat a*round*,

Such sophisticated manipulation of rhyme indicates the dual pull that poetry can effect on its listeners: disrupting our desire to divorce reasoned sense from stimulated senses, poetry's appeal to the eyes and ears forces – or delights – us into recognizing how our encounters with the world, and our development of value and appreciation, are not always logical or coherent, but are overtly and covertly influenced by the simultaneous appeal of sensory and intellectual stimulation.

A word on accent and dialect

The examples discussed here have presumed that all English speakers agree on how words are pronounced or stressed. Of course, this is not always the case in English or in any other language. Therefore, it is worth being mindful of what sort of assumptions we make when we identify rhymes and non-rhymes in poems. What are traditionally considered 'imperfect' rhymes are often used in folk writing, dialect verse or English verse influenced by other indigenous languages, such as Celtic tongues: names such as Yeats, Hopkins and Dylan Thomas often occur in discussion of imperfect rhymes, for example. On the one hand this might suggest a 'counter-culture' of poetry, one that only half-conforms to recognized English tradition, suggesting the experience of being an English-speaking Celt. Slanted relationships with Received Pronunciation suggest slanted relationships with received values and ideals, and imperfect rhymes might celebrate the speech spoken and shared in marginalized or silenced communities.

On the other hand, we must allow that what one person calls consonance or pararhyme is actually perfect rhyme in the accent of the person who wrote the poem, or in the mouths of those who recite them. It is worth trying to read a poem aloud so that eye rhymes and imperfect rhymes do, in fact, become perfect ones. It is possible to uncover older usages and changing traditions and cultures by revealing these now-lost (or simply unfamiliar) sound pairs. Similarly, we can 'hear again' the accents of long dead poets and, in doing so, think more sophisticatedly about their relationships with their contemporary cultures.

For example, you might think of Tennyson as a royal favourite, having been Poet Laureate, and therefore imagine him to have spoken the 'Queen's English'. His rhyming of 'crannies' with 'man is' in 'Flower in the Crannied Wall', however, reveals a different voice. The rhyme is not necessarily a case of consonance: shortening the 'i' vowel sound in 'crannies' not only brings out a perfect rhyme but also gives a sense of the poet's Lincolnshire accent. You might then hear all his poems from an altered soundpoint, and so an altered cultural perspective:

> Flower in the crannied wall,
> I pluck you out of the crann*ies*,
> I hold you here, root and all, in my hand,
> Little flower—but if I could understand
> What you are, root and all, and all in all,
> I should know what God and man *is*.

Alfred Tennyson (1869), 'Flower in the Crannied Wall'.

Jonathan Pritchard has traced a similar 'accent' in poetry by Jonathan Swift (1667–1745), whose rhymes tend to be described as imperfect to modern ears. Put into context with the dynamic changes in seventeenth-century pronunciation, however, you can hear how they record an 'Irish English' timbre in Swift's voice. We can hear that accent again by listening to how it makes 'deceit' and 'great', for example, into perfect rhymes as the Irish style pronounces 'deceit' as 'desate'.

Reference

Pritchard, J. (2007), 'Swift's Irish Rhymes', *Studies in Philology* 104, 123–58.

Stanzas

5

Chapter Outline

> ## Stanza
> A group of poetic lines, defined by its arrangement of **metre** and **rhyme**.

Feet, lines and rhymes of poetry have been considered; now we come to how all of these features come together into particular poetic arrangements. 'Stanza' is the name given to a block of formal poetry; commonly these blocks are called 'verses' (especially with reference to songs), but stanza is clearer. (Note however that in **blank verse** such divisions are known as *verse paragraphs*.) 'Stanza' is often etymologically linked via Latin to the Italian for 'stopping place', but the term also applies in Italy to a chamber or room and this latter root is more helpful in thinking about the definition of a stanza of poetry. We may think that a room is most obviously defined by its function and content (beds in bedrooms; ovens in kitchens). Framing this functional definition, however, is a room's dimensions (the length of its walls) and its decor. A stanza's line lengths may be likened to its 'walls' (which form a particular set of dimensions on the page) and the **rhyme scheme**, which decorates the line lengths, becomes the wallpaper.

In this section stanzas are arranged primarily in terms of their dimensions – the number of lines included in each – since all stanzas may be described most simply in this way. In certain fixed or named stanza arrangements the rhyme scheme or metre is specified, so these are also given in each definition.

5.1 One-line stanzas and refrains

> ## One-line stanza
> Monostich or refrain.

One-line stanzas are very rare and in practice only really occur as occasional instances in **free verse**. However, the contemporary poet Ian Findlay Hamilton wrote poems of just one line, some of which featured in 'The sonnet is a sewing machine for the monostich' (shown at the Victoria Miro Gallery, London, 2007). However, the refrain is arguably the closest that traditional English verse comes to a monostich, although even then refrains are often absorbed into the body of a longer stanza.

A *refrain* is a line of poetry that is repeated either exactly or in very slight variation at regular intervals throughout a longer poem, usually as the final line of each stanza, or in a line on its own. Its purpose is to create a pulsing return to a poem's keynote. The refrain may be a melancholic intonation or a rousing chorus. It is particularly prevalent in the **ballad** tradition, and in the fixed French forms such as the **villanelle** and the **ballade**, but they also feature in **lyric** poems as a case of heightened or concentrated emotion. A famous example is Alfred Tennyson's 'Lady of Shalott' (1832), in which the subject's name is repeated as a refrain in the final line of every **stanza**. Note how Rossetti's refrains become increasingly disturbing – or devoutly committed – with each appearance:

> I have no wit, no words, no tears;
>   My heart within me like a stone
> Is numbed too much for hopes or fears;
>   Look right, look left, I dwell alone;
> I lift mine eyes, but dimmed with grief
>   No everlasting hills I see;
> My life is in the falling leaf:
>   *O Jesus, quicken me.*
>
> My life is like a faded leaf,
>   My harvest dwindled to a husk;
> Truly my life is void and brief
>   And tedious in the barren dusk;
> My life is like a frozen thing,
>   No bud nor greenness can I see:
> Yet rise it shallóthe sap of Spring;
>   *O Jesus, rise in me.*
>
> My life is like a broken bowl,
>   A broken bowl that cannot hold
> One drop of water for my soul
>   Or cordial in the searching cold;
> Cast in the fire the perished thing,
>   Melt and remould it, till it be
> A royal cup for Him my King:
>   *O Jesus, drink of me.*
>
> Christina Rossetti (1862), 'A Better Resurrection'.

5.2 Two-line stanzas (couplets)

> ## Two-line stanza
> A couplet.

Although the shortest of the English stanza forms, the couplet comes in many different styles that vary in line length, rhyme scheme and line integrity. Most commonly couplets are *rhyming couplets* (their scheme being *a-a b-b c-c* and so on) and, although they have an obvious identity as pairs, they are often run together in printed poetry. In terms of arranging content within these pairs couplets may fall into two camps:

- *Closed couplets*: each couplet expresses a 'complete' phrase and line-ends are generally marked with punctuation – they are **end-stopped** lines.
  Example:

  > And yet, believe me, good as well as ill,
  > Woman's at best a Contradiction still.
  >
  > Alexander Pope (1735), 'Epistle 2: To a Lady', ll. 269–70.

- *Open couplets*: phrases run across line endings and punctuation doesn't fall in with line length – they use **enjambment**.
  Example:

  > Round and round, like a dance of snow
  > In a dazzling drift, as its guardians, go [...]
  >
  > Robert Browning (1855), 'Women and Roses', ll. 4–5.

The couplet was popular in the eighteenth century, in line with a vogue for fixed and regular elegance in poetry. Its sense of balance or 'question-and-answer' shape is perfectly suited to the **epigrammatic** or aphoristic style exemplified by Alexander Pope (1688–1744). Following the Augustan period's enthusiasm for closed couplets, English poetry turned more towards the unfurling effect of the open couplet. In Keats' **romance**, *Endymion*, (the **epigraph** to which is, 'The stretchèd metre of an antique song', adapted from Shakespeare's 'Sonnet 17') open couplets draw attention to the sense of excess that characterizes this poem of more than 4,000 lines. As the lines' enjambment bursts open each otherwise closed pairing of rhymes they capture the insistent-yet-languorous pursuit of imaginative development undertaken by the protagonist, who crosses 'a space of life between [boyhood and manhood], in which the soul is in a ferment, the character undecided, the way of life uncertain' (from Keats' preface to the poem):

> Nor do we merely feel these essences
> For one short hour; no, even as the trees
> That whisper round a temple become soon
> Dear as the temple's self, so does the moon,
> The passion poesy, glories infinite,
> Haunt us till they become a cheering light
> Unto our souls, and bound to us so fast,
> That, whether there be shine, or gloom o'ercast,
> They alway must be with us, or we die.
>
> John Keats (1818), 'Book 1', *Endymion*, ll. 25–33.

This half-fixed form is often particularly effective in couplet verse: a suggestion of regularity is more attractive than a slavish attachment to it. An even number of **feet** in a couplet (as in **tetrameter** couplets) can be difficult to sustain since they tend to split into two equal parts. When joined with two rhymes in quick succession a 'doubling-up' effect can fall into a sing-song rhythm; but this does mean that the best examples are especially attractive as they create sophisticated variation within regularity. Note Milton's handling of this arrangement here, where punctuation **caesuras** alternate between appearing mid-foot (line 28) and throughout lines (line 32), **iambs** are switched to a run of **trochees** (in line 32) and **alliteration** and **assonance** breach the gap between the first and second pairs of feet (lines 27 and 29):

> Oft in glimmering bowers and glades
> He met her, and in secret shades
> Of woody Ida's inmost grove,
> While yet there was no fear of Jove.
> Come, pensive Nun, devout and pure,
> Sober, steadfast, and demure,
>
> John Milton (1645), 'Il Penseroso', ll. 27–32.

Read more

- Browning's open couplets in his **dramatic monologues** are particularly effective as they mark the precarious line between control and anarchy that his protagonists tread under pressure.
- Tennyson's **trochaic octameters** in 'Locksley Hall' (1842) and 'Locksley Hall Sixty Years After' (1886) are in closed rhyming couplets. Both poems struggle to contain rage and disillusion within (albeit lengthy) couplets that range between backward-looking regret and remembrance and ranting and raging at the present.
- Craig Raine's 'A Martian Sends a Postcard Home' (1979) uses irregular couplets – some rhyming, some unrhymed, all of varied length – to make the reader share the Martian's experience of the earth's familiar as strange. Just as the poem repeatedly introduces obscured images ('like engravings under tissue paper', l. 10), so the poem's unusual couplets give the impression that a familiar poem is present but somehow masked.
- Forms that use couplets include the **epigram** and the Shakespearean **sonnet**.

> ## Heroic couplets
> Closed, rhyming couplets of **iambic pentameter**.
> Rhyme scheme: *a-a-b-b-c-c-d-d* and so on.

The heroic couplet is very rigid: it has a fixed rhyme scheme, a fixed line length, a fixed arrangement of **feet** and a fixed line integrity. Unsurprisingly, therefore, it is associated with control and circumscription, as Pope often wittily acknowledges in his frequent uses of the form. Heroic couplets are first recognized in Chaucer's 'The Legend of Good Women' [c. 1380–1387] and subsequently in some of his *Canterbury Tales*, but are now associated with the Augustan poetry of the eighteenth century. We might speculate that because a **heroic couplet** is never left open-ended it is the stanza par excellence for an age registering the spread of intellectual notions of the 'Enlightenment':

> Expatiate free o'er all this scene of man;
> A mighty maze! but not without a plan;
> A wild, where weeds and flowers promiscuous shoot,
> Or garden, tempting with forbidden fruit.
> Together let us beat this ample field,
> Try what the open, what the covert yield;
> The latent tracts, the giddy heights, explore
> Of all who blindly creep, or sightless soar;
> Eye Nature's walks, shoot folly as it flies,
> And catch the manners living as they rise;
>
> Alexander Pope (1733), 'Epistle 1', from *An Essay on Man*, ll. 5–14.

However – especially given the brilliant variety of substitutions that Pope uses (sometimes even stretching 'couplets' to three lines of rhyme) – we might want to remember that the heroic couplet doesn't necessarily achieve stability, but it acknowledges a desire for it. While they are sometimes thought of as smug and too quick to reduce human complexity to mechanical repetition, heroic couplets can sometimes gather a striking sense of running pressure in long stretches, as though they want to grasp at life to capture and attempt to understand it. Indeed, although Pope's use is often breezy or even irreverent (see *The Rape of the Lock*, 1714), the heroic couplet can also be serious and solemn, unbending in its pursuit of significance in human endeavour (which is all the more moving when it almost admits defeat: 'Must helpless man, in ignorance sedate, | Roll darkling down the torrent of his fate?', Samuel Johnson, 'The Vanity of Human Wishes' (1749), ll. 345–6). Perhaps because of its apparent unwillingness to bend, even under intense pressure, however, the heroic couplet was criticized by some for a lack of inspiration and its air of assimilation, even of the most horrifying of human cruelties.

In the move to Romanticism, the couplet was somewhat overtaken by the looser forms that flourished in the wake of a more obvious emphasis on the individual character of the imagination and emotion. A poem that sits between these impulses is Barbauld's passionate plea for an end to years-long British conflict with France. Here Barbauld describes those who look in newspapers to discover the fate of loved ones. In 'bending' over a map that divides up land and the lives of people struggling to live in it, the 'soft one' does what the heroic couplet cannot. Regularity hints rather at the systematic gunning down of 'husband, brothers, friends', while also suggesting the crassness of reducing human experience and sacrifice to arbitrary shapes on a page. That this is done in almost fully sustained heroic couplets (the exploration of line 35 does create an instance of a half-open couplet) attests to Barbauld's insistence that her anger is heard in public seriousness, not in private woe:

> Oft o'er the daily page some soft one bends
> To learn the fate of husband, brothers, friends,
> Or the spread map with anxious eye explores
> Its dotted boundaries and pencilled shores,
> Asks *where* the spot that wrecked her bliss is found,
> And learns its name but to detest the sound.
>
> Anna Laetitia Barbauld (1812), 'Eighteen Hundred and Eleven: A Poem',
> ll. 33–8.

Read more

- See David Caplan (1999), 'Why Not the Heroic Couplet?', *New Literary History* 30.1, 221–38 for consideration of the heroic couplet's modern fate. As Caplan mentions, it has been used by modern poets such as Thom Gunn and Marilyn Hacker, but it has reduced in popularity considerably since the nineteenth century.
- Yeats (1899), 'The Secret Rose' unusually employs heroic couplets in a poem of dreamy wistfulness.

5.3 Three-line stanzas (tercets)

Three-line stanza

A tercet.

Three-line stanzas are less common in English verse than even-numbered ones. Perhaps because of their inherent imbalance, these stanzas may intertwine with each other even as the stanza distinction is clear on the page (this is especially true of **terza rima**, because of the rhyme scheme). Philip Larkin (1922–1985) frequently employed tercets, undermining their integrity with a jaded sense of the absurd as the lines' content reaches across stanza breaks, drawing attention to their aspirant poeticism ('There's something laughable about this,' 'Sad Steps' (1974), l. 6). Rossetti employed tercets in some of her most rigorously 'reserved' poetry that works through her religious impulses and desire to ready herself for liberation by God. She resists their intertwining impulse, however, and uses the tercets to meditate on construction, constraint, and confinement. This weight of rhythmic reserve will only finally lift with divine intervention:

> God harden me against myself,
> This coward with pathetic voice
> Who craves for ease, and rest, and joys:
>
> Myself, arch-traitor to myself;
> My hollowest friend, my deadliest foe,
> My clog whatever road I go.
>
> Yet One there is can curb myself,
> Can roll the strangling load from me,
> Break off the yoke and set me free.
>
> Christina Rossetti (1875), 'Who Shall Deliver Me?', ll. 16–24.

See the **villanelle** for a fixed use of tercets.

Triplet

Three lines of regular length.

Rhyme scheme: *a-a-a b-b-b c-c-c* and so on.

The triplet's boxed-in rhymes make a strong structure around the stanza's odd-numbered imbalance. Even so, this tight repetition can be difficult to sustain, as testified by the fragmentary length (and quick demise) of Tennyson's triplet poem:

> The wrinkled sea beneath him crawls:
> He watches from his mountain walls,
> And like a thunderbolt he falls.
>
> Alfred Tennyson, 'The Eagle: A Fragment' (1851), ll. 4–6.

Herbert used the stanza to illustrate the protective, enclosing presence of a benevolent God, likened to a gardener whose judicious pruning (seen in the clipped **masculine rhymes** that define each triplet) strengthens the integrity of the plant/faithful follower:

Such sharpness shows the sweetest FREND:
Such cuttings rather heal than REND:
And such beginnings touch their END.

George Herbert (1633), 'Paradise', ll. 13–15.

Hardy's disarrayed triplets (written on hearing of the loss of the ocean liner, the *Titanic*) meanwhile demonstrate the driving force of an 'Immanent Will' (l. 18) that cares little for those whose fate it dictates:

Over the mirrors meant
  To glass the opulent
The sea-worm crawls—grotesque, slimed, dumb, indifferent.

Jewels in joy designed
  To ravish the sensuous mind
Lie lightless, all their sparkles bleared and black and blind.

Thomas Hardy (1914), 'The Convergence of the Twain', ll. 7–12.

Read more

- Robert Herrick's Christmas drinking song, 'The Wassaile' (1648) uses triplets to wish for prosperity and bounty in the coming year.
- The triplets in Browning's 'A Toccata of Galuppi's' (1855) emphasize the three-dimensional character of this three-voiced exhibition piece.

Terza rima

Three lines of regular length, usually **tetrameter** or **pentameter**.

Rhyme scheme: *A-b-A B-c-B C-d-C D-e-D* and so on.

This version of the tercet takes advantage of how three-line stanzas tend to reach forwards to the next tercet in the sequence. It is an Italian form, used by Dante in his **epic** poem, *La Divinia Commedia*. The stanzas effectively form a flowing stream of rhyme which surfaces in waves across each grouping: the central rhyme sound of one stanza shoots outwards to form the outside rhymes of the next stanza in an image of repeated bursts of growth. This shape perfectly suits Shelley's purpose as he employs a sustained organic **metaphor** that likens the stirring of a revolutionary spirit to the spreading and budding of seeds, so characterizing revolution as full of potential and strength (despite its pestilential setting) yet naturalized and benevolent – a cyclical change that emerges miraculously from within a diseased society rather than being imposed upon it:

Oh wild west wind, thou breath of autumn's being;
Thou from whose unseen presence the leaves dead
Are driven, like ghosts from an enchanter feeling,

Yellow, and black, and pale, and hectic red,
Pestilence-stricken multitudes; oh thou
Who chariotest to their dark wintry bed

The winged seeds, where they lie cold and low,
Each like a corpse within its grave, until
Thine azure sister of the spring shall blow

Her clarion o'er the dreaming earth, and fill
(Driving sweet buds like flocks to feed in air)
With living hues and odours plain and hill –

Wild spirit, which are moving everywhere,
Destroyer and preserver, hear, oh hear!

Percy Bysshe Shelley (1820), 'Ode to the West Wind', ll. 1–14.

As the poem develops this revolutionary potential so it more tightly maps such change onto the spirit of poetry (and the poet) itself. The poem transpires to be a series of five quasi-**sonnets** forged from terza rima, orchestrated and held together by a poet who will become 'The trumpet of a prophecy!' (l. 69). In doing so, the terza rima (itself shaped like a trumpet, or clarion) represents the action of the poet himself.

Morris used terza rima for his dramatization of the trial of King Arthur's Queen Guenevere. Here Guenevere faces her accusers and speaks with great eloquence and intimated sensuality. The terza rima follows the line of her gathering strength and defiance as she demands to be heard:

Yea also at my full heart's strong command,
See through my long throat how the words go up
In ripples to my mouth; how in my hand

The shadow lies like wine within a cup
Of marvelously coloured gold; yea now
This little wind is rising, look you up,

William Morris (1858), 'The Defence of Guenevere', ll. 229–34.

Compare this treatment with Tennyson's contemporaneous account of a wife burdened with guilt: 'Guinevere' from *Idylls of the King* (1859).

Read more

- Elizabeth Jennings' sonnets feature an interlocking version of this rhyme scheme in their **sestets**, which rhyme *e-f-e f-e-f*. See also 'At the Source'

(1989) or 'Time for the Elegy' (1989), both of which respond energetically to the terza rima premise (that growth issues from small beginnings): the first in the poem's sense of expansive adult love traced back to childhood sources; the latter in windows joyfully flung open at the first hint of spring.

5.4 Four-line stanzas (quatrains)

Four-line stanza

A quatrain.

The quatrain is extremely common in English poetry, perhaps because it is so flexible. The addition of one line to the **tercet** allows pattern varieties to increase exponentially. There is now enough length to create space, echo and repetition. This may be taken in the direction of pressurized containment (there are, after all, only four lines), or it may branch out into ringing peals of sound that replicate their pattern over and again. Rhymes can breathe a little more easily (rather than necessarily being squashed up against each other, as in the **couplet** or **triplet**), but they will be answered within the stanza itself (unlike **tercets** or **terza rima**). Lines can lengthen and shorten regularly (rather like a squeezebox, which may indeed accompany a quatrain poem such as a **ballad**) and pairings can be emphasized by doubling-up into four. On the other hand, the four-wall shape may suggest solidity or impenetrability as all line up equally together and pairs of sounds or images stand in orderly convoy, near but not converging with their partners. There is no one particular tradition or style associated with the quatrain: they appear across genres and several forms feature quatrains in their fixed make-up (Shakespearean **sonnets**, **ballads**, **villanelles**). In the first instance quatrains can be identified by rhyme scheme:

a-a-a-a: monorhyme quatrain

In Rossetti's example the close repetition of stuck rhymes suggests how the grief-ridden speaker stalls when trying to gather meaning from this emotional experience:

> From perfect grief there need not be
> Wisdom or even memory;
> One thing then learned remains to me—
> The woodspurge has a cup of three.

> Dante Gabriel Rossetti (1870), 'The Woodspurge', ll. 12–15.

> **a-a-b-b:** essentially paired couplets

Burns' example uses this scheme to create a rippling effect that replicates the movement of the water that inspires the poem:

> Flow gently, sweet Afton, among thy green braes,
> Flow gently, I'll sing thee a song in thy praise;
> My Mary's asleep by thy murmuring stream,
> Flow gently, sweet Afton, disturb not her dream.
>
> Robert Burns (1789), 'Afton Water', ll. 1–4.

> **a-b-b-a:** envelope rhyme (see *In Memoriam stanza; sonnets*)

In Yeats' example this rhyme scheme's enclosed shape adds poignancy to the poem's talk of holding transient, youthful love:

> When you are old and grey and full of sleep,
> And nodding by the fire, take down this book,
> And slowly read, and dream of the soft look
> Your eyes had once, and of their shadows deep;
>
> William Butler Yeats (1892), 'When You are Old', ll. 1–4.

> **a-b-a-b:** cross rhyme (the most common quatrain rhyme scheme)

Vaughan uses this alternating rhyme scheme to switch between the painful contradictions of Christian grief: joy at loved ones' entry to heaven and gloom at the poet's abandoned state:

> They are all gone into the world of light!
>   And I alone sit ling'ring here;
> Their very memory is fair and bright,
>   And my sad thoughts doth clear.
>
> Henry Vaughan (1655), 'They are all gone into the world of light', ll. 1–4.

However, certain quatrain arrangements have become especially established and attached to particular traditions, whether in response to collective use, or in acknowledgement of particularly prominent examples.

> ## Ballad stanza
>
> Four lines of alternating **tetrameter** and **trimeter**.
>
> Rhyme scheme: *a-b-x-b* or *a-b-a-b* (cross rhyme).

Strictly the ballad stanza only rhymes in lines 2 and 4 and, particularly in ballads with a strong narrative sense, this suggests progression as well as repetition: each tetrameter–trimeter pair can introduce a new aspect to the story while still bringing it into line with the characteristic sound of the whole poem. Often this 'in and out' shape will use **refrains** for emphasis: the long lines keeping the story moving, the short ones providing interjections or undercurrents to pulse throughout the narrative. In Cowper's tale of John Gilpin's farcical horse ride the tetrameters seem to push the narrative forward while the trimeters pull at the reins:

> Now see him mounted once again
>   Upon his nimble steed,
> Full slowly pacing o'er the stones,
>   With caution and good heed.
>
> But finding soon a smoother road
>   Beneath his well-shod feet,
> The snorting beast began to trot,
>   Which galled him in his seat.

William Cowper (1782), 'The Diverting History of John Gilpin', ll. 77–84.

However, perhaps in order to emphasize these effects, ballad stanzas in fact very often allow the first and third lines also to rhyme, creating an overtly rocking rhythm. This is sometimes so dominant that the sound pattern is even more memorable than the ballad's content. When our ears are so enchanted, a poet may catch us unawares, and deliver a series of emotional blows or cultural clashes whose ripples of effect destabilize the ballad's stable arrangement. This may be seen in Wordsworth's 'We Are Seven' (1799), or in Hemans' famous 'Casabianca', which treads a precarious path between invoking pacifist sympathy and falling into line with tales of military heroism (the poem here engaging with the **ballad** tradition's history of sea faring stories):

The boy stood on the burning deck
   Whence all but he had fled;
The flame that lit the battle's wreck
   Shone round him o'er the dead.

Yet beautiful and bright he stood,
   As born to rule the storm;
A creature of heroic blood,
   A proud, though childlike form.

Felicia Hemans (1829), 'Casabianca', ll. 1–8.

Most commonly poets vary the ballad stanza by making all of the lines tetrameters, a version that is sometimes known as *long measure* (see below). This keeps the ballad's simplicity and aural appeal, but often shifts away from rushing narrative. Blake's 'songs' in long measure evoke the ballad's simple pulsing rhythm in order to bring readers to a new perspective rather than to the end of a story. This example recalls the ballad tradition of community culture and wandering minstrels only to sing a bitter and jaded tale of social degradation and stifling mental restriction; these long measures (hinted at by the repeated 'chartered') are the first stage (recognition) in a process of reshaping imaginative life:

I wander through each chartered street
Near where the chartered Thames does flow,
And mark in every face I meet
Marks of weakness, marks of woe.

William Blake (1794), 'London', ll. 1–4.

Johnson's **elegy** uses long measure to remember a physician valued for his modest enactment of Christian virtue. The stanza form hints at a history emotional content (ballads can be sentimental or overt in their expression of grief) but, like the man it remembers, it lengthens the lines to an orderly regularity and restrains itself to use 'The power of art without the show':

His virtues walked their narrow round,
   Nor made a pause, nor left a void;
And sure the Eternal Master found
   The single talent well employed.

Samuel Johnson (1783), 'On the Death of Dr Robert Levet', ll. 25–9.

Ballad stanzas in hymns

Ballad stanzas in all their varieties are commonly used for hymns, where they are known as 'measures'. Many hymns are adaptations of poems originally written in ballad stanzas (such as Blake's lines from *Milton* (1804) which are sung as the hymn 'Jerusalem'). The equivalent measures for ballad stanzas are given here:

- standard ballad stanza: *common measure*
- *a-b-a-b* ballad stanza: *common hymnal measure*
- four tetrameters, *a-b-c-b*: *long measure*
- four tetrameters, *a-b-a-b*: *long hymnal measure*.

Hymnody (the study and technique of hymns) has a final formal variation to the ballad stanza called 'short measures'. Here the first tetrameter of a standard ballad stanza is replaced with a trimeter, making a foot pattern 3-3-4-3:

- 3-3-4-3, rhymed *a-b-c-b*: *short measure*
- 3-3-4-3, rhymed *a-b-a-b*: *short hymnal measure*.

A poetic example of short measure is Felicia Hemans' 'England's Dead' (1822); a traditional example is found in Doddridge:

> Ye Servants of the Lord,
>   Each in his Office wait,
> Observant of his heav'nly Word,
>   And watchful at his Gate.
>
> Philip Doddridge (1755), 'The Active Christian', in *Hymns founded on Various Texts in the Holy Scriptures*, ll. 1–4.

Read more

- Emily Dickinson (1830–1886) wrote many poems in ballad stanzas that echo with the almost-hypnotic quality of Protestant hymns. Taking these two traditions (stories and faith) as structural presences, Dickinson's poetry evokes ritualism and faith in purpose, but applies that to expressions, observations and actions of disarming asceticism or even cruel repression.
- Particularly in his earlier collections, Yeats explores cultural pasts and cultural identities through verse and stanza form, with ballad stanzas often framing the pursuit of poetic voice. See the collections *Crossways* (1889), *The Rose* (1893) and *The Wind Among the Reeds* (1899).

> ## Heroic or elegiac stanza
>
> Four end-stopped lines of iambic pentameter.
>
> Rhyme scheme: cross rhyme (*a-b-a-b*).

By lengthening the lines of the ballad stanza, the heroic or elegiac stanza seems to increase its sense of purpose and lastingness. Gray's **elegy** is the most famous use of an elegiac stanza. This poem uses a classical genre (the elegy) to memorialize humble subjects (commoners who are not normally given formal remembrance): the combination of the formal, stately **iambic pentameter** with the short shape of the ballad stanza encapsulates this dual identity formally. The extra foot slows the pace while the alternate rhymes suggest a continued rippling of movement, a combination precisely invoked by the twilight setting at the elegy's start: a space for calm reflection, away from the distant sounds of life:

> Now fades the glimmering landscape on the sight,
> And all the air a solemn stillness holds,
> Save where the beetle wheels his droning flight,
> And drowsy tinklings lull the distant folds;
>
> Thomas Gray (1751), 'Elegy Written in a Country Churchyard', ll. 5–8.

In the wake of Gray's treatment the quatrain has an air of emotional solemnity, as seen in Yeats' 'The Sorrow of Love' (1895, revised 1924), which echoes Gray by attempting to find man's emotional experience marked in the natural world. Yet Gray was himself engaging with tradition when he chose this stanza. It was first used by the innovator Henry Howard, Earl of Surrey in a poem that remembered his lost friend Henry Fitzroy ('Prisoned in Windsor, He Recounteth His Pleasure There Passed', 1557), but it gained particular prominence as the vehicle for stately public poems such as Dryden's *Annus Mirabilis*. This poem celebrates the defiance and steadfastness of London in a year of repeated disaster (1666 saw war, plague and fire). The quatrains (which derive from Classical metre used by writers such as Virgil) appear to create order and grandeur from chaos as they narrate the mighty rise of London phoenix-like from the fire (note that 'August' is pronounced as an **iamb**):

> Already, labouring with a mighty fate,
> She shakes the rubbish from her mounting brow,
> And seems to have renewed her charter's date,
> Which Heaven will to the death of time allow.
>
> More great than human, now, and more August
> New deified she from her fires does rise:

Her widening streets on new foundations trust,
And, opening, into larger parts she flies.

John Dryden (1667), 'London Reborn', *Annus Mirabilis*, ll. 1173–80.

Given this Classical and public heritage, the significance of Gray's decision to use the quatrain to remember the unremembered becomes clear.

A variant on the heroic quatrain is that used by Fitzgerald in his translation of Omar Khayyám's poetry which rhymes *a-a-x-a*. In this version the lines exchange stateliness or solemnity for the more immediate pleasures of sensual indulgence. A very tipsy poem, its swirling rhyme scheme – that seems to try to pirouette on one rhyme sound – repeatedly puts out a non-rhymed line as though to steady itself before ploughing on to insist, yet again, that you must drink (as does wise nature) while you can:

As then the Tulip, for her morning sup
Of Heav'nly Vintage, from the soil looks up,
   Do you devoutly do the like, till Heav'n
To Earth invert you—like an empty Cup.

Perplexed no more with Human or Divine,
Tomorrow's tangle to the winds resign,
   And lose your fingers in the tresses of
The Cypress-slender Minister of Wine.

Edward Fitzgerald, 'The Rubáiyát of Omar Khayyám' (1889), ll. 157–64.

Read more

- Like Surrey, Michael Drayton remembered Virgil in the heroic quatrain, but in his **pastoral vein**: see 'Pastorals' (1619).
- Anna Laetitia Barbauld used heroic quatrains for her angry response to Mary Wollstonecraft's criticism: 'The Rights of Woman' (1825).

In Memoriam stanza

Four **iambic tetrameter** lines.

Rhyme scheme: envelope rhyme (*a-b-b-a*).

This stanza is named after Tennyson's elegy, *In Memoriam A. H. H.* (1850), but it appeared very occasionally before this, for example in Ben Jonson's elegies. However, Tennyson's use is the most prominent example of this stanza, and few have followed his lead. Certainly, few have conformed to its rigidity so vigorously.

The stanza's shortish lines, short feet and rhyme scheme based on the quatrains in a Petrarchan **sonnet** may give the impression of simplicity, but many insightful observations have been made about its multilayered effect in Tennyson's elegy: see Sarah Gates' discussion particularly. Most strikingly, it creates an impression of terse enclosure. In a poem of such seriousness, the iambic beat might lead us to expect an expansive **pentameter** line. Indeed, a reader may have expected the poet to use the elegiac stanza's longer lines and forward-moving rhyme scheme. Tennyson's decision to lop off that final foot jolts us into appreciating how, despite the elegy's great length, the grief is expressed painfully, even reluctantly. The rhyme scheme adds to the air of restraint and reticence, even as it is a clear gesture at formal artistry. The effects of holding two b-rhymes within a 'bracket' of a-rhymes are manifold: it suggests that the elegist wishes to move forwards (we are listening out for the a-rhyme to return), but we also sense that he can't help but look backwards to the past (the fourth line's return to the first line's sound doesn't really convey a sense of progression). Within this circling movement two b-rhymes are cocooned within a protective frame of sound, suggesting a shielding impulse in the elegist, who is after all seeking to preserve the memory of a lost friend:

> I sometimes hold it half a sin
>   To put in words the grief I feel;
>   For words, like Nature, half reveal
> And half conceal the Soul within.
>
> But, for the unquiet heart and brain,
>   A use in measured language lies;
>   The sad mechanic exercise,
> Like dull narcotics, numbing pain.
>
> In words, like weeds, I'll wrap me o'er,
>   Like coarsest clothes against the cold:
>   But that large grief which these enfold
> Is given in outline and no more.
>
> Alfred Tennyson (1850), 'Lyric V', *In Memoriam A. H. H.*

These effects are especially apparent in Tennyson's handling because of his frequent use of monosyllables and **masculine rhymes**, which emphasize the uniformity, and even monotony, that holds his elegy together throughout its 133 separate **lyrics**. Yet, there is a purpose to such simple repetition: the stanza's measured, careful tone and shape acts as a kind of healing for Tennyson, but it also produces a calming, softening effect in the reader as we are lulled along on its restrained, lilting patterns of sound. This puts us temperamentally at one with the poet, allowing us to experience the grief and its consolation at once. Yet, as the lyric ends ambivalently, we see a further effect of the shortened tetrameter and reclusive rhyme scheme: it leaves us always listening for more. Even this great, lengthy elegy is only an 'outline', within which is enfolded a 'large grief', apparently beyond expression.

Read more

- Dante Gabriel Rossetti in fact used the *In Memoriam* stanza just before Tennyson's publication, in 'My Sister's Sleep' (1847).
- Oscar Wilde wrote many **lyrics** in this stanza in *Poems* (1881). Partly because they recall *In Memoriam A. H. H.* and partly because of the formal effects of the stanza itself such lyrics have a mournful, aching tone. Many touch on grief for a lost man (see 'Lotus Leaves' for example), echoing Tennyson's poem in form and content.
- This notion is further developed by looking at Wilfred Owen's 'On Shadwell Stairs': again the *In Memoriam* stanza reappears, making the poem echo with previous expressions of love between men. Consider how the form shapes how we might interpret the poem's rather oblique and obscure content.

Sapphic stanza (Classical)

Three **hendecasyllablics** (11-syllable lines) and one Adonic (five-syllable line of fixed feet).

Foot scheme: trochee-trochee-dactyl-trochee-trochee (three times); dactyl-spondee (or sometimes dactyl-trochee).

Sapphic stanza (English)

Three lines of 11 syllables followed by one of five syllables.

tro	chee	tro	chee	dac	tyl	lic	tro	chee	tro	chee
			dac	tyl	lic	spon	dee			

This stanza is named after the Greek female poet Sappho (see **lyric**), although several Classical writers used it. Although it seems complex and unfamiliar, in practice it flows surprisingly naturally. The central **dactyl** makes for a slight loosening of the reins, a moment to swallow your breath before re-energizing to complete the line. This makes for an attractively robust poetic rhythm that seems to strengthen natural speech patterns rather than distort them. Strictly, being a **quantitative metre** form, a trochee should be thought of as 'long-short' and a dactyl 'long-short-short', but in English this is likely to fall into the stress-unstress pattern of **accentual-syllabic** metre. Swinburne used Sapphics to write about Sappho herself (stressed syllables are bolded):

Heard the flying feet of the Loves behind her
Make a sudden thunder upon the waters,
As the thunder flung from the strong unclosing
    Wings of a great wind.

So the goddess fled from her place, with awful
Sound of feet and thunder of wings around her;
While behind a clamour of singing women
    Severed the twilight.

Algernon Charles Swinburne (1866), 'Sapphics', ll. 17–24.

Rachel Wetzsteon uses the stanza to 'serve as a sharp contrast to [her] contemporary subject' (see *The Other Stars*, 1994) and, despite their restrictions, describes Sapphics as addictive, pointing out how the final Adonic line fits with familiar English phrase patterns – 'shave and a haircut'; 'over and over'. Sometimes the shape and proportion of Sapphics are used but the very strict foot patterns are altered to fit with English stress patterns, or, as in Cowper's tortured poem, to contrast their strict shape with the expression of pain and disarray:

Hatred and vengeance, my eternal portion,
Scarce can endure delay of execution,
Wait, with impatient readiness to seize my
    Soul in a moment.

[. . .]
Him the vindictive rod of angry Justice
Sent quick and howling to the centre headlong;
I, fed with judgment, in a fleshy tomb, am
    Buried above ground.

William Cowper (1816), 'Lines Written during a Period of Insanity', ll. 1–4; 17–20.

The blunt slashing of line to make an Adonic often sounds like a harsh ruling. In keeping with its origin (the line pattern was devised to mourn the death of Adonis) the line may also vocalize melancholy or lament as the second foot thuds home with a painful inevitability. See George Herbert's 'Virtue' (1633), a poem of modified Sapphics (the ratio is eight syllables to four, rather than 11 to five) that uses curtailed Adonics to deliver a series of crushing blows.

Read more

- Other twentieth-century poets who have attempted the Sapphic stanza include W. H. Auden, John Hollander, Marilyn Hacker and Timothy Steele.

5.5 Longer-length stanzas

Five-line stanza: a *quintain* (or *cinquain*)

Six-line stanza: a *sextet* (or occasionally *sestain*)

Seven-line stanza: a *septet*

Eight-line stanza: an *octet*

Longer-length stanza forms are very common in English verse, and they feature many variations in pattern. Sometimes longer stanzas simply fuse shorter stanzas together – so an eight-line stanza may be arranged in rhyming terms into two quatrains (say, *a-b-a-b-c-d-c-d*); a six-line stanza may fall into three couplets, as in Ben Jonson's 'Still to be Neat' (1609), or into a quatrain and a couplet, as in the **Venus and Adonis stanza**. In other instances regular rhymes may stretch to accommodate more bursting variety than a quatrain could contain, such as Browning's 'Meeting at Night', in which each stanza's rhymes fan open from a central meeting point in an *a-b-c-c-b-a* formation, creating in sound the sensual meeting that the stanza describes:

> Then a mile of warm sea-scented beach;
> Three fields to cross till a farm appears;
> A tap at the pane, the quick sharp scratch
> And blue spurt of a lighted match,
> And a voice less loud, thro' its joys and fears,
> Than the two hearts beating each to each!
>
> Robert Browning (1845), 'Meeting at Night', ll. 7–12.

Odd-line stanzas can be unpredictable to follow – they may extend the number of lines without extending the number of rhymes, creating 'bottom-heavy' and claustrophobic stanzas, as in Dante Gabriel Rossetti's 'The Orchard-Pit' (1886) which rhymes *a-b-a-a-b*; or they may introduce unpredictable disruptions to the rhyme, as in Housman's 'Bredon Hill', which rhymes *x-a-x-a-a*. The sprightly arrangement at first seems to fall in with the chiming church bells that the speaker hears from the hilltop (the fifth line echoing as do the bells); but the use of only one rhyme turns out to have a more solemn portent: as the poem ends it sounds the single intonation of a funeral bell:

> They tolled the one bell only,
> Groom there was none to see,
> The mourners followed after,
> And so to church went she,
> And would not wait for me.
>
> A. E. Housman (1896), 'Bredon Hill', ll. 26–30.

Seven-line stanzas are fairly unusual in English verse and they are usually employed in the **rime royale** style. However, Wilmot uses them in a concentrated arrangement when he seeks to convince his mistress that he should leave her so that she is free to capture several rather than just one male heart. Perhaps, like the speaker himself, the triplet that follows the quatrain does not want to stay around long enough to make an equal pair?

> 'Tis not that I am weary grown
> Of being yours, and yours alone;
> But with what face can I incline
> To damn you to be only mine?
>   You, whom some kinder power did fashion,
>   By merit and by inclination,
>   The joy at least of one whole nation.
>
> John Wilmot, Earl of Rochester (1680), 'Upon Leaving his Mistress', ll. 1–7.

See also Donne's 'Love's Deity' (1633) which uses the lopsided seven-line stanza to interrogate love as a series of paradoxes. Eight- and nine-line stanzas are often used for narrative poems as they have enough room to contain episodes while devising a regular shape in repetition, creating consistency across an entire story. Sometimes these will be written in **ottava rima,** but note innovative uses such as John Clare's 'The Flitting' (1908 [c. 1832]), which uses eight-line stanzas to narrate the psychological distress caused by forced removal from a familiar landscape. The regularity of the eight-line stanza, however, sees it employed in many other contexts: the double-quatrain shape may produce a 'double ballad' such as George Wither's 'A Love Sonnet' (1620), which fuses ballad stanzas together to bemoan the loss of a love with a double refrain, 'But now alas she's left me, | *Falero, lero, loo*'. Other eight-line poems move around indulgently within this capacious room, devising their own orders of lines and rhymes.

As well as creating space for unusual rhyme, all of the longer-length stanzas also provide the opportunity for experiments with line length. This may be especially effective when there is room for a pattern to emerge and to be broken within the same stanza. Shelley's 'To a Skylark', for example, devises a cinquain that uses four **trimeters** to evoke rippling natural harmonies before leaping to an **Alexandrine** to demonstrate the superior ability of the 'song bird':

Sound of vernal showers
  On the twinkling grass,
Rain-awakened flowers,
  All that ever was
Joyous and clear and fresh, thy music doth surpass.

Teach us, sprite or bird,
  What sweet thoughts are thine;
I have never heard
  Praise of love or wine
That panted forth a flood of rapture so divine:

Percy Bysshe Shelley (1820), 'To a Skylark', ll. 56–65.

When considering longer-length stanzas simply be aware of the opportunities they provide and notice how poets inhabit the rooms they have chosen with subtlety, variety and elaboration. Do they appear encumbered by a complex or lengthy stanza formation, or is the stanza's shape and presence helpful, a tool that works as hard as the poet to convey expression, emotion and narration?

The most common and fixed arrangements of longer-length stanzas are considered below.

Mad-song stanza

Five lines in three **tetrameters** (lines 1, 2, 5) and two **dimeters** (lines 3 and 4).

Rhyme scheme: *x-a-b-b-a*.

This stanza derives from folk tradition and was used for songs or poems spoken by a 'mad man', most notably the anonymous 'Tom o'Bedlam's Song'. Its jaunty rhythm and rhyme scheme was adapted and fixed for the **limerick**, but the original has more flexibility. Furthermore, although its snappy lines and fixed rhyme are suited to **light verse**, the stanza can imply a dangerous or disturbing 'madness'. Examples from Percy's *Reliques* (see **ballad**), for example, allude to religious mania, and social restraint:

They bound me like a bedlam,
They lash'd my four poor quarters;
  While this I endure,
  Faith makes me sure
To be one of Foxes martyrs.

Bishop Corbett (1767 [c. 1600]), 'The Distracted Puritan', ll. 15–19.[1]

In Herrick's handling the stanza becomes a flirtatious mode of persuasion:

> Let not the dark thee cumber;
> What though the moon does slumber?
>   The stars of the night
>   Will lend thee their light
> Like tapers clear without number.
>
> Then, Julia, let me woo thee,
> Thus, thus to come unto me:
>   An when I shall meet
>   Thy silv'ry feet,
> My soul I'll pour into thee.
>
> Robert Herrick (1648), 'The Night-Piece, to Julia', ll. 11–20.

In Shakespeare's *Hamlet*, Ophelia sings in mad-song stanzas with painful aptness when she becomes deranged by life at the Danish court (see *Hamlet* (1623), IV: 5, ll. 187–96).

Read more

- Wordsworth's five-line stanzas (see 'The Idiot Boy' (1798) and 'Peter Bell' (1819)) are sometimes considered variations of the mad-song stanza. The final stanza of 'We are Seven' (1799), in which the narrator despairs of a small girl's emotional logic, also breaks out into a variation of the mad-song stanza (the rest of the poem is written in **ballad stanzas**).

Note

1. Textual source: spelling modernized from text in Percy's *Reliques*, Vol. 2.

Rime couée

Six lines rhymed *a-a-b-c-c-b*: the two b-rhymes must occur in short lines, the a- and c-rhymes in longer lines.

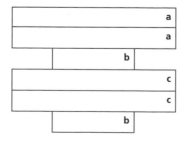

'Rime couée' is a French term for 'tail rhyme': these stanzas have a final rhyme in a short line that acts as a 'tail'. It may be seen in longer stanzas, but six lines are the fewest that can demonstrate this apparently complex pattern. It has several rules and its definition is often very complicated to follow, but in practice it is a stanza form that is harmonious and even sing-song in its shifts between long and short lines and its regularly recurring rhymes. These are its requirements:

- The stanza must finish on a short line that rhymes with the only other short line in the stanza.
- Between these two short lines there must be at least one long line.
- In the stricter definition this is arranged so that each short line is preceded by long-line rhyming couplets.

In a traditional six-line rime couée stanza this essentially means that the stanza makes two T-shapes, with b-rhymes forming each stem, as seen in the table above. This division is made clear in a dialogue poem by the Countess of Pembroke (a great prosodic experimenter), which takes place between two shepherds. The two voices each provide the two halves of the rime couée shape. Thenot establishes the pattern with great flourish as he claims his language is fit to praise Astrea; Piers' answers complete the rime couée pattern, but they reveal his deep mistrust of all linguistic praise, made all the more ironic by the elaborate stanzas they create between them:

> THENOT: I sing divine Astrea's praise,
> O Muses! help my wits to raise,
> And heave my Verses higher.
> PIERS: Thou need'st the truth but plainly tell,
> Which much I doubt thou canst not well,
> Thou art so oft a lier.

> Mary Herbert, Countess of Pembroke (1602), 'A Dialogue between two shepherds, Thenot and Piers', ll. 1–6.

The rime couée form was often used for Middle English **romance** tales, and is sometimes known as a *romance six*. Chaucer ironically used this carefully constructed stanza in the doggerel tale spoken by 'Chaucer' in *The Canterbury Tales*, 'The Tale of Sir Thopas' [c. 1396–1400]. Michael Drayton responded with an extended version in eight-line stanzas (see also his 'Nymphidia', 1621), which replaces the stipulated couplets with triplets:

Fair stood the wind for France,
When we our sails advance,
Nor now to prove our chance,
    Longer will tarry;
But putting to the main
At Kaux, the mouth of Seine,
With all his martial train,
    Landed King Harry.

Michael Drayton (1606), 'Ode to the Cambro-Britons and their Harp, His Ballad of Agincourt', ll. 1–8.

Read more

- Shelley's 'To Jane (The keen stars were twinkling)' (1832) fuses two rime couée movements together into 12-line stanzas: the rise and swell of the alternating lines suggest the harmony between Jane's voice and the 'tinkling' guitar.
- George Herbert uses a particularly tight form of rime couée that rhymes *a-a-b-a-a-b* in 'The British Church' (1633).

Burns stanza (originally standard Habbie, or Scottish Stanza)

Three iambic tetrameters, one dimeter, one iambic tetrameter and a final dimeter.

Rhyme scheme: *a-a-a-b-a-b*.

The most common variation of the traditional rime couée stanza sees the short-long-short dance pushed nearer to the end of the stanza and the rhymes reduced to just a- and b-. The Scottish poet Robert Burns used this arrangement in his many celebrated songs in Scots dialect, hence its name. However, the stanza remembers French troubadour songs, and was also known as the 'standard Habbie', after an eighteenth-century **epitaph** for a piper, Habbie Simson, written by Robert Sempill. Burns often used these stanzas for noisy, 'spoken' poems using dialect related to an oral culture of performed entertainment. The three consecutive rhymes allow the poems to build in intensity (and comedy), as in this address to a louse seen on a lady's bonnet at church:

Ye ugly, creepan, blastet wonner,
Detested, shunn'd, by saunt an' sinner,
How daur ye set your fit upon her,
    Sae fine a *Lady*!
Gae somewhere else and seek your dinner,
    On some poor body.

Robert Burns (1785), 'To a Louse', ll. 7–12. [1]

Yet these poems are not simply 'rough': the stanza's tight rhyming and short lines demand precision and sustained artistry and Burns often varied the rhyme between **masculine**, **feminine** and **triple** rhymes, as in this satirical 'prayer':

What was I, or my generation,
That I should get such exaltation?
I, wha deserve most just damnation,
    For broken laws,
Sax thousand years, 'foe my creation,
    Through Adam's cause.

Robert Burns (1785), 'Holy Willie's Prayer', ll. 13–18.

This splicing together of dialect terms with scholarly Latinate ones in fact says much about the 'standard Habbie' stanza. Although they may seem to evoke a naive and even 'peasant' diction, scholars such as Fiona Stafford and Murray Pittock suggest that the stanza breached high and low culture in the eighteenth century, appearing across genres such as **elegy**, **pastoral** and **lyric** as well as in the more boisterous **broadside ballad**.

Read more

* See 'The Eemis Stane' (1925) or 'The Watergaw' (1925) by Hugh MacDiarmid (pen-name of Christopher Murray Grieve): they register a contentious relationship to tradition in their half-remembrance of the Burns stanza (notice the changed rhyme schemes or proportions).

References

Pittock, M. (2007), 'Allan Ramsay and the decolonisation of genre', *The Review of English Studies*.

Stafford, F. (2005), 'Scottish poetry and regional literary expression' in *The Cambridge History of English Literature, 1660–1780*, ed. J. Richetti (Cambridge: Cambridge University Press), pp. 340–62.

Sesta rima

Six lines divided into a **quatrain** and a **couplet**.

Rhyme scheme: *a-b-a-b-c-c*.

This attractive arrangement of rhymes has often been used in English poetry, perhaps because a quatrain together with a couplet allows the stanza to create a soundscape and then to linger there in a final double rhyme. In Wordsworth's famous example the poem ends by reflecting back to when the poet witnessed a dance of floral abundance. As the memory infuses his present state of mind (this is 'emotion recollected in tranquillity') the cross-rhymed quatrain followed by a rhyming couplet intimates the sense of growing and then achieved significance that this simple scene attains when remembered and manifested in verse:

> For oft, when on my couch I lie
> In vacant or in pensive mood,
> They flash upon that inward eye
> Which is the bliss of solitude;
> And then my heart with pleasure fills,
> And dances with the daffodils.

William Wordsworth (1807), 'I wandered lonely as a cloud', ll. 19–24.

In other treatments the lilting, sprightly beat of the tetrameter is solemnized by using the rhymes and short regulated lines to denote not so much growing joy as melancholic limbo or even stasis: see Matthew Arnold's 'Stanzas from the Grande Chartreuse' (1855). George Herbert, a brilliant manipulator of sesta rima, uses **tetrameter** lines to personify time as a gardener who prunes the mortal in preparation for meeting with God after death, a process suggested by the shift from quatrain to couplet: 'An usher to convey our souls | Beyond the utmost stars and poles' ('Time', 1633, ll. 17–18). Christina Rossetti engages with something of this ordered anticipation of death in her use of sesta rima for a poem that explores a widow's pining after loss, 'Death's Chill Between' (1848).

Yet sesta rima may also be used in stanzas of irregular line length. Again, Herbert is an innovator here, using a diminishing arrangement of pentameter, tetrameter and trimeter in 'Home' (1633), but perhaps especially movingly Clare uses irregular sesta rima in a poem that yearns not only after a lover but also after liberty and mental freedom:

Stanzas

Mary, or sweet spirit of thee,
  As the bright sun shines to-morrow
Thy dark eyes these flowers shall see,
  Gathered by me in sorrow,
In the still hour when my mind was free
To walk alone—yet wish I walked with thee.

John Clare (1924 [c. 1840]), 'Mary', ll. 13–18.

Venus and Adonis stanza

Six lines of **iambic pentameter**.

Rhyme scheme: *a-b-a-b-c-c*.

This established form of sesta rima is named after Shakespeare's narrative poem, 'Venus and Adonis'. The pentameter lines fall in with narrative tradition, as seen in Chaucer or in Shakespeare's own blank verse, while the rhymes provide a tripping, more lyrical quality. The poem takes the story of Venus and Adonis, as told in Ovid's *Metamorphoses*, and refashions it in various ways, most notably casting the mortal Adonis as a gauche teenager alarmed by the fevered advances of the older Venus, the goddess of love. This contrast is demonstrated in Shakespeare's handling of the stanza: on one occasion the couplet serves Venus in her determination to linger in Adonis' presence; the next it serves the boy, giving him just the snappy escape route he needs:

Look how he can, she cannot choose but love;
And by her fair immortal hand she swears
From his soft bosom never to remove
Till he take truce with her contending tears,
  Which long have rained, making her cheeks all wet;
  And one sweet kiss shall pay this countless debt.

Upon this promise did he raise his chin,
Like a divedipper peering through a wave
Who, being looked on, ducks as quickly in—
So offers he to give what she did crave,
  But when her lips were ready for his pay,
  He winks, and turns his lips another way.

William Shakespeare (1593), 'Venus and Adonis', ll. 79–90.

Read more

- Felicia Hemans used the stanza for some of her *Records of Woman* (1828) – see 'Pauline' for example. The Venus and Adonis stanza allows her to evoke with iambic pentameter the presence of her influence, Wordsworth (who

207

used that line to address his own personal history in *The Excursion*, 1814) and a tone of public recognition (using a line favoured by male Augustan poets), but then shape this with rhyme, to sound 'the last note of that wild horn [...] Which haunts the exile's heart with melody' ('The Switzer's Wife', l. 5–6).

Rime royale

Seven lines of **iambic pentameter**.

Rhyme scheme: *a-b-a-b-b-c-c*.

Chaucer devised this stanza shape and used it in his long poem, *Troilus and Criseyde* [c. 1382–1386], the tragic love story that, like the stanza it is written in, derives from Continental sources. He also used it in the more varied dream vision *The Parlement of Foules* [c. 1380–1382], a strange **allegory** that uses a gathering of birds to address the pursuit of scholarly enquiry. Shakespeare later used the stanza for 'The Rape of Lucrece', a poem that redirects the eroticism of 'Venus and Adonis' into the murkier and tragic waters of violence, suicide and political upheaval. The stanza's dovetailing movement from an open cross-rhymed quatrain into claustrophobic heroic couplets is especially troubling here, towards the end of the poem:

> Poor broken glass, I often did behold
> In thy sweet semblance my old age new born;
> But now that fair fresh mirror, dim and old,
> Shows me a bare-boned death by time outworn.
> O, from thy cheeks my image thou hast torn,
>   And shivered all the beauty of my glass,
>   That I no more can see what once I was.

William Shakespeare (1594), 'The Rape of Lucrece', ll. 1758–64.

Lucrece's father, despairing over her dead body, remembers how he used to see his youthful self in her face, but now their images only converge as hers becomes as aged as his: they are grotesquely fused (as couplets fuse together after a quatrain) into one image of 'bare-boned death'.

Such solemn subjects have given the stanza a reputation for seriousness and high-minded subject matter with an air of scholarly endeavour, bolstered by the suggestion that it was King James I's preference for the stanza that gave it its name. Yet poems in this stanza frequently impart a more specific sense of the tragic, dangerous or repercussive in matters of love, as have been seen in the examples so far. Wyatt used the stanza unusually in a short **lyric** rather than a narrative poem that suggests a simmering sense of resentment even as it thrills in remembrance of erotic pursuits:

> They flee from me that sometime did me seek
> With naked foot stalking in my chamber.
> I have seen them gentle, tame, and meek
> That now are wild and do not remember
> That sometime they put themself in danger
> To take bread at my hand; and now they range,
> Busily seeking with a continual change.
>
> Thanked be fortune, it hath been otherwise
> Twenty times better, but once in special,
> In thin array after a pleasant guise,
> When her loose gown from her shoulders did fall
> And she me caught in her arms long and small,
> Therewithal sweetly did me kiss
> And softly said, 'Dear heart, how like you this?'
>
> Thomas Wyatt (1557), 'LXXX: They flee from me that sometime did me seek', ll 1–14 [2]

Wyatt also produced a radically curtailed form of the stanza in 'What should I say' (1815 [c. 1542]), which uses the rhyme scheme, but in lines of iambic dimeter.

Read more

- Wordsworth's 'Resolution and Independence' (1807) struggles to reconcile opposing impulses: despair and the need to continue developing; his own solipsistic struggle and the equally lonesome yet worldly experience of the leech-gatherer; the poet's work of the mind and the leech-gatherer's work in the field. This is reflected in the poem's rime royale stanzas, which shift between humble and 'natural' philosophy and elaborate coded language: 'Choice word and measured phrase, above the reach | Of ordinary men; a stately speech;' (ll. 95–6). Note that the poem adds an extra foot in every seventh line, arguably moving towards the **Spenserian stanza**.
- Morris used rime royale for *The Earthly Paradise* (1868–1870), the 'Apology' to which contrasts the speaker's humility with his ambitious literary form: 'Let it suffice me that my murmuring rhyme | Beats with light wing against the ivory gate;' (ll. 24–5).

Ottava rima

Eight lines of **iambic pentameter**.

Rhyme scheme: *a-b-a-b-a-b-c-c*.

This stanza is Italian in origin, but was developed in English by Thomas Wyatt (c. 1503–42). The stanza has two prominent impulses: on the one hand the series of neatly alternating lines followed by a distinct couplet (whose rhymes have not so far appeared) make it almost a miniature **Shakespearean sonnet**. In other treatments it may gallop along with a drumming energy, accounting for its appearance in many narrative poems. This defence of Eve, written by Aemilia Lanyer (a woman resident in England but of Italian Jewish descent) beautifully demonstrates its affinity with sonnet-style argument. The alternating a- and b-rhymes set up an argument in which Lanyer turns Adam's claim to superiority into an accusation; she then employs the couplet to encapsulate that argument and drive the point home:

> But surely Adam cannot be excus'd,
> Her fault, though great, yet he was most too blame;
> What Weaknesse offerd, Strength might have refus'd,
> Being Lord of all, the greater was his shame:
> Although the Serpents craft had her abus'd,
> Gods holy word ought all his actions frame:
>   For he was Lord and King of all the earth,
>   Before poore Eve had either life or breath.

Aemilia Lanyer (1611), *Salve Deus Rex Judæorum*, ll. 15–22.

John Harington on the other hand delights in the dashing energy of a run of iambic cross rhymes in his translation of Ludovico Ariosto's **romance**, *Orlando Furioso* (1532). Here his protagonists (and his readers) are carried along on lilting pentameters that lead us through the spectacular landscape before gradually slowing down and grinding to a halt in the face of the unknown, captured in the terrifying rhyme of 'confused' with 'abused':

Twere infinit to tell what wondrous things
He saw, that passed ours not few degrees,
What towns, what hills, what rivers and what springs
What dales, what Pallaces, what goodly trees:
But to me short, at last his guide him brings,
Unto a goodlie vallie, where he sees,
A mightie masse of things straungely confused,
Things that on earth were lost, or were abused.

John Harington (1591), 'Book 34' from *Ariosto's Orlando Furioso*, ll. 33–40.

Despite these elegant early experiments in English, ottava rima has not received an overwhelming number of treatments. It had a revival during the Romantic period, however (Shelley translated Homer's *Hymns* in ottava rima), but today it is generally associated with Byron's rough-and-ready treatment in his irreverent narrative, *Don Juan* (1819). This alternates between using the stanza's potential for speed, where the narrative pushes along with as little regard for consequence as its protagonist, and episodes where the narrative stalls, filling the stanza's relatively capacious room with waspish comment and pointed gibes.

Read more

- Yeats' collection, *The Tower* (1928) features many poems in ottava rima. Why might Yeats be interested in reviving this form in this collection? How far does it simply suit a present purpose (its rhyme scheme being especially attractive) and how far does it engage with literary tradition? Does Yeats celebrate such tradition, or rewrite it?

Spenserian stanza

Eight lines of **iambic pentameter** plus one **Alexandrine**.
Rhyme scheme *a-b-a-b-b-c-b-c-c*.

Edmund Spenser devised this form for *The Faerie Queene*. By adding the ninth extended line he introduced a bold disruption to an otherwise regular rhythm and rhyme scheme that might have divided the stanza into couplets (*ab ab bc bc*) or neat quatrains (*abab bcbc*). The force of that last **Alexandrine**, with its indulgent extra c-rhyme, dynamically disrupts any sense of restrained balance. Our eye loses sight of regularity, and our ear is enchanted by this now languorous and elegant display of echoing repetition. Part of Spenser's **invocation** at the start of *The Faerie Queene* demonstrates some of the stanza's effects.

> Helpe then, O holy Virgin chiefe of nine,
> Thy weaker Novice to performe thy will,
> Lay forth out of thine everlasting scryne
> The antique rolles, which there lye hidden still,
> Of Faerie knights and fairest Tanaquill,
> Whom that most noble Briton Prince so long
> Sought through the world, and suffered so much ill,
> That I must rue his undeservèd wrong:
> O helpe thou my weake wit, and sharpen my dull tong.

Edmund Spenser (1590–1609), *The Faerie Queene*, Book 1, ll. 10–18.

Here Spenser addresses his muse (Clio), and pleads for help in telling the tale of the noble Briton Prince (Arthur). The stanza (an intricate, enclosed and fixed shape on the page) functions rather like Clio's 'scryne' (a chest for papers) by being a vessel for a story. So the poet asks that 'antique rolles' reveal their hidden tales of knights and ladies, and the Spenserian stanza allows this to happen. We can see the rhyme scheme slowly unravelling just as the stories will do. At first the b-rhymes appear in tight pairs with a-rhymes, but they soon pick up the newcomer c-rhymes. In the end, the rhymes unpeel completely, leaving the c-rhymes to take over as they end the stanza with an extra echo, which is emphasized by the additional **foot** of the last line. It is Spenser's innovative use of the final Alexandrine that will be the key to his success, and this is cleverly acknowledged in line 18, which uses an Alexandrine to ask the muse to 'sharpen my dull tong [tongue]'.

This form has inspired many imitators (although it is rarely used in latter years), particularly among Romantic poets, most notably John Keats. 'The Eve of St Agnes' (1820) – an unearthly tale of magic visions – is distinguished by Keats' deft handling of the final Alexandrine. Look to Stanza XLI, for example. Here the phantom-like lovers are threatened with imprisonment, but because the Alexandrine is longer it effectively gives them time to act and the stanza creaks on to let them free with the line, 'The key turns, and the door upon its hinges groans'. The stanza was used to celebrated effect again in Keats' **elegy** by Percy Bysshe Shelley, 'Adonais' (1821).

This longer-length stanza is especially suited to narrative, often of a fantastic or visionary kind that fits with the Spenserian's elaborate style. It harks back to courtly cultures that revelled in innovative wordplay and prettifying structures. However, the so-called 'Peasant' poet, John Clare, disrupts its association with 'high' art in his impressive use of the form in 'St Martin's Eve'. Set in the winter, when 'woods are desolate of song', it tells of villagers who create their own music in raucous gatherings by the fireside. The poem adopts the perspective of an onlooker, who intriguingly views such an apparently humble scene through a sophisticated literary frame:

And such a group on good St Martin's Eve
Was met together upon pleasure bent,
Where tales of fun did cares so well deceive
That the old cottage rung with merriment,
And even the very rafters groaned & bent;
Not so much, it would seem, from tempest's din,
That roared without in roaring discontent,
As from the merry noise and laugh within,
That seemed as summer's sports had never absent bin

John Clare (1920 [c. 1832]), 'St Martin's Eve', ll. 37–45.

As the villagers are drawn inside, the building's frame stretches to accommodate its new occupants. Similarly, the poetic frame contorts to meet the dual demands of Clare's colloquial speech and his knowledge of literary tradition. The rafters groan, and we might too as 'bent' is used twice in order to 'bend' to the rules of the Spenserian stanza. As the stanza closes, the extra foot's slowing reluctance to end and move on is echoed in the remembrance of summer sun at a time of winter storm. In this final moment, Clare conforms to the elaborate form with the dialect 'bin', so putting an idiosyncratic stamp on a recognized mode.

Read more

- Byron's *Childe Harold's Pilgrimage* (1812–1818) uses the Spenserian stanza to record Childe Harold's roamings across contemporary Europe. Note how his use of the form changes across the poem – an early deferential attachment to Spenserian archaisms (e.g. 'hight' for named; 'Whilome' for once upon a time) moves to bravado and assurance later in the poem. Why would Childe Harold wish to record his particular journey in this way? What is the tone of Byron's admission, in a poem of Spenserian stanzas, that 'Nor florid prose, nor honied lies of rhyme | Can blazon evil deeds, or consecrate a crime?' (Canto 1, ll. 26–7).
- The young Elizabeth Barrett Browning acknowledged Byron's association with the Spenserian stanza when she used it for 'Stanzas on the Death of Lord Byron', published in the periodical, *The Globe and Traveller* in June 1824.
- Wordsworth used Spenserian stanzas to frame the 'artless story' (l. 2) of 'The Female Vagrant' (1798). Is it employed to evoke a literary tradition, or simply as a sympathetic shape for a gradually unravelling tale?

Notes

1. Textual source: *The Poems and Songs of Robert Burns*, ed. James Kinsley (1968), three volumes (Oxford: Clarendon Press).
2. See *Sir Thomas Wyatt: The Complete Poems*, ed. R. A. Rebholz (1978) (London: Penguin), pp. 45–58 for consideration of Wyatt's variable metre in his use of the stanza. This is also the source edition for the text.

Wordplay

Chapter Outline

> ## Wordplay
>
> Employing a flexible and imaginative approach to meanings and arrangements of words.

As has been seen throughout this book, poetry excels at making readers encounter words in new and enriching ways. This may be achieved by giving words or phrases strange applications (such as when a woman rather than a bird is said to 'fly', or even 'have wings'), by creating ambiguities (such as when a word refers to two objects at once, for example 'glass' might be a drinking vessel or a mirror (looking glass)), or by using words in a sense that is grammatically unusual (such as when a noun is used as a verb – 'I've laddered my tights'). These tricks of language all play on the *meaning* of words: they are tropes. Tropes occur everywhere and in all linguistic communication. Poetry does not 'stand apart' (a metaphor itself) from other forms of language because it uses such devices, but whereas in everyday speech figurative language is often absorbed and accepted so fully that we do not even notice its presence, in poetry tropes are interrogated and sustained; it is one form of communication notable for the attention it draws to the strange effects of language. Becoming increasingly alert to poetic uses of figurative language can give you a new awareness of wordplay in all your encounters with the world.

While all of these figurative effects are exciting and enlightening, poetry does more than concentrate on meaning and content: it also provides us with particular arrangements of words – arrangements that are just as vital to a poem's import as the individual words themselves. Poetry's use of **metre**, **rhyme** and **stress** may importantly dictate (or simply shape) these arrangements (as seen in the discussion of rhyme, usual word order may be reversed in order to fit with a rhyme), but this original requirement has become a point of principle: poetry not only tolerates unusual arrangements, but encourages or indeed insists on them. This contributes to poetry's ability to provide alternative, slanted perspectives on the world. A poem may start every line with the same word for a particular effect ('And … And … And'), it may present an adjective before a noun ('her cheeks red and glowing' rather than 'her red cheeks glowed'), or it may repeat words in forwards and backwards order ('I broke the horse before the horse broke me'). These tricks of language play on the *ordering* of words: they are schemes.

6.1 Tropes

Here some of the more common tropes and schemes are explained along with some examples. Poems often use several tropes at once, or they might combine tropes with schemes. Some of these combinations are also considered here. Of course both tropes and schemes occur in all forms of writing (especially in fictional prose) and speaking (especially in formal speeches), and many more exist than those considered here (for a useful introduction to rhetorical schemes, for example, see the website, http://rhetoric.byu.edu). These examples are simply those that occur most frequently in this book and illustrate poetry's willingness and aptness to make us rethink linguistic expression. To recap:

- *tropes*: wordplay based on the meaning of words
- *schemes*: wordplay based on the order of words.

Simile

A comparison drawn between two distinct objects or ideas connected with 'as' or 'like'.

Similes characterize something by comparing it with another idea or object and drawing attention to that by using 'as' or 'like'. 'O My Luve's like a red, red rose' is a famous example (Burns (1796), 'A Red, Red Rose', l. 1). In Shakespeare's 'Sonnet 21' the speaker likens his love to the beloved child who is always thought beautiful: 'my love is as fair | As any mother's child' (ll. 10–11). These comparisons often heap praise (or spite) on a subject, but they may also make an unfamiliar or complex idea more understandable by likening it to something familiar. In this way they bring a distant notion closer to our experience. In Shakespeare's example the speaker reassures his beloved that his love is not dangerous or false; it is as innocent and sincere as that between a mother and child.

In a recent collection Fiona Sampson drew the arresting comparison, 'Slim as a nun, I lie along | the margin of a borrowed bed' ('Hay-on-Wye' (2007), ll. 1–2). The simile works on several levels – the figure of a slim nun suggests religious denial of food, and a certain unwillingness to take up space either in the world or in the bed: a kind of humility that insists on bodily control (this comparison will be made ironic later in the poem). Having used simile to characterize the speaker, the lines go on to echo that device: the borrowed bed emphasizes the action of 'borrowing' involved in simile (an idea from one area of life is borrowed to illuminate another one) and the fact that the speaker doesn't quite inhabit the borrowed space illustrates how simile uses comparisons, but it maintains a distinction between the two ideas: the two parts are *like* each other, but are not the same.

Metaphor

A comparison that speaks of an idea or object as if it is another.

At its simplest level, metaphor is the figure of speech in which one thing is said actually to be another:

- 'I was a stricken deer, that left the herd' (William Cowper (1785), 'Book III', *The Task*, l. 108).
- 'Sappho? But thou – thy body is the song, | Thy mouth the music' (Algernon Charles Swinburne (1866), 'Anactoria', ll. 74–5).

Metaphor goes further than simile: comparisons are drawn, but the two objects are converged and are now indistinguishable. As with simile, this trope may work by adding character to an object, or making it more understandable for a reader. For relatively familiar uses of metaphor (and simile) see the love **blazon**. The metaphor becomes more complex, however, either when the comparison is not made obvious by use of the verb 'to be', or when the distinction between the object described and the object used for comparison becomes unclear. I. A. Richards usefully labelled these two ideas (p. 96):

- *tenor*: the object or idea described in a metaphor
- *vehicle*: the object or idea called upon to illuminate that object.

So, in the Cowper example above the tenor would be the speaker and the vehicle the deer; in the Swinburne example Anactoria is the tenor and music is the vehicle. In these figures one object is brought into view through another: the speaker's fear is indicated rather than described by the metaphor; Anactoria's centrality to Sappho's song is asserted by the almost-accusatory metaphor.

Metaphor may also emerge (in fact it does so more frequently) 'silently', that is without explicit attention being drawn to it, by describing one object in terms that properly refer to another. This form of metaphor frequently exists in a verb, such as in Carew's 'A Rapture' that opens, 'I will enjoy thee now, my Celia, come | And fly with me to love's Elysium', l. 1–2. Here the metaphor is located in 'fly', with the tenor being the lovers' movement and the vehicle being a bird; the verb attached to the tenor is one that strictly only relates to the vehicle.

Later in the same poem the speaker only states the vehicles in a series of metaphors (the tenor in this section being Celia's body); this allows him to express explicit sexual desire by implication:

> I'll seize the rosebuds in their perfumed bed,
> The violet knots, like curious mazes spread
> O'er all the garden, taste the ripened cherry,
> The warm, firm apple, tipped with coral berry.
>
> Thomas Carew (1640), 'A Rapture', ll. 63–6.

Often an image or idea will be presented apparently literally in a poem only to reveal itself as the vehicle for a metaphor as the lines continue. This moving example from Tennyson's elegy begins as a description of the confluence between the rivers Wye and Severn. Yet that tidal movement becomes the vehicle for a metaphor for the poet's grief, seen in the metaphoric 'brim' (l. 12). 'Brim' properly refers to a vessel for fluid – here the river valley that fills with tidal water – but applied metaphorically to the speaker it allows sorrow to materialize in the poem. The white space on the page between the final two **stanzas** also arguably stands as a metaphor for the choked silence that the experience produces in the speaker:

> There twice a day the Severn fills;
>   The salt sea-water passes by,
>   And hushes half the babbling Wye,
> And makes a silence in the hills.
>
> The Wye is hushed nor moved along,
>   And hushed my deepest grief of all,
>   When filled with tears that cannot fall,
> I brim with sorrow drowning song.
>
> The tide flows down, the wave again
>   Is vocal in its wooded walls;
>   My deeper anguish also falls,
> And I can speak a little then.
>
> Alfred Tennyson (1850), 'Lyric XIX', *In Memoriam A. H. H.*, ll. 4–15.

Having absorbed the metaphoric connection between grief and the river we read of falling water levels, but we sense the passing tension of unspoken grief; our lump in the throat is swallowed as the tide flows down.

Metaphor and philosophies of language

Both metaphor and simile, as has been seen, not only draw out comparisons between two known objects or ideas (deers and men; birds and movement; apples and breasts), but they also make the less well known, the abstract or the elusive available for us (and the poet) to experience and understand (fear, love, grief). In each case we identify two elements (encouraged by the epithets vehicle and tenor): there is the thing described and the means used to describe it. However, even just this explanation installs a kind of hierarchy: the metaphor (the means used) implicitly takes up a secondary position in relation to the 'reality' that exists behind it (we indicate this position when we say, 'the apples in this poem "really" refer to breasts'). The idea that this distinction – between the 'thing' itself and the means used to articulate it – can be maintained, and that metaphor can be 'imported' into common language (in poetry, for example) to achieve a specific end (to illuminate the tenor) is what Terence Hawkes names the 'classical' view of metaphor (p. 92). However, this position has been richly interrogated, not least by Romantic writers and their readers. The other proposition – which Hawkes terms the 'romantic' view (p. 92) – is that metaphors aren't unusual events of language, occurring in specific circumstances, but they are the underlying principle of all language. It asserts that language is itself metaphorical, indeed vitally so, as a metaphorical interaction occurs between words and the 'hurrying of material' (life, experiences and so on) that they encounter. This interaction, when deliberately invoked (as in poetry), has the potential to create 'new' realities. The work of many late-twentieth-century commentators, especially 'deconstructionists', has been to interrogate these two positions, bringing them closer together. Paul de Man, for example, in his reading of Nietzsche, identifies something akin to the 'romantic' view when he claims that 'the trope [including metaphor] is not a derived, marginal, or aberrant form of language but the linguistic paradigm par excellence. The figurative structure is not one linguistic mode among others but it characterizes language as such' (p. 105). The implication, however, is that the special case of poetry (which is still held onto via the notion of intensification in the 'romantic' view) is increasingly absorbed as a point of principle in all language.

The result of entertaining the possibility that all language is metaphorical is that the fallibility of the 'reality' that metaphor describes (the tenor) is put into question: no longer does it is exist independently, merely waiting for a vehicle occasionally to draw attention to it, but it is now understood to rely precisely on the metaphor's action to bring it into being. The tenor is therefore fused with the vehicle, and indeed the vehicle conditions that tenor.

Some of these complexities – the differing status of vehicle and tenor and the implications for perception, reality and ultimately belief – can be seen in Arnold's poetic meditation on metaphor and simile in an age when scientific and geological knowledge increasingly appeared to encroach on religious belief. In 'Dover Beach' there is a wavering sense that there may be no stable 'truth' behind metaphors and the possibility that faith is itself a figure of speech (think of the metaphorical nature of the Christian maxim, 'God is Love') emerges in Arnold's likening of faith to the sea:

> The Sea of Faith
> Was once, too, at the full, and round earth's shore
> Lay like the folds of a bright girdle furl'd.
> But now I only hear
> Its melancholy, long, withdrawing roar,
> Retreating, to the breath
> Of the night wind, down the vast edges drear
> And naked shingles of the world.
>
> Matthew Arnold (1867), 'Dover Beach', ll. 21–8.

The extract opens with a metaphor that suggests gravity and stability, particularly through capitalization, and yet it characterizes faith as fluid, fluctuating and unstable, like the sea. Looking back to a time predating religious doubt, that sea (and so the faith it points to) was understood as protective, bright and unbroken, remembered by being likened through simile to a fabric belt ('girdle') that encircles the waist. Returning to the present ('But now') however, metaphor persists ('I hear [...] [its] roar'), but the tenor is now the sea itself (faith has slipped away), which is accessed through the vehicle of a roaring wild animal. The poet turns to the beach. In a context that likened the sea to faith he might have hoped that the presence of a beach could point (as in the metaphoric method) to the presence of a creator God. However, just as the sea no longer seems to refer to anything beyond the sea in this poem, so the beach cannot function metaphorically either: the beach is simply a collection of naked shingles, no longer the vehicle for the tenor of a present God.

The final element that Arnold's poem serves to illustrate is how the vehicle of a metaphor can leave traces behind, irreversibly colouring our experience of the tenor. Unlike the 'classical' position, which implicitly suggests that the tenor is merely illuminated but essentially untouched by a metaphoric vehicle, Arnold demonstrates that the use of the sea as a vehicle for faith precisely fuses the two together, making faith vulnerable to the fluctuating fortunes of that sea. This articulates something of the discomfort and fear that metaphor may provoke. Metaphor may begin to bring something into view, but it may also snatch it away: it is reassuring and disarming simultaneously.

Metonymy

When something associated with an object or idea stands in for the idea itself.

Whereas metaphor and simile are based on resemblance – the tenor is understood to be like or even the same as the vehicle – metonymy is based on association, a slightly looser arrangement. It occurs in everyday speech when we talk about government or monarchy as 'Westminster', 'the White House' or the 'crown'. All of these buildings and objects are *associated* with (rather than being the same as) government or monarchy; so they serve as metonymic 'shorthand' for the larger notion itself. Keats uses this trope in 'Ode to a Nightingale', where he evokes a metonymy, and then revels in and develops it:

> O, for a draught of vintage! that hath been
>   Cool'd a long age in the deep-delvèd earth,
> Tasting of Flora and the country green,
>   Dance, and Provençal song, and sunburnt mirth!
> O for a beaker full of the warm South,
>   Full of the true, the blushful Hippocrene,
>   With beaded bubbles winking at the brim,
>   And purple-stainèd mouth;
>   That I might drink, and leave the world unseen,
>   And with thee fade away into the forest dim—

John Keats (1820), 'Ode to a Nightingale', ll. 11–20.

Here Keats' call for a gulp of wine ('vintage!') brings to mind an entire culture of song. We understand the wine to have been produced in Provence, an area of France with a particularly strong poetic heritage, being the area associated with troubadours, **romance** and **courtly love**. Keats pursues this association such that the wine (one of the elements associated with this part of France) becomes a sensual metonymy for the whole culture of troubadours, dancing and singing. So Keats makes a 'draught of vintage', which existed in mediaeval Provence and which exists in nineteenth-century England, stand in for a culture it was associated with, and which the poet may now participate in, even from a distance. Metonymy thus sets up a chain of association in which its present user can be absorbed into its larger associated culture. As the **stanza** progresses the metonymy progresses to metaphor: a 'beaker full of [...] the blushful Hippocrene' is a metaphor for inspiration (Hippocrene being the fountain of the Muses). A beaker is not a part of inspiration (in the way that wine was a part of Provencal culture); rather it is a metaphoric vehicle for inspiration: the earlier association between wine and song now fuses together such that wine *is* song. The metonymy has infused the stanza, staining what follows: since it is wine (an intoxicant) that is evoked by association in the beaker, inspiration is also intoxication and from intoxication comes oblivion (the 'purple-stained mouth' leads inexorably to the disappearance of the poet from the world). The metonymy-metaphor of wine for song may have made abstract inspiration materially present in the poem, but it also threatens to dissolve it away.

Synecdoche

A form of metonymy in which one part of an object or idea stands in for the whole of that object or idea.

Synecdoche is very close to metonymy and sometimes the terms are used synonymously. However, synecdoche uses an inextricable part of a larger abstract idea (rather than just something associated with it) to stand in for that idea. In everyday speech we speak of 'the stage' to refer to theatre culture (a stage is a necessary physical part of the theatre) or 'motoring' to refer to a whole leisure pursuit involving cars (obviously cars must have motors). An especially famous literary example comes from Marlowe's *Dr Faustus*:

> [*Enter* Helen]
> Faustus: Was this the face that launched a thousand ships,
> And burnt the topless towers of Ilium?
> Sweet Helen, make me immortal with a kiss:
> Her lips sucks forth my soul, see where it flies!
>
> Christopher Marlowe (1604), *Dr Faustus*, Scene 12, ll. 81–4.

The passage occurs when Helen of Troy makes a fleeting appearance in this play, almost as a mirage. As told in Homer's *The Iliad* (see **epic**) Helen was married to Menelaus, King of Sparta. Paris (a Trojan prince) fell in love with her renowned beauty and captured her to take back to Troy. This effective plundering of 'treasure' provoked the Greeks into launching a sea attack on Troy and so began the Trojan wars. In Marlowe's play Helen's face is a synecdoche for her whole body's beauty (and its devastating effect); the 'thousand ships' are a synecdoche for the whole Grecian army and so for the wars themselves; the 'topless towers of Ilium' are a synecdoche for the whole of Troy, all its buildings and all its inhabitants destroyed in battle. Each is an inextricable physical part not only of an event but also of a whole culture of myth and storytelling. By grafting his play onto Classical heritage in this way Marlowe allows his writing to become a portal to an entire culture, like Faustus himself, who kisses Helen in order to gain her abstract immortality. We might say then that synecdoche illustrates the wider practice of poetry, which is to evoke multiple associations and larger ideas from immediate and individual ideas and words.

Pun

Wordplay that depends on a similarity in sound but a difference in meaning.

Puns (also known as 'paranomasia', the Greek for 'equal word') occur when a word is understood in at least two different ways at once; for example, when 'die' is understood as both death and orgasm in seventeenth-century poems such as John Donne's 'The Canonization' (1633): 'We die and rise the same, and prove | Mysterious by this love' (l. 26–7). Puns are nowadays often considered humorous devices used by risqué comics who rely on audience recognition of *double entendre*. However the sense that a word may be understood in two ways simultaneously can have a disturbing effect, not only in overt uses (as when 'grave' is understood as both serious and as a tomb, for example), but also in line with the principle that lies behind punning: the meaning of words is arbitrary, dependent on context and escapes the complete control of the speaker. The use of puns has variously been celebrated or admired as evidence of intellectual prowess or denigrated as evidence of a poet's willingness to stoop to bawdy irreverence. Puns take advantage of a number of different word similarities:

Homonyms: words that are spelt and pronounced identically, but which have different meanings, allowing for perfect puns. Andrew Marvell employs several in his reserved commentary on Oliver Cromwell, who he describes as having 'cast the kingdom old | Into another mould' ('An Horatian Ode' (1681), ll. 35–6), with 'mould' implying both a new form and a decaying one.

Homophones: words that are pronounced identically but are spelt differently (such as 'pour' and 'poor'). This form of pun is common in spoken poetry as it is a pun that is clear to the ear as well as the eye. Many occur in Shakespeare's plays, for example in the famous opening to *Richard III* (1597): 'Now is the winter of our discontent | Made glorious summer by this son of York' (Act 1 Scene 1), which puns on 'son' and 'sun'.

Homographs: words that are pronounced differently but spelt identically (such as 'bow' for an arrow and 'bow' taken at the end of a performance).

Etymological puns: puns that refer to the etymological source of a word. A famous example comes from the Bible: 'And I say also unto thee, That thou art Peter, and upon this rock I will build my church' (Matthew 16.18). In Greek 'Peter' is *Petrus* and 'rock' is *petra*, so the two become a pun here. Felicia Hemans' collection *Records of Woman* (1828) arguably operates as an etymological pun because it records the history of women's lives, but it does so through telling the stories of their 'hearts' or emotions ('records' links to 'cor' meaning heart). Ben Jonson puns on the Latin *fallo* (to make a mistake) in his ode on Cary and Morison (see **ode**): 'He never fell, thou fall'st, my tongue' (l. 45).

Paronomasia: although often used to mean 'pun' this strictly refers to a play on similar rather than identical-sounding words. Emily Dickinson (1890) [c. 1862] suggests this in poem 328, on the subject of a bird: 'And then he drank a Dew | From a convenient Grass' (ll. 5–6), with grass punning on glass.

Conceit

When a metaphor is extended and explored so that it becomes the governing idea of a poem.

A trope may used to serve an immediate purpose (for example to describe the extreme beauty of a beloved or express a speaker's sorrow at leaving a lover) but a conceit will extend this so that it becomes a principle of the poem's logic. So, if a woman's cheeks are compared to roses at one point this might start a whole conceit for the poem in which flowers always indicate a part of woman or women in general. Sometimes this is also called an 'extended metaphor', seen in poems such as Coleridge's 'The Eolian Harp' (1834), which considers Aeolus' harp as a metaphor for perception and goes on to ask: 'what if all of animated nature | Be but organic Harps diversely framed, | That tremble into thought' (ll. 44–6).

A conceit usually indicates an especially ingenious type of comparison in which two divergent ideas are surprisingly brought together to produce apt and successful tropes. These are especially associated with seventeenth-century poets such as John Donne, known as 'Metaphysical poets', and so these strange and apparently illogical conceits are sometimes known as *metaphysical conceits*. To prove that these odd likenesses are suitable and indeed constitute a special kind of insight metaphors are extended and explored, and the resulting passage is known as a metaphysical conceit. In this poem, Donne likens two lovers to a pair of drawing compasses, a comparison which allows him not only to suggest how they are inextricably tied together but also to characterize their relative movements, and suggest an erotic pull of desire:

> If they be two, they are two so
>   As stiff twin compasses are two;
> Thy soul, the fixed foot, makes no show
>   To move, but doth, if th'other do.
>
> And though it in the centre sit,
>   Yet when the other far doth roam,
> It leans and hearkens after it,
>   And grows erect, as that comes home.
>
> Such wilt thou be to me, who must,
>   Like th'other foot, obliquely run;
> Thy firmness makes my circle just,
>   And makes me end where I begun.

John Donne (1633), 'A Valediction: Forbidding Mourning', ll. 25–36.

Elsewhere, such as in Donne's 'Hymn to God My God, in My Sickness' (1635), a metaphysical conceit (here that the speaker's dying body is a map) allows an abstract or terrifying unknown (here the afterlife) to be explored (literally); exploring the exact proportions and nature of the vehicle of such a metaphor allows for the tenor to be explored by implication.

Petrarchan conceits are comparisons used originally in the Italian poet's love poetry, but which have since become clichéd or hackneyed. They are used in the conventional love **blazon**, or they may involve exaggerated claims of the beloved's beauty (or cruelty) and the lover's despair. Common Petrarchan conceits include likening the woman to the sun and the lover's despair to a life threatening fever or a terrible storm.

Personification

When an abstract concept or inanimate object is given human attributes.

Personification operates as an extended metaphor by treating an object or concept as though it were human. So in the second lyric of *In Memoriam A. H. H.* (1850), Tennyson describes a yew tree as 'sullen' and 'stubborn' (ll. 13, 14); in the next lyric he personifies sorrow as a 'Priestess in the vaults of death' (l. 2). In strict categorization the former example is of personification and the latter one *prosopopoeia*, which (according to Fontanier) is when the absent, supernatural or inanimate is treated as real. However, the two terms are often used synonymously. By addressing something alien in human terms (it is a form of anthropomorphism), personification makes something available for human interaction. It may then excite emotions, such as anger, sympathy and empathy (which especially suggest various forms of fellow feeling) that might not be possible if the object is radically 'other' to the speaker or reader. The trope is importantly shaped by Classical myth, in which abstract concepts are repeatedly 'personified' through acquiring a god (so Venus as the god of love, Mars as the god of war) that then demonstrate some human (and some super-human) attributes. Keats performs several personifications in his *Odes*, either of non-human but still material objects (the nightingale, the Grecian urn) or of abstract concepts (melancholy, indolence) or of interrelations between the two such as Psyche (a nymph from Classical myth who personifies the soul) and Autumn, which is materially present in the world but which Keats also makes into a mood and attitude, personified here as a drowsy labourer:

> Who hath not seen thee oft amid thy store?
>   Sometimes whoever seeks abroad may find
> Thee sitting careless on a granary floor,
>   Thy hair soft-lifted by the winnowing wind;
> Or on a half-reaped furrow sound asleep,
>   Drowsed with the fume of poppies, while thy hook
>   Spares the next swath and all its twinèd flowers;

> John Keats (1820), 'To Autumn', ll. 12–18.

Francis Thompson's late-nineteenth-century poem 'The Hound of Heaven' (1893) performs a complex version of personification. Its conceit – that God may be likened to a dog – terrifyingly shifts the custom of giving God human attributes by implying that his are so menacing that they reach beyond the human into the animal. This indicates how personification or prosopopoeia not only impacts on the object personified; it also produces an entity within a poem that can react to (or chase) the speaker or poet. Fontanier proposes that these objects and notions can become 'confidants, witnesses, accusers, avengers, judges'. In a world of chaos and desperate cruelty, such as that seen in the trenches of the First World War, personification might be a last resort. Surveying the partisan divisions of the battlefield, it is only in a rat that Rosenberg identifies anything resembling civilized human attributes:

> Droll rat, they would shoot you if they knew
> Your cosmopolitan sympathies.
> Now you have touched this English hand
> You will do the same to a German
> Soon, no doubt, if it be your pleasure
> To cross the sleeping green between.

> Isaac Rosenberg (1922), 'Break of Day in the Trenches', ll. 7–12.

Apostrophe

A 'vocalized' address within a poem directed at an inanimate object, abstract concept or an absent figure.

Many poems of course are addressed to a person, but apostrophe is the name for those moments when an address is made directly to an absent figure (often in fact dead or not yet living), to a notion that is abstract, or to an object that is inanimate, or animal but not human. The oddity of addressing such a figure is made more obvious in apostrophe as it is 'vocalized', often with 'O' or 'Oh!' Since a response is impossible (because the addressee is absent or abstract), apostrophes are understood as moments of pure address on the speaker's part. Examples include Wordsworth's 'Milton! thou should'st be living at this hour' ((1807), 'London, 1802', l. 1); Samuel Wesley's 'Harmonious Hog draw near!' ((1685), 'A Pindaric on the Grunting of a Hog', l. 1); or in prose Charlotte Brontë's famous, 'Reader, I married him' (1848, *Jane Eyre*).

Clearly personification or prosopopoeia is implied by the very presence of apostrophe: for something to be addressed you imply that it has the human capacity to listen. To follow Jonathan Culler, apostrophe is therefore one way in which the poet tries to bring a state of affairs into being: when Shelley addresses the west wind, 'O wild West Wind, thou breath of Autumn's being' ((1820), 'Ode to the West Wind', l. 1) he asserts that the wind is able to listen, and so is sentient, and so may be implored to behave in a certain way. However, Culler goes on to assert that although apostrophe would seem make the addressee present in the poem it also importantly helps to constitute the poet themselves: 'the object is treated as a subject, an *I* which implies a certain type of *you* in its turn' (p. 142). Something of this effect arguably occurs in Graves' address of the reader:

> You, reading over my shoulder, peering beneath
> My writing arm—I suddenly feel your breath
>   Hot on my hand or on my nape,
> So interrupt my theme, scratching these few
> Words on the margin for you, namely you,
>   Too-human shape fixed in that shape:—
>
> All the saying of things against myself
> And for myself I have well done myself.
>   What now, old enemy, shall you do
> But quote and underline, thrusting yourself
> Against me, as ambassador of myself,
>   In damned confusion of myself and you?
>
> Robert Graves (1938), 'The Reader Over My Shoulder', ll. 1–12.

Although Graves conjures a reader into being by addressing them, this immediately leads to an experience of himself as breathed upon and touched. The rest of the poem's jousting tone indicates that to address a figure is to create a figure who can now perceive you too, so apostrophe is a trope in which both addresser and addressee are present and authority passes between the two.

Allegory

An extended metaphor in which events and actions within a narrative imply a separate series of events and actions 'outside' the poem.

Allegories use many of the tropes discussed in this section in order to create a sustained comparison: a poem proceeds as though it is describing one set of events or occurrences but it implies that such events actually refer to a different set of circumstances not directly stated within the poem. So allegories imply two simultaneous meanings – the literal one that takes place within the text and the symbolic one that points to events or ideas outside the text. Edmund Spenser's *The Faerie Queene*, is a famous example: ostensibly it is a **romance** tale about knights, dragons and princesses, but as an allegory it symbolizes Christian ideals and routes to salvation. Other allegories, such as John Dryden's *Absalom and Achitophel* (1681) allegorize contemporary political and historical events. In this case, Dryden addresses the contemporary Exclusion Crisis (which threatened British political and religious stability) through the filter of the biblical narrative of David and Absalom from 2 Samuel. Such distant-yet-implied connections allow Dryden to maintain a sustained critique of events while keeping an even, politic hand.

The key is that allegory's symbolic treatment of an abstract or historical complexity allows difficult, contentious or abstract conundrums to be interrogated and investigated in accessible (or safer) terms. This is not to say that they cannot be risky, however: allegories can be satirical as well as contemplative. Although personifications are sometimes called allegories (because humanizing an abstract notion implies an allegorical connection), allegories may be distinguished from that trope because they tend to reach a coherent conclusion on a subject through sustained comparison; in fact this is part of their purpose.

References

Culler, J. (1981), 'Apostrophe' in *The Pursuit of Signs: Semiotics, Literature, Deconstruction* (London: Routledge and Kegan Paul), pp. 135–54.

de Man, Paul (1979), *Allegories of Reading: Figural Language in Rosseau, Nietzsche, Rilke, and Proust* (New Haven and London: Yale University Press).

Fontanier, Pierre (1821), *Les Figures du discours*, quoted in Michel Riffaterre (1985), 'Prosopopeia', *Yale French Studies* 69, 107–23.

Hawkes, Terence (1972), *Metaphor: The Critical Idiom* (London and New York: Methuen).

Richards, I. A. (1936), *The Philosophy of Rhetoric* (New York and London: Oxford University Press).

6.2 Schemes

Anaphora

Repeating words at the beginning of successive phrases or clauses.

Anaphora draws the attention of listeners and readers through repetition. James Fenton uses anaphora in 'A German Requiem' (1981), which remembers the Jewish Holocaust of the twentieth century by devising a series of phrases that open 'it is not' and answer 'it is', 'It is not the streets that exist. It is the streets that no longer exist' (l. 3). Not only does this shift attention from presences to absences, but it also intimates the relentlessness of the loss by making this occur again and again. Indeed, anaphora often appears in listing poems, as in Shakespeare's 'Sonnet 66' which lists all the sins and deceptions that spoil the speaker's life, and would make death welcome, were it not for his desire to stay with his love:

> Tired with all these, for restful death I cry,
> As to behold desert a beggar born,
> And needy nothing trimm'd in jollity,
> And purest faith unhappily forsworn,
> And gilded honour shamefully misplaced,
> And maiden virtue rudely strumpeted,
> And right perfection wrongfully disgraced,
> And strength by limping sway disabled
> And art made tongue-tied by authority,
> And folly, doctor-like, controlling skill,
> And simple truth miscall'd simplicity,
> And captive good attending captain ill:
> Tired with all these, from these would I be gone,
> Save that, to die, I leave my love alone.

> William Shakespeare (1609), 'Sonnet 66'.

Epistrophe

The repetition of words at the ends of successive phrases or clauses.

Epistrophe reverses anaphora: it retains the coherence and steadiness of any repetition, but it allows that each time you reach that phrase you bring to it a new idea, image or sound. Whitman's sensual and erotic catalogue epistrophe

sounds a note of defiance: these fragments of same-sex union (that are anticipated, but suggest previous experience) *will* be orchestrated into a wholeness
that may be seen and worshipped:

> If I worship any particular thing it shall be some of the spread of my
>   body;
> Translucent mould of me it shall be you,
> Shaded ledges and rests, firm masculine coulter, it shall be you,
> Whatever goes to the tilth of me it shall be you,
> You my rich blood, your milky stream pale strippings of my life;
> Breast that presses against other breasts it shall be you,
> My brain it shall be your occult convolutions,
> Root of washed sweet-flag, timorous pond-snipe, nest of guarded
>   duplicate eggs, it shall be you,
> Mixed tussled hay of head and beard and brawn it shall be you,
> Trickling sap of maple, fibre of manly wheat, it shall be you;
> Sun so generous it shall be you,
> Vapors lighting and shading my face it shall be you,
> You sweaty brooks and dews it shall be you,
> Winds whose soft-tickling genitals rub against me it shall be you,
> Broad muscular fields, branches of liveoak, loving lounger in my
>   winding paths, it shall be you,
> Hands I have taken, face I have kissed, mortal I have ever touched,
>   it shall be you.
>
> Walt Whitman (1865), '23', *Leaves of Grass*, ll. 529–44.

Chiasmus

Two successive phrases or clauses switched around to create a cross
shape.

'Chiasmus' derives from the Greek for the letter X, hence its supposed cross
shape. It occurs when words are arranged to suggest symmetry on either side
of a central crossover point. So in two consecutive clauses the arrangement of
words is reversed, as in 'Whoso sheddeth man's blood, by man shall his blood be
shed' (Genesis 9:6). In a perfect chiasmus only the syntax of a phrase is reversed
while content changes. For example, 'apples are red and purple are grapes'
parallels the points being made (this fruit is this colour, that fruit is that colour)
but syntactically the parts of the phrase are reversed: 'subject-verb-adjective /
adjective-verb-subject'. Note that chiasmus occurs only in syntax as reversal is
achieved without the repetition of any single word. Something similar occurs in
Samuel Johnson's 'By day the frolic, and the dance by night' ((1749), 'The Vanity
of Human Wishes, l. 326).

This strict action is not always demonstrated, however; chiasmus is often used in a looser sense, occurring in meaning rather than syntax. So a concept is reversed or referents are swapped around an identical action, as seen in Donne's 'Love's Deity'. This features a series of chiastic **refrains** that illustrate schematically a series of paradoxes through which the 'God of Love' exerts 'tyranny' on his subjects:

> I must love her, that loves not me...
> Love, till I love her, that loves me...
> I should love her, who loves not me...
> If she whom I love, should love me.

John Donne (1633), 'Love's Deity', ll. 7, 14, 21, 28.

John Hollander loosens the strictures on chiasmus further, suggesting it is simply a 'patterning of two pairs of elements, which might be vowel-sounds or syntactical', which allows for **internal rhyme** to add to the cross shape evoked.

If we allow chiasmus to name a loosely 'criss-cross' arrangement, John Milton's famous phrase, 'He for God only, she for God in him' ((1667), Book IV, *Paradise Lost*, l. 299) may be usefully included. Although its syntactically parallel clauses suggest a sequential or contiguous action (Eve looks to Adam who looks on to God), the placement of Adam at either end of the phrase with Eve at the centre and God between her and Adam on either side creates a cross shape that installs a patriarchal dynamic between man, woman and God even at a schematic level within the poem.

Chiasmus clearly draws attention to parallels, which may suggest uniformity and stable truth, but it may equally be made absurd by the action of reversal or swap-over: suddenly a cherished aphorism may be shown to be entirely arbitrary. For these reasons chiasmus often features in **epigrams**. The action of reversal may also create less amusing confusion as categories are swapped and implicitly merged before the reader's eyes, as seen in the chiasmus that closes Shakespeare's 'Sonnet 20' (1609, l. 14): 'Mine be thy love and thy love's use thy treasure' (see **sonnet**). This instance demonstrates how, by rearranging words schemes may rearrange cultural assumptions, such as gender categories in the case of this poem. So a poet may recruit chiasmus to serve an agenda of political or ideological radicalism.

Note that when a chiasmus uses the *same* words in reverse order it is called *antimetabole*. 'Antimetabole' comes from the Greek for 'turning around' and this is precisely what the scheme enacts. It emphasizes the cross shape of chiasmus by reversing the words used in one phrase more or less exactly in the next. Christina Rossetti's 'For one is both and both are one in love' ((1880), '4' of *Monna Innominata*, l. 11) uses the scheme to reverse not only the words but also the ideology of sonnet convention, replacing the lover–beloved pairing with a radical notion of equality. Rogers' is a comic example (italicized). Here the speaker recounts the whining complaints of Montrioli, a figure of immense wealth and power but who speaks only of the toil and tedium it brings him:

> When, ah when,
> The leisure and the liberty I sigh for?
> Not when at home; at home a miscreant-crew,
> That now no longer serve me, mine the service.
> And then that old hereditary bore,
> The steward, his stories longer than his rent-roll,
> Who enters, quill in ear, and, one by one,
> *As though I lived to write and wrote to live*,
> Unrolls his leases for my signature.

Samuel Rogers (1830), 'A Character' from *Italy, A Poem*, ll. 9–17.

The antimetabole of line 16 encapsulates his boredom and ennui as his lack of imagination or empathy traps him into absurd hyperbole. (Note that line 12 includes an implied antimetabole as Montrioli's servants become his master.)

Anastrophe

The jumbling of parts of a sentence or phrase.

Anastrophe is simply a scheme in which the parts of a sentence appear in an unusual order, such as when a noun appears before an adjective ('the branches green and budding', or Christina Rossetti's disturbing phrase, 'Brooding in an anguish dumb', (1896), 'Introspective', l. 11). Or when a predicate comes before a subject: 'Upward I fly;' (Sarah Flower Adams (1841), 'Nearer, My God, To Thee' l. 32).

Anastrophe can sound a little stiff and overwrought, suggesting that a writer is trying too hard to be 'poetic', or even farcical, as when phrases are rearranged to fit rhythm or rhyme. Yet it can serve the poet too, by allowing unusual emphases to occur, or for disturbing acts to be suggested. The lines, 'her hair | In one long yellow string I wound | Three times her little throat around,' from Robert Browning's 'Porphyria's Lover' (1836, ll. 38–40) would have far less impact if anastrophe had not been used to perform this action by making 'little throat' sit suffocated between the rhymes of 'wound' and 'around'. In Pope's use, the anastrophes (italicized) demonstrate the very 'fraughtness' that Pope mocks in writers' lazy rhymes (but he wryly sets up easy rhymes for himself):

While they ring round the same unvaried chimes,
With sure returns of still expected rhymes;
Where'er you find 'the cooling western breeze,'
In the next line, it 'whispers through the trees'
If crystal streams *with pleasing murmurs creep,'*
The reader's threatened (not in vain) with 'sleep';
Then, at the last only *couplet fraught*
With some unmeaning thing they call a thought
A needless Alexandrine ends the song
That, like a wounded snake, drags its slow length along.

Alexander Pope (1709), 'Essay on Criticism', ll. 348–56.

The moment in Milton's *Paradise Lost* when Adam hears of Eve's transgression is littered with anastrophe, overtly demonstrating the awful disruption that it causes. Milton controls the character of the verb before it arrives (astonishment and amazement feeds into the monosyllables 'stood' and 'blank'; the roses are already faded before they are shed) and installs a period of 'slow motion' from 'slack hand' onwards by describing the garland before allowing it to drop in an **alliterative spondee**:

Thus Eve with countenance blithe her story told;
But in her cheek distemper flushing glowed.
On th'other side, Adam, soon as he heard
The fatal trespass done by Eve, amazed,
Astonied stood and blank, while horror chill
Ran through his veins, and all his joints relaxed;
From his slack hand the garland wreathed for Eve
Down dropped, and all the faded roses shed:
Speechless he stood and pale, till thus at length
First to himself he inward silence broke:

John Milton (1667), 'Book IX', *Paradise Lost*, ll. 886–95.

Zeugma

When one word refers in the same way to two or more other words in a phrase.

Zeugma derives from the Greek for 'yoking' and in this scheme two words are yoked together under one other word that may refer to either. The scheme suggests multiple effects without repeating grammatical structures, since one will stand in for many. In this discussion the governing word is **bolded** and those to which it refers are *italicized*.

An example of zeugma is William Cowper's 'In ages past, old Proteus, with his droves | Of sea-calves, **sought** the *mountains* and the *groves*' ((1803), 'Translation on the Ice Islands', ll. 3–4). Here Proteus seeks both the mountains and the groves, but zeugma allows Cowper to avoid repeating 'sought', so the phrase fits neatly within the **heroic couplet**. In Landon's example zeugma allows intensity to build:

> If song be past, and hope undone,
> And *pulse*, and *head*, and *heart*, are **flame**;
> It is thy work, thou faithless one –
> But no I will not name thy name!
>
> Letitia Elizabeth Landon (1824), 'Sappho's Song', ll. 153–5.

Zeugma converges each of the speaker's physical signs (their pulse, head and heart) together by translating them all simultaneously into a fiery **metaphor**. Arguably 'heart' also functions metaphorically here to suggest intense emotion since 'pulse' refers to the organ that pumps the blood and 'heart', following 'head', refers to the combination of mental and physical experience that constitutes love.

Syllepsis

A zeugma in which the governing word applies differently to each of the referent words.

Syllepsis is an especially lively form of zeugma because it subtly shifts how the governing word refers to each of its referents. Whereas in the examples given for zeugma 'sought' and 'flame' meant the same thing to each of the referents, in syllepsis its meaning will be different for each one, usually because it is literal in one case and metaphoric in the other. Alexander Pope is celebrated for his use of syllepsis:

> This day black omens threat the brightest fair,
> That e'er deserved a watchful spirit's care;
> Some dire disaster, or by force of slight,
> But what, or where the Fates have wrapped in night:
> Whether the nymph shall break Diana's law,
> Or some frail china jar receive a flaw,
> Or **stain** her *honour* or her new *brocade*,
> Forget her prayers, or miss a masquerade,
> Or **lose** her *heart*, or *necklace*, at a ball;
>
> Alexander Pope (1714), *The Rape of the Lock*, Canto 2, ll. 101–9.

In both these examples the function of the governing word slips from **metaphor** (your honour is only metaphorically stained; your heart is lost without it leaving your body) to literal truth (brocade – a fabric – can be stained; necklaces are often lost at balls). In each of these instances we see a miniature act of puncture as Pope introduces lofty ideas but then returns them to the every day. So syllepsis schematically performs the whole poem's larger comic purpose of puncturing pomposity and grandiosity. The syllepsis' wry yoking together of the literal with the figurative (or the small with the large) is the scheme par excellence for a poem that delights in how 'mighty contests rise from trivial things' (Canto 1, l. 2).

PART III: PRACTICE

Part III Overview

Close reading

Chapter Outline

As we reach the end of this guide to studying poetry, it is time to think about putting the ideas, vocabularies, terms and traditions considered into practice with some sustained close reading. In this section two examples of close reading essays are given: one of a nineteenth-century, fairly regular poem and one of a late-twentieth-century, less regular, although still tightly constructed, poem. The second one in particular spends a great deal of time with the poem, feeling for its rhythms, sounds, images and ideas. Of course, this length of commentary is pretty uncommon, but the poem can sustain it and, particularly when a poem seems to hold back its meaning, it is fruitful to spend a good deal of concentration trying to 'get to know' a poem, to explore it from the inside, to try to sense what makes it tick.

Following these two example essays, a small group of poems are printed for you to try out your own close reading. At the end some pointers (not answers) are given suggesting forms, images, sounds and traditions that you may have spotted in the poems. The directions you follow in close reading, however, are not fixed: they are up to you. So, how to go about close reading a poem?

Some poems suggest their content fairly obviously — we could say that Wordsworth's 'Old Man Travelling' (1798), for example, is simply about an old man walking along a road. Why stop at that, however? Why would he have caught a poet's eye? This is when it is worth spending a good deal longer with apparently simple poems. When you trace the sound and pace of the poem, pick out the images and figures, follow the poem's path of association, think about its arrangement on the page, notice speech, contrast it with silence and so on, the significance of the scene begins to dawn. You can then move outwards, think about the poem's context and ask yourself, why this arrangement? Why this association? Before long you might feel that the poem intrigues you as you read just as the old man intrigues its narrator. Perhaps the poem is about reading poems?

To reach this kind of textured, multilayered reading – especially if you will be writing about it – you need a copy of the poem that you can annotate, and indeed draw all over. A pencil is vital. Even if you think you know what the poem is about, it's worth starting with basics. How many lines are there? How are they arranged? Is there a rhyme scheme? Are the lines the same length? Does it fit with any forms you know?

Read it aloud. Is it easy to read? What kind of language does it use, in what style? Do you feel comfortable reading it? Or embarrassed? Is it natural? Or is it stagey, self-conscious, 'poetic'? Can you sense a rhythm? Listen for stresses. Mark them. Do these stresses converge into metre? Or is it a free verse poem? Is the sound of the poem attractive? Which sounds dominate? Are there perfect rhymes? Imperfect ones?

Underline similar sounds. Think about why they might be linked in this way. How often does the same sound occur? Don't just list rhymes and sounds, think about them. What impression do they create? Which words rhyme, or receive rhythmic emphasis? How does this affect how you understand them? Do they fit with what the poem is saying?

Now start looking at the words themselves – notice particular groups of association. Are there colours in this poem? Is it light? Or dark? Does that change in different parts of the poem? Do the images come from one particular area of life – the natural world? Industry? Fashion? Science? Are there any words you don't understand? Look them up – a good dictionary is another excellent thing to have on hand.

Start to look in detail at the arrangement on the page – which words are given a prominent position? Follow the grammar of the poem in detail. Follow the exact path of the poem's 'sentences' and phrases – who is doing what to who and when? Here you may find it helpful to draw a map of the poem by its side – how does each of its parts fit together? You may find unusual and exciting arrangements – what you thought had happened has not, when you look carefully. Imagine you are inside the poem – think about where it takes place. Are there any indications of location? What about timescale? Is time mentioned? Look out for words such as 'now', 'then', 'before', 'after'. Be aware of the tense of verbs – past, present, future, continuous? Try to conceive of a timeline for the poem.

Think about making sense of the poem on its own terms – if it suggests one idea in the beginning, how does that impact on what it suggests at the end? If it makes a particular comparison at the start, is that sustained? Or does it change over the course of the poem?

Having examined the poem in this detail you may now feel more comfortable about taking it as a whole. What is its dominant idea? Is it a love poem? Does it tell a story? Express emotions? Is it thoughtful? Or angry? Or comic? What kind of people does it feature? What might you guess about their lives from what is shown here? Does it fit with any of the broad traditions you've come across here, or elsewhere? Does it overlap them?

Particularly if you are developing this reading into a research essay, you should now start moving outwards ... Who wrote the poem? When was it written? What other ideas were prevalent at the time it was written, in terms of content *and* form or tradition? Was this a popular form of poetry? Or an unusual or radical one? How would the poem have seemed to its contemporary readers? What about the history of this poem's reception? Has it always been valued? Or did it fit with some periods' values and not with others? Are you able to find something valuable in a poem that had been dismissed? Or are you finding reasons why a celebrated poem should perhaps be reconsidered?

In the essays that follow the working notes are included – see the annotated copies of the poems – to help demonstrate how a close reading might be undertaken. Don't be put off by the technical vocabulary used here – it is all explained elsewhere in this guide. And try not to be concerned by how poems seem to become complicated by their commentary. All readings of poems begin simply and can be undertaken by anyone who has the time and inclination. You may find, though, that once you start spending time with a poem, it is difficult to leave off and come to an end.

7.1 Sample close reading of Felicia Hemans

'Twas but a dream! I saw the stag leap free   1
    Under the boughs where early birds were singing;
I stood o'ershadowed by the greenwood tree,
    And heard, it seemed, a sudden bugle ringing
Far through a royal forest: then the fawn   5
Shot, like a gleam of light, from grassy lawn
To secret covert; and the smooth turf shook,
And lilies quivered by the glade's lone brook,
And young leaves trembled as, in fleet career,
A princely band with horn and hound and spear,   10
Like a rich masque swept forth. I saw the dance
Of their white plumes that bore a silvery glance
Into the deep wood's heart, and all passed by
Save one – I met the smile of *one* clear eye,
Flashing out joy to mine. Yes, *thou* wert there,   15
Seymour! A soft wind blew the clustering hair
Back from thy gallant brow, as thou didst rein
Thy courser, turning from that gorgeous train,
And fling, methought, thy hunting-spear away

And, lightly graceful in thy green array,   20
Bound to my side; and we, that met and parted,
  Ever in dread of some dark watchful power,
Won back to childhood's trust and, fearless-hearted,
  Blent the glad fullness of our thoughts that hour,
Even like the mingling of sweet streams beneath   25
Dim woven leaves, and midst the floating breath
Of hidden forest flowers.

Felicia Hemans (1828), 'Arabella Stuart: Part I', ll. 1–27.

Working notes

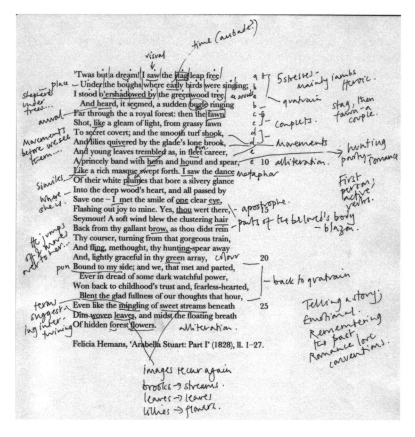

Arabella Stuart captured Felicia Hemans' imagination just as she captured, as this passage remembers, her lover Seymour's 'clear eye' (l. 14). Stuart was imprisoned and divided from Seymour, however, because she married him without the king's permission. Although Stuart had a recorded history of a sort – she was related to James I, who imprisoned her in the Tower of London – Hemans stated that she 'meant [this poem] as some record of her fate, and the imagined fluctuations of her thoughts and feeling' (Preface to the poem). As such this passage relates not merely the fact of her meeting with her lover Seymour – which is retold here as a memory recalled from prison – but also relates, indeed evokes in the reader, the emotional experience of that meeting: it is a history written as lyric. This is achieved through a wonderful display of artistic control and harmonious evocation that deftly weaves sensual immediacy together with imaginative dream vision. Yet Hemans goes further: this is not only a passage of striking eroticism, framed by the shadow of imprisonment and restraint; it also integrates this part-remembered, part-enacted, part-imagined scene in the historical life of Stuart with the tropes and patterns of literary tradition with ingenuity and some daring.

The scene is littered with the conventions of love poetry: the pastoral setting ('Under the boughs' [...] I stood o'ershadowed by the greenwood tree'), the dawn-time opening as in an aubade ('early birds were singing'), the hunting metaphor from romance tales, the blazon that lovingly enumerates the beloved's features. On first reading this intimates a sense of passionate intensity: all the tropes and symbols of previously known and celebrated passions chime together to frame the account of one hidden narrative of desire. The natural setting is then enlivened in rhythm with the sensual awakening that Stuart undergoes in her movement from shadowed observer to desirous participator in love: first the stag leaps, next the fawn shoots, the turf shakes, the lilies quiver, the leaves tremble and finally the hunt appears, converging this natural setting, and its many indicators of forthcoming erotic pairing and sensual embodiment, with the human drama that this version of history seeks to record.

Yet such abundance of conventions indicates the complexity of Stuart's method of remembrance. She is given impressive command of the narrative and the entire passage is dictated purely by her experience of the action: we experience the hunt with her, and as it passes out of her sight so it passes out of our hearing too. However, this immediacy is framed all the while with literary devices that render it unclear how far this is an event remembered and how far it is a desire imagined, a dream spun from literary rather than actual experience. This is emphasized by the uncertainty that appears at either end of the passage's main action, '"Twas but a dream!' (l.1); 'it seemed' (l. 4); 'methought' (l. 19). At these points in the passage the keynote is simile: 'the fawn | Shot, like a gleam of light' (l. 5–6); 'Like a rich masque' (l. 11); 'Even like the mingling of sweet streams' (l. 25). Although Stuart reaches out to suggest a broad, impressive significance for these small actions the tenor does not quite converge with the vehicle. That level of certainty, or achieved stability, is reserved for when Seymour comes into Stuart's view: 'I saw the dance | Of their white plumes' (ll. 11–12). This heralds the moment of meeting, which is infused with intimations of light and clarity – 'I met the smile of *one* clear eye, | Flashing out joy to mine' (ll. 14–15) – that prompt a reverie of visual delight. It is as though Stuart's eye, now awakened to sensual stimulation, eagerly develops this into an aesthetic prowess, creating a coherent picture from a series of parts:

> A soft wind blew the clustering hair
> Back from thy gallant brow, as thou didst rein
> Thy courser, turning from that gorgeous train,
>
> (ll. 16–18)

Yet, at the heart of this transformative process – where what had been anticipated in sound and rhythm is manifested before her – is a moment that jumps back from the immediacy of the scene to resound within the walls of the prison where Stuart is now languishing: 'Yes, *thou* wert there, | Seymour!' As Isobel Armstrong has pointed out (1996, p. 257), this is not the cry she uttered when she met him; it is the cry she utters now, in the real time of the poem rather than that of the action: it is a bid for reassurance that she is not dreaming. Just as the poem seemed to have fallen back to the time it is remembering, we are reminded that this is a double-framed poem, a simultaneous holding together of then and now. Suddenly the passage's narrative line and its attachment to Stuart's experience are not so clear-cut; her experience is both in the past and in the present.

This level of duality is permeated through the passage via its frequent use of homonym puns. 'Fleet' suggests both the speed and the quantity of men; enjambment allows that 'glance' shifts between a noun (a flash of light) and a verb (to look, into the forest); 'Bound' (l. 21) may immediately describe the sprightly movement of the would-be hunter, but it seeps into a metaphor for the strength of feeling that Stuart implies was immanent in this leap: he is now bound to her side. Evidently this is a poem that systematically rejects singularity either at the level of timeframe or in the intricacies of language, predicting the image of interdependency as the passage ends with the two lovers' thoughts 'ming[led]' not only together, but also with their natural setting. This double-framing alerts the reader to the poem's dynamic handling of evocation and performance more generally. Returning to the series of love tropes that the poem used to frame this scene with longstanding traditions of poetry and romance, it is apparent that just as the scene is simultaneously evoked and rewritten through Stuart's remembrance so are these literary traditions evoked and re-characterized in the poem.

It is tempting to read the hunt not only as a hint at the knight's pursuit of a lady in romance tales but also as an intimation of Stuart's larger predicament – the stag has leapt free, but the fawn (like Stuart herself) is hidden in the royal forest at the mercy of hunters (predicting the royal prison where she is now kept). Yet, this is not quite the case. The hunt passes by – just as the hunters' helmets merely glance at the wood, so their hunt only deals Stuart (and the fawn) a glancing blow. Seymour abandons the chase and is drawn into a space that Stuart controls, under the trees, where hers is the active principle – 'I met the smile' (l. 14). Retaining this command, it is Stuart's gaze that conducts the blazon dissection as her eye moves across Seymour's smile, eye, hair and brow before settling on his green garments (hers are not described). In this version of the romance it is the knight who is light, graceful, visually pleasing and attended by a 'gorgeous' train; the woman is the steadfast lover. This steadfastness is not figured as passive submission; rather it is given an almost masculine strength – he is bound to her side, not she to his. By recounting the experience in this way Stuart can set the terms for her present situation as prisoner and yearning lover: she may now, as then, be circumscribed in a space of murky darkness, but that position in fact affords her the power to love and be loved. We see then that Hemans has called on traditional motifs and traditions but also analysed them and reconditioned them for her present purpose. This fits enough with cultural expectation to be recognized, but it carries within it the potential for radical reconsideration of history, politics and gender.

Yet all of this is something of an intellectual, analytic reading of the passage. What keeps us reading, and what appeals to our imaginative and sensual experience as well as Stuart's is Hemans' superlative handling of pace, sound and rhythm. The passage opens with a well-modulated elegiac quatrain, recalling Thomas Gray's 'Elegy written in a Country Churchyard' not only through form, but also in content as Stuart takes her place in the hidden corners of a scene. However, from a quatrain that invested long vowel sounds in 'e' (dream, free, seemed, green, tree) there issues a clamorous long 'u' in 'bugle' and suddenly the restrained spacing of the elegiac quatrain is collapsed into rumbling couplets. The line length suggests these as heroic couplets, and for a time we sense they will conform: lines 7 to 11 appear to be end-stopped, although the repeated appearance of 'And' at front- and mid-line positions delivers such an accumulative drive that their integrity is stretched almost to breaking point. The thundering pace of the iambic rising metre thrills through the lines, galloping in intensity with the huntsmen it hears until its power spills over in to the first spondee ('rich masque', l. 11) and the movement predicted in the fawn's early dash across line endings is reprised with a run of exuberant enjambment as Stuart encounters her lover and the lines' heroic couplets spill over into open ones:

> I saw the dance
> Of their white plumes that bore a silvery glance
> Into the deep wood's heart, and all passed by
> Save one –
>
> (ll. 11–14)

Line 11's spondee is quickly reiterated in 'white plumes' of line 12 (perhaps distantly remembering the bugle of line 4) and the movement between iambs and substituted feet and open and closed couplets serves a scene that excitingly pits restraint and demureness against desire and erotic awakening. Yet the soundplay is not restricted to end-rhymes. Hemans maintains a startlingly consistent game of alliteration and assonance in these lines too: almost every line repeats sounds across its length, encouraging us to modulate our hearing between marked line lengths and endings in the Augustan tradition and a sensual excess that intimates the late-Romanticism of Keats. These tight couplets cannot help but mirror the couple as they are drawn together and, as the tension rises and Seymour casts aside his spear to turn to Stuart, the rhymes escalate into the feminine 'away | array'. Here Stuart's visual awakening is expressed through aural stimulation as our ear listens out for the repeated coming together of closer and closer rhymes. However, propriety steps in just as the lovers meet and suddenly, appropriately with the phrase 'met and parted', the tight couplets step apart as the heroic quatrain is revived: the lovers remember themselves and convert their pulsing togetherness into the shape of a civilized foursquare dance. All the potential for passion is established and remembered, but this is rearranged into a poignant performance of loving ritual, conducted under surveillance rather than enacted in private:

> And, lightly graceful in thy green array,
> Bound to my side; and we, that met and parted,
>   Ever in dread of some dark watchful power,
> Won back to childhood's trust and, fearless-hearted,
>   Blent the glad fullness of our thoughts that hour,
>
> (ll. 20–4)

As the passage draws to a close Hemans demonstrates an impressive consistency of metaphor and figurative line – the young leaves trembling and the lone brook of lines 8–9 recur at the end as the mingling of dim woven leaves and sweet streams of lines 25–6. She has absorbed him into her world. His presence steadies the scene, but it is her landscape that remains.

Reference

Armstrong, I. (1996), 'A Music of Thine Own: Women's Poetry – an Expressive Tradition?', in *Victorian Women Poets: A Critical Reader*, ed. A. Leighton (Oxford: Blackwell), pp. 245–76.

7.2 Sample close reading of Peter McDonald

Now it starts:
the music being played on glasses,
'unearthly', echoing itself, up in the air,
dividing into separate, ringing parts
that make feints and passes
at each other like a courting pair
alone, together alone,
sounding the resonance of one another's hearts.

(But of this world all along:
that these had grown
above themselves, were wrong
and overblown
parts of a voiceless song,
is easily shown.)

Like a tulip-bud
the smallest glass, the highest note,
is lead-painted with the rest in its own shade,
and of all the *virtuosi* in the flood
of players who had by rote
each composition, the last has played
his last, and waits alone
in quiet now, with all the music in his blood.

Peter McDonald (1996), 'The glass harmonica'.

Working notes

Peter McDonald's 'The glass harmonica', an alluring and moving piece of poetry, draws attention to ideas of performance. What is being performed here, however, is difficult to pin down. Its stark opening stress on 'Now' (the heavy downbeat suggesting the first fall of the conductor's baton) leads us to expect the opening bars of a musical composition. This fits with the poems' subject: a glass harmonica is an 'instrument' made up of glasses of various sizes. A player elicits a remarkable harmony from this by running his or her finger around the rims of the glasses, each size producing a different pitch. Yet, in the poem, what follows 'Now starts' is more complex. We have been wrong-footed if we expect things to begin at the beginning. Rather, line 2 demonstrates that the poem opens *in medias res*: music is already 'being played on glasses'. If the music is already in progress, what is it that 'starts' in the first line?

Reminiscent of a child's painting of a butterfly, the poem's two octaves issue from a central, tightly bracketed pivot, creating a shape that is strikingly

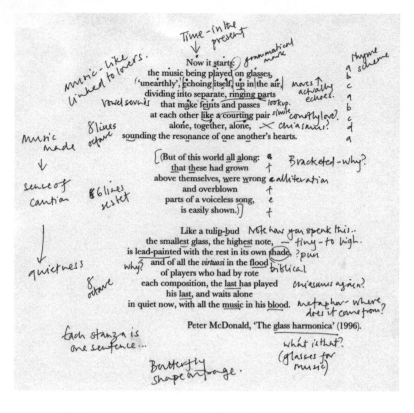

The annotated poem reads:

Now it starts: *[grammatical mark]*
the music being played on glasses,
'unearthly', echoing itself, up in the air,
dividing into separate, ringing parts
that make feints and passes
at each other like a courting pair
alone, together, alone,
sounding the resonance of one another's hearts.

[(But of this world all along:
that these had grown
above themselves, were wrong
and overblown
parts of a voiceless song,
is easily shown.)]

Like a tulip-bud
the smallest glass, the highest note, —
is lead-painted with the rest in its own shade,
and of all the *virtuosi* in the flood
of players who had by rote
each composition, the last has played
his last, and waits alone
in quiet now, with all the music in his blood.

Peter McDonald, 'The glass harmonica' (1996).

Handwritten annotations include: "music-like, linked to lovers.", "Time — in the present", "vowel sounds", "music made", "8 lines octave", "sense of caution", "8 6 lines sestet", "quietness", "octave", "moves actually echoes.", "simile constly love?", "chiasmus?", "Bracketed — why?", "alliteration", "Note how you speak this... tiny — to high.", "?pun", "why?", "biblical", "chiasmus again?", "metaphor — where does it come from?", "rhyme scheme", "a b c a b c d a", "a b c c e f", "Each stanza is one sentence...", "what is that? (glasses for music)", "Butterfly shape on page."

symmetrical (suggesting repetition) and yet dynamic (suggesting change). Moving around the parenthetical fulcrum are two halves of one story of poetry and harmony. Above the central twist is a beautiful poetic invocation of the mesmerizing sound of music drawn magically from the tops of drinking vessels. Below it is a shadowy story of artistic risk and demise.

The bracketing sibilance of 'starts' (l. 1), returning in 'glasses' (l. 2), begins a pattern of repetition and encirclement that predicts the poem's central concern with elicited and controlled sound. After the opening trochee, this settles into an iambic rhythm, reminiscent of simple singing. Yet the third line's 'unearthly', set off from the poem as its sense dictates, disrupts this order: this humpbacked amphibrach breaks through serenity (shatters it even, as glass) in its reach for the otherworldly, almost imperceptible, pitch that vibrates from the glasses' rims. Suspended, alone and unqualified between commas, it casts a charm over the octave as a whole.

Line 3's paced caesurae then begin the work of separation that line 4 describes, producing packets of sound that perform the echoes they evoke. '[E] choing itself' institutes a dactyl-iamb mirroring that recurs in curtailed form in the trochee-iamb of 'up in the air', so creating the diminishing sound of music rising almost out of earshot. Line 4, however, begins to reel such harmony back to earth. The return of 'arts' in the rhyme of 'parts' with 'starts', establishes a larger pattern for these moments of repeated sound: the first three line endings are now recognized as the beginning of a rhyme scheme (*a-b-c a-b-c*) that is played out across lines 4 to 6, with the added anchorage of the alliterative 'parts', 'passes', 'pair'. This repeated patterning illustrates poetically the musical phenomenon of 'ringing parts' (l. 4), alluding to different members of a choral group singing the same phrase in different keys: the pattern 'starts', 'glasses', 'air' is taken up and intensified into 'parts', 'passes', 'pair'. Within the lines, vowel sounds resonate in shimmering pairs (the assonance of 'm*a*ke' and 'f*ei*nts'; 'parts' distantly remembering 'separate'), playing out in miniature the octave's fascination with harmony and echo. These various suggestions of intimacy, as rhymes and rhythms cleave together, are then made real by being likened to a 'courting pair' (l. 6), where courting puns on the humble notion of 'stepping out' and the more elevated tradition of courtly ritual. Suddenly the brittle, ethereal quality of the music is given a human heart, heard beating falteringly in the iamb-amphibrach-iamb of line 7's chiastic 'alone, together, alone'. Having been enchanted and delighted by the light touch of carefully orchestrated 'a'-, 'e'-, and 'i'-sounds, the deeper intoning of line 7's 'alone', which then reverberates in the lengthy assonance of line 8, ('resonance' produces 'of one another's'), sounds the first hint of a warning. Every moment of joining that occurs within this couple's flirtatious aural dance occurs against a backdrop of isolation, the stillness of which makes more moving and effective these intermittent intrusions of sound.

That warning may have been heard earlier: the octave's only spondee (the lines in general trip lightly between stressed and unstressed syllables) falls in line 5: 'make feints'. A feint is a term used in boxing or fencing for a pretend (feigned) attack on your opponent. The line's unexpected rhythm jolts the poem out of a naturalized iambic pace to draw attention to the art of deception: what appears natural, right or even real is manufactured. This is discomforting when delivered at the end of a *virtuoso* act of poetic evocation (the second octave's *virtuosi* reflected in the first's performance). The reader was lulled into hearing the sounds of the harmonica in the poet's words; now this spondee hints at what the bracketed phrase reveals: this is a feint itself, a teasing jab at the reader's senses, designed to confuse seeing for hearing.

Pausing for a moment we find that a clue to the poem's knowing shifts between sight and hearing appeared in the colon of line 1. This typographical point of control draws attention to the material presence of the poem as a series of marks on the page. Unlike the music, which is 'up in the air' (l. 3), the poem exists in black and white before the reader and abides by grammatical rules (the octave is one sentence sustained by careful punctuation). Following the colon, as grammar dictates, comes amplification as the main clause's present tense, 'starts', modifies into the present continuous of 'being', 'echoing', 'dividing', 'ringing', 'courting' and 'sounding'. While referencing the delicate sound of the glass harmonica, this echoing and dividing gesture (the colon has a semantic and a rhythmic purpose) draws attention to the symbiosis between the poet's method of controlling the placement and spacing of words and that of the musician who uses the separate tones elicited from different glasses to create an ethereal sound-scape. This is not so much poetry as overflowing feeling as poetry as the ordering of experience. Which is not to suggest that poetry is characterized as cold and logical – far from it. As well as being warm and sensual, the poem replaces the sequential progress of logic with the more sprawling shapes of association, echo and allusion. Rather, 'ordering' here is shaping and realizing: a method that both preserves an experience and elicits one again from its reader. What 'starts' in line 1 then is the poetic experience of the musical composition; vitally, part of that experience is a painful knowledge of its end, and, as the second octave shows, the poem holds together the immediacy of hearing music with the backward glance of sorrow. What unnerves us, after all, is that what begins with almost imperious noise ('Now it starts') will end 'in quiet now' (l. 22).

Directing this shift is the central bracketed phrase. As prose this reads, 'But of this world all along: that these had grown above themselves, were wrong and overblown parts of a voiceless song, is easily shown.' If 'these' is understood to refer either to the glasses themselves, or to those who hear them, this is a puncturing phrase that sharply points out that to hear glass music as 'unearthly', ethereal and somehow mystical is to mistake the source of this music and to become carried away, 'overblown', above oneself. The phrase voices the poem's anticipation of its own critical reading in this respect, implicitly lampooning the absurd over-reader while also getting in first with a strike against itself, pre-empting the sceptical reader's imperviousness to its aural and visual design. Its parentheses act here as a drawing in, this under-breath functioning as shield. Yet, the arrangement of the phrase as poetry complicates this reverse movement: in execution the phrase escalates its harmoniousness. Working against the drive to enjambment, with its push for the prosaic, rhyme comes to the fore: triplets and assonance become couplets of perfect rhyme (*e-f e-f e-f*); 'o'-sounds ring off each other, denying the voicelessness they claim, and echoing alliteration causes the phrase to rise off the page into a breathless incantation: '*all al*ong' '*th*at *these*', '*w*ere *w*rong'. Furthermore, the poem cannot extract itself from the figurative effects of language. The glib 'is easily shown' (l. 14) belies the sentence's particular investment in paronomasia, as 'overblown' puns on the production of glass itself and 'grown above themselves' is a metaphor that recalls the music spun up and off the rims of glasses evoked in the first octave. As such, the dance of 'feints and passes' (l. 5) is recast as a game the poem plays with itself: rigorously adhering to its own pattern of sound while all the while threatening to dismantle the ideology that such patterning seeks to promote (that poetry is akin to music, that poems render an experience 'more real' through their linguistic method).

Yet what especially jars this poem's investment in sound is the notion of a 'voiceless song' (which could describe the poem itself) and the visual demonstration in 'easily shown', indicating most overtly that we are to see rather than hear this poem. Seeing it, we then are inclined to analyse it. Just as the final octave uses the filtering device of the glass harmonica to examine unflinchingly the compromises behind that instrument, the poem's wry self-naming draws attention to the work behind its own structure.

Opening with a simile that plays off the diminutive (the plosives of 'tulip-bud' (l. 15) demanding a delicate differentiation in the mouth) against the superlative ('smallest' versus 'highest', l. 16), the second octave addresses the notion of small beginnings unravelling into catastrophic ends. Reprising the mirroring effect seen in line 3, line 17 begins and ends with spondees, empha-sized by the assonance of 'painted' with 'shade', that beat out an ominous prediction. '[L]ead-painted' refers to the practice of painting glasses with different colours according to the pitch they produce, aiding the player. This act of pragmatism, however, handed out death sentences to those who used them. In order to produce a clearer sound, players would lick the tip of their finger before running it around the glasses' rims; in doing so, over time, it's thought they ingested dangerous quantities of lead from the paint, causing eventual madness and death. The instrument that promised such ingenious harmony thus gradually fell silent as practitioners became terrified of the consequences of producing 'unearthly' music. The assonance in 'paint' and 'shade' therefore prompts the dark punning that makes the colourful shade of the glasses produce the blackened tones of the ghostly shade. The rest of the octave unravels the consequences of this turn, as the sprightly '*virtuosi*' (l. 18) unleashes a flood of musicians (alluding to the biblical flood that wiped out a whole civilization) who had, in learning compositions by rote, in fact only programmed their own demise.

In acknowledgement of its own status as container of sound, like the harmonica, however, the poem allows its patterns to continue replicating. The faltering quality noted in line 7's chiastic 'alone, together, alone' is almost broken by the enjambment of line 20 to 21, but still it retains the repetition, echo and reprise that structure the poem as a whole. In fact 'the last has played | his last' uses the pause of the line break to pre-empt the agonizing waiting intimated by the delivery of the final 'last' in its answering chiasmus. That this schematically recalls the earlier 'alone, together, alone' installs a moment of moving nostalgia in our experience of the poem, intimating in this echo the larger perspective of backward-looking regret that characterizes the desire to draw attention to the fate of these lost players. At this final moment the player has not only ingested the fatal substance but, being the last in a line, is assumed to know his own fate. The final line's 'with all the music in his blood' thus shimmers between the metaphorical (lionizing the player as one with a specialized gift for music) and metonymy (music is associated with, and so stands in for, lead poisoning) coursing a dangerous potential through his veins. The poem's larger investment in figures of potential (the courtship that becomes love, the bud that becomes a flower, the glass that holds 'unearthly' music, the player that can conjure such music into being) is returned in this serene and hushed finish (the final line relinquishes soundplay) with a sobering revelation of inherent danger that the player, vessel-like, now harbours within himself. Looking back across the poem, it is apparent that it is the players themselves who were 'of this world all along', and this poem is their elegy as they leave it.

7.3 Exercises

Exercise A

Alas how barbarous are we,
Thus to reward the courteous Tree,
Who its broad shade affording us,
Deserves not to be wounded thus;
See how the Yielding Bark complies
With our ungrateful injuries.
And seeing this, say how much then
Trees are more generous than Men,
Who by a Nobleness so pure
Can first oblige and then endure.

Katherine Philips (1667), 'Upon the Graving of her Name upon a Tree in *Barnelmes* Walks.'

Exercise B

I

That is no country for old men. The young
In one another's arms, birds in the trees,
– Those dying generations – at their song,
The salmon-falls, the mackerel-crowded seas,
Fish, flesh, or fowl, commend all summer long
Whatever is begotten, born, and dies.
Caught in that sensual music all neglect
Monuments of unageing intellect.

II

A aged man is but a paltry thing,
A tattered coat upon a stick, unless
Soul clap its hands and sing, and louder sing
For every tatter in its mortal dress,
Nor is there singing school but studying
Monuments of its own magnificence;
And therefore I have sailed the seas and come
To the holy city of Byzantium.

III

O sages standing in God's holy fire
As in the gold mosaic of a wall,
Come from the holy fire, perne in a gyre,
And be the singing-masters of my soul.
Consume my heart away; sick with desire
And fastened to a dying animal
It knows not what it is; and gather me
Into the artifice of eternity.

IV

Once out of nature I shall never take
My bodily form from any natural thing,
But such a form as Grecian goldsmiths make
Of hammered gold and gold enamelling
To keep a drowsy Emperor awake;
Or set upon a golden bough to sing
To lords and ladies of Byzantium
Of what is past, or passing, or to come.

William Butler Yeats (1927), 'Sailing to Byzantium'.

Exercise C

Bless'd as the Immortal Gods is he,
The Youth who fondly sits by thee,
And hears and sees thee all the while
Softly speak and sweetly smile.

Twas this depriv'd my Soul of Rest,
And rais'd such Tumults in my Breast;
For while I gaz'd, in Transport toss'd,
My Breath was gone, my Voice was lost:

My Bosom glow'd; the subtle Flame
Ran quick through all my vital Frame;
O'er my dim Eyes a Darkness hung;
My Ears with hollow Murmurs rung:

In dewy Damps my Limbs were chill'd;
My Blood with gentle Horrours thrill'd;
My feeble Pulse forgot to play;
I fainted, sunk, and dy'd away.

Ambrose Philips (1732), 'A Fragment of Sappho'.

Exercise D

> If there were any power in human love,
> > Or in th'intensest longing of the heart,
> > Then should the oceans and the lands that part
> Ye from my sight all unprevailing prove,
> Then should the yearning of my bosom bring
> > Ye here, through space and distance infinite;
> And life 'gainst love should be a baffled thing,
> > And circumstance 'gainst will lose all its might.
> Shall not a childless mother's misery
> > Conjure the earth with such a potent spell –
> > A charm so desperate – as to compel
> Nature to yield to her great agony?
> > Can I not think of ye till ye arise,
> > Alive, alive, before my very eyes?

> Frances Anne Kemble (1847), 'If there were any power in human love'.

Suggestions for Exercise A

- Form: epigram, but perhaps also epigraph (it is carved onto a tree); maybe even epitaph (it will remain after the poet's death)
- Metre: iambic tetrameter ([Thus **to**] [re**ward**] [the **court**-] [eous **Tree**,])
- Rhyme: rhyming couplets, using masculine rhymes
- Trope: personification (of the tree)
- Other: images of yielding, and generous accommodation are linked to endurance and steadiness; the tree appears to hold a lesson for man; writing is associated with violence; meditation on poetry, lastingness, imposition and accommodation. Is the tree in opposition to or in coalition with human endeavour?

Suggestions for Exercise B

- Form: ottava rima
- Metre: generally iambic pentameter ([The **sal**-] [mon-**falls**,] [the **macke**-] [rel-**crow**-] [ded **seas**,]); where does this vary? End-stopped lines and enjambment
- Rhyme: many perfect rhymes, but where are there less perfect ones? Alliteration; pararhyme; assonance
- Tradition: what kind of wanderer is evoked here? A balladeer? An epic traveller?
- Words to clarify: Byzantium; gyre; perne
- Other: evocations of music; images of artistry (mosaics, hammered gold, enamelling); 'artifice of eternity' – contradictory or complimentary?; movements between tattered clothes and golden splendour; monuments; fire – divine or artistic?

- What does Byzantium represent in the logic of the poem? Distinction? Or oblivion?

Suggestions for Exercise C

- Tradition: lyric (Classical reference); love poetry
- Metre: iambic tetrameter ([The **Youth**] [who **fond**-] [ly **sits**] [by **thee**,]); are there any foot substitutions?
- Stanza: quatrains made up of rhyming couplets
- Rhyme: perfect, masculine rhymes. Assonance
- Tropes: metaphors of fire, light, bodies, storms (glowing bosom, a body in flame, tumults in the breast, 'horrified' blood)
- Other: trace the sense and arrangement of this poem carefully – who is looking at whom? Where are each of the figures placed? What ignites the speaker's passion?
- Passion and emotion felt in the body – trace how the body is evoked in different parts; the premise (that this is a poem so it implies a speaker, or at least expression) is contradicted by the content (repeated suggestions that the speaker has lost their voice, become silent, even died at the end). How are the reader's senses stimulated along with the speaker's?

Suggestions for Exercise D

- Form: sonnet, unusually arranged into a hybrid between Petrarchan and Shakespearean – three quatrains and a couplet. Quatrains 1 and 3 show the Petrarchan rhyme scheme, quatrain 2 the Shakespearean. Where is the volta?
- Tradition: love poetry, evoking distance between lovers and 'agony' of the lover, as in courtly love; Petrarchan conceit in distance over the ocean
- Metre: iambic pentameter, as in sonnet form ([Then **should**] [the **oce**-] [ans **and**] [the **lands**] [that **part**]). Are there any substituted feet? End-stopped lines and enjambment
- Trope: metaphors associated with magic (conjuring, charms, spells). 'Childless mother': a contradiction?
- Other: strangeness of using the courtly love tradition to characterize the yearning for a child rather than a lover; conjuring a child's presence through poetry; contradictions, paradoxes and contrasts (life against love; circumstance against will; space and distance); the notion of a 'childless mother'.

Sources and suggestions for further reading

Here is a list of sources for the poetry mentioned or discussed in this guide. Where possible an easily accessible print edition of a writer's work is given (older publications may need to be found in a good library). However, more obscure examples need to be tracked down in anthologies or online. Particularly useful anthologies are listed here. Unfortunately some of these have gone out of print or have been replaced with new editions; do try to track those given down in libraries or in second-hand bookshops though, as they include impressive collections of materials. The internet is an increasingly useful resource for poetry readers, but do be careful: many websites publish poems from unacknowledged sources, often in very unreliable editions. Websites are recommended here for their ease of use, the organization of materials, searchability and authority. Some of them require subscription: ask your library if they can help you access these materials.

Anthologies and online sources

Cunningham, V. (ed.) (2000), *The Victorians: An Anthology of Poetry and Poetics* (Oxford: Blackwell Anthologies).

Greenblatt, S. (2006), *The Norton Anthology of English Literature*, two volumes, 8th edn (New York: W. W. Norton & Co.).

Greer, G., S. Hastings, J. Medoff and M. Sansone (eds) (1988), *Kissing the Rod: An Anthology of Seventeenth-Century Women's Verse* (London: Virago Press).

Grigson, G. (ed.) (1973), *The Faber Book of Love Poems* (London: Faber and Faber).

Jay, P. and C. Lewis (eds) (1996), *Sappho through English Poetry* (London: Anvil Press).

Leighton, A. and M. Reynolds (1995), *Victorian Women Poets: An Anthology* (Oxford: Blackwell Publishing).

Norbrook, D. (ed.) (1993), *The Penguin Book of Renaissance Verse: 1509–1659* (London: Penguin Classics).

Percy, T. (ed.) (1996), *Reliques of Ancient English Poetry*, three volumes, with an introduction by N. Groom (London: Routledge/Thoemmes Press).

Spengemann, W. C. and J. F. Roberts (eds) (1997), *Nineteenth-Century American Poetry* (London: Penguin Classics).

Literature Online: http://lion.chadwyck.co.uk/marketing/index.jsp

The Poetry Foundation: www.poetryfoundation.org

Project Gutenberg: www.gutenberg.org

Representative Poetry Online: http://rpo.library.utoronto.ca

The Brown University Women Writers Project: www.wwp.brown.edu (texts from between 1400 and 1850)

The Victorian Women Writers Project: www.indiana.edu/~letrs/vwwp/

Sources for all authors

Abse, D. (2002), *New and Collected Poems* (London: Hutchinson).

Apollinaire, G. (2007), *Selected Writings of Guillaume Apollinaire*, trans. R. Shattuck (Whitefish, MT: Kessinger Publishing).

Ayres, P. (2008), *With These Hands: A Collection of Work* (London: Weidenfeld and Nicholson).

Armitage, S. (2006), *Sir Gawain and the Green Knight* (London: Faber and Faber; New York: W. W. Norton & Co.).

Arnold, M. (1979), *The Poems of Matthew Arnold*, ed. K. Allot, 2nd edn, ed. M. Allott (London: Longman).

Auden, W. H. (2002/2007) *Collected Poems*, ed. E. Mendelson (London: Faber and Faber; London: Modern Library).

Bailey, P. J. (1860), *Festus: a poem* (Michigan: Scholarly Publishing Office, University of Michigan Library).

Baillie, J. (2000), *De Montfort*, in *Five Romantic Plays, 1768–1821*, ed. P. Baines (Oxford: Oxford World Classics).

Barbauld, A. L. (2002), *Selected Poetry and Prose*, ed. W. McCarthy and E. Kraft (Peterborough, ON: Broadview Press).

Barrett Browning, E. (1995), *Aurora Leigh and Other Poems*, J. R. G. Bolton and J. Bolton Holloway (eds) (London: Penguin Classics).

Basho, M. (1990), *Basho's Haiku: Literal Translations*, trans. T. Oseko (Tokyo: Maruzen Co. Ltd).

Bayles, J. C., see Project Gutenberg.

Betjeman, J. (2006), *Collected Poems* (London: John Murray; New York: Farrar, Straus, and Giroux).

Blake, W. (1977), *The Complete Poems*, ed. A. Ostriker (London: Penguin).

Borek, B. (2007), *Donjong Heights* (Norwich: Egg Box Publishing).

Bottomley, G. (1922), *Gruach and Britain's Daughter: Two Plays* (London: Constable & Co.).

Bradstreet, A. (2007), *The Works of Anne Bradstreet*, ed. J. Hensley (Cambridge, MA: Harvard/Belknapp Press).

Browne, W., see Literature Online.

Browning, R. (2005), *The Major Works*, ed. A. Roberts (Oxford: Oxford World's Classics).

Burns, R. (1993), *Selected Poems*, ed. C. McGuirk (London: Penguin Classics).

Burnside, J. (2005), *The Good Neighbour* (London: Jonathan Cape).

Byron, Lord (George Gordon) (2000), *The Major Works*, ed. J. J. McGann (Oxford: Oxford World's Classics).

Carew, T., see Literature Online

Carroll, L. (2002), *The Nonsense Verse*, illus. L. Hussey (London: Bloomsbury Children's Classics).

— (2003) *Alice's Adventures in Wonderland; and Through the Looking Glass*, ed. H. Haughton (London: Penguin Classics).

Carson, A. (2001), *The Beauty of the Husband* (London: Jonathan Cape).

Chaucer, G., quotations taken from *The Riverside Chaucer*, L. D. Benson and F. N. Robinson (eds) (1987) (Oxford: Oxford University Press).

Clare, J. (2004), *Major Works*, E. Robinson and D. Powell (eds) (Oxford: Oxford World's Classics).

Clough, A. H. (2003), *Selected Poems* ed. S. Crew (Manchester: Fyfield Books).

Coleridge, S. T. (1997), *The Complete Poems*, ed. W. Keach (London: Penguin Classics).

Collins, W. (2006), *The Complete Poetical Works of William Collins, Thomas Gray, and Oliver Goldsmith*, with notes by E. Sargent (Michigan: Scholarly Publishing Office, University of Michigan Library).

Cook, E. (2006), *The Poetical Works of Mary Howitt, Eliza Cook and L.E.L.* (Michigan: Scholarly Publishing Office, University of Michigan Library).

Cope, W. (2001), *Making Cocoa for Kingsley Amis* (London: Faber and Faber).

— 'Lissadell', see The Poetry Foundation.

Cowley, A. (2004), *The Poems of Abraham Cowley*, ed. A. R. Waller (Whitefish, MT: Kessinger Publishing).

Cowper, W. (1994), *The Task, and Selected Other Poems*, ed. J. Sambrook (London: Longman).

Cummings, E. E. (1994), *Complete Poems 1904–1962*, ed. George J. Firmage (New York: Liveright; New York: W. W. Norton & Co.).

Dante (1999), *La Vita Nuova*, trans. M. Musa (Oxford: Oxford World's Classics).

— (1998), *The Divine Comedy*, trans. C. H. Sisson (Oxford: Oxford World's Classics).

Davies, J., see Literature Online.

Davidson, L. A. (1982/1991 and 1996), *The Shape of the Tree: New York New York* (Wind Chimes; rpt. Miami, DLT Association Inc.).

— (2003 and 2007), *bird song more and more* (Northfield, Mass.: Swamp Press).

de la Mare, W. (2006), *Selected Poems*, ed. M. Sweeney (London: Faber and Faber).

Deloney, T., see Literature Online.

Dickinson, E. (1988), *The Complete Poems*, ed. T. H. Johnson (London: Little, Brown & Co.).

Dobell, S., see Literature Online.

Donne, J. (2000), *The Major Works*, ed. J. Carey (Oxford: Oxford World's Classics).

Dryden, J. (2003), *The Major Works*, ed. K. Walker (Oxford: Oxford World's Classics).

Dunn, D. (1985), *Elegies* (London: Faber and Faber).

Eliot, G. (1991), *Selected Essays, Poems, and other writings*, A. S. Byatt and N. Warren (eds) (London: Penguin Classics).

Eliot, T. S. (1969), *The Complete Poems and Plays* (London: Faber and Faber).

Fenton, J. (2006), *Selected Poems* (London: Penguin).

Field, M. (2008), *Michael Field, The Poet: Published and Manuscript Materials*, M. Thain and A. Parejo Vadillo (eds) (Peterborough, ON: Broadview Press); see also Literature Online.

FitzGerald, E. (1997), *Rubáiyát of Omar Khayyám: A Critical Edition*, ed. C. Decker (Charlottesville, VA: University of Virginia Press).

Ford, J. (1999), *'Tis Pity She's a Whore and other plays*, ed. M. Lomax (Oxford: Oxford World's Classics).

Frost, R. (2001), *The Poetry of Robert Frost*, ed. F. Connery Lathem (London: Vintage Books).

Gay, J., see Representative Poetry Online.

Ginsberg, A. (2007), *Collected Poems: 1947–1997* (New York: Harper Perennial Modern Classics).

Gray, T. (2006), *The Complete Poetical Works of William Collins, Thomas Gray, and Oliver Goldsmith*, with notes by E. Sargent (Michigan: Scholarly Publishing Office, University of Michigan Library).

Graham, W. S. (2004), *New Collected Poems* (London: Faber and Faber).

Graves, R. (2003), *The Complete Poems*, B. Graves and D. Ward (eds) (London: Penguin Modern Classics).

Gunn, T. (1994), *Collected Poems* (London: Faber and Faber).

Hacker, M. (1995), *Love, Death, and the Changing of the Seasons* (New York: W. W. Norton & Co.).

Hall, L., see Project Gutenberg.

Hardy, T. (2001), *The Complete Poems*, ed. J. Gibson (Basingstoke: Palgrave Macmillan).

Harington, J., see Literature Online.

Hart Crane, H., see The Poetry Foundation.

Hartill, G. (2004), in *The Hare That Hides Within: Poems about St Melangell*, A. Cluysenaar and N. Schwenk (eds) (Ceredigion/Carmarthen: Parthian Books).

Heaney, S. (1999), *Beowulf* (London: Faber and Faber).

Hemans, F. (2002), *Selected Poems, Prose and Letters*, ed. G. Kelly (Peterborough, ON: Broadview Press).

Herbert, G. (2004), *The Complete English Poems*, ed. J. Tobin (London: Penguin Classics).

Herbert, M. (Countess of Pembroke), see Literature Online.

Herrick, R. (2003), *Selected Poems*, ed. D. Jesson-Dibley (Manchester: Fyfield Books).

Hill, G. (1985), *Collected Poems* (London: Penguin).

Hogg, J. (2007), *A Queer Book: The Collected Works of James Hogg*, ed. P. Garside (Edinburgh: Edinburgh University Press).

Hollander, J. (1991), *Types of Shape*, 2nd edn (New Haven, CT: Yale University Press).

Homer (2003a), *The Iliad*, trans. E. V. Rieu, P. Jones and D. C. H. Rieu (eds) (London: Penguin Classics).

— (2003b), *The Odyssey*, trans. E. V. Rieu, P. Jones and D. C. H. Rieu (eds) (London: Penguin Classics).

Hopkins, G. M. (2002), *The Major Works*, ed. C. Phillips (Oxford: Oxford World Classics).

Housman, A. E. (1995), *Collected Poems*, ed. J. Sparrow (London: Penguin Poetry Library).

Howard, H. (Earl of Surrey) (2006), *Selected Poems*, ed. D. Keene (Manchester: Fyfield Books).

Howard, R. (1984), *Untitled Subjects: Poems* (New York: Atheneum).

Hutchinson, L., see Literature Online.

Jennings, E. (2002), *New Collected Poems*, ed. M. Schmidt (Manchester: Carcanet Press).

Johnson, S. (2000), *The Major Works*, ed. D. Greene (Oxford: Oxford World's Classics).

Jones, D. (2002), *Wedding Poems* (London: Enitharmon Press).

— (2003), *In Parenthesis* (New York: The New York Review of Books).

Jonson, B. (1981), *The Complete Poems*, ed. G. Parfitt (London: Penguin Classics).

Keats, J. (1988), *The Complete Poems*, ed. J. Barnard, 3rd edn (London: Penguin Classics).

Kerouac, J. (2008), *Blues and Haikus* [CD] (Zonophone).

King, H., see Literature Online.

Kyd, T. (2003), *The Spanish Tragedy*, ed. J. Mulryne (New Mermaids edn, London: Methuen).

Landon, L. E. (1997), *Selected Writings*, J. McGann and D. Reiss (eds) (Peterborough, ON: Broadview Press).

Lanyer, A. (1993), *The Poems of Aemilia Lanyer: Salve Deus Rex Judaeorum*, ed. S. Woods (Oxford: Oxford University Press).

Larkin, P. (2004), *Collected Poems*, ed. A. Thwaite (New York: Farrar, Straus, and Giroux).

Lear, E. (2006), *The Complete Nonsense and Other Verse*, ed. V. Noakes (London: Penguin Classics).

Lennon, J. (1965), *A Spaniard in the Works* (London: Simon and Schuster).

Levy, A. (2004), *A London Plane Tree and other verse* (Whitefish, MT: Kessinger Publishing).

Logue, C. (1981–), *War Music*, five volumes (London: Faber and Faber).

Longfellow, H. W. (2000), *Poems and Other Writings* (New York: Library of America).

Lowell, A. (2002), *Selected Poems* (Piscataway, NJ: Rutgers University Press).

Lowell, J. R., see Spengemann and Roberts (eds).

MacDiarmid, H. (2000), *Complete Poems*, M. Grieve and W. R. Aitken (eds), two volumes (Manchester: Carcanet Press).

MacDonald, P. (1996), *Adam's Dream* (Tarset: Bloodaxe Books).

MacNeice, L. (2007), *Collected Poems*, ed. P. MacDonald (London: Faber and Faber).

Mallarmé, S. (2006), *Collected Poems and other verse*, trans. E. H. Blackmore and A. M. Blackmore (Oxford: Oxford World's Classics).

Mallet, D., see Percy's *Reliques*.

Malory, T. (1998), *Le Morte D'Arthur*, ed. H. Cooper (Oxford: Oxford University Press).

Marlowe, C. (2003), *The Complete Plays*, F. Romany and R. Lindsey (eds) (London: Penguin Classics).

— (2007), *Complete Poems and Translations*, ed. S. Orgel (London: Penguin Classics).

Marvell, A. (2005), *The Complete Poems*, ed. E. Story Donno (London: Penguin Classics).

Master, E. L. (2007), *Spoon River Anthology*, ed. R. Primeau (New York: Signet Classics).

McCrae, J. (2005), *In Flanders Fields and Other Poems* (Dodo Press).

Meredith, G. (2005), *Modern Love* (Whitefish, MT: Kessinger Publishing).

Middleton, T. (1988), *Five Plays*, B. Loughrey and N. Taylor (eds) (London: Penguin Classics).

Milton, J. (2003), *The Major Works*, S. Orgel and J. Goldberg (eds) (Oxford: Oxford World's Classics).

Miller, E. (2004), *The Go-Go Boy Sonnets* (Portland, OR: Inkwater Press).

Morgan, E. (1996), *Collected Poems* (Manchester: Carcanet Press).

Moore, T. (2007), *Poems* (Whitefish, MT: Kessinger Publishing).

Moore, M. (2005), *The Poems of Marianne Moore*, ed. G. Schulman (London: Penguin Classics).

Morris, W., see Literature Online.

Motion, A. (2003), *Public Property* (London: Faber and Faber).

Sources and suggestions for further reading

Muldoon, P. (1994), *Annals of Chile* (London: Faber and Faber).

— (2002), *Moy, Sand, Gravel* (London: Faber and Faber).

Murray, L. (2000), *Fredy Neptune: A Novel in Verse* (New York: Farrar, Straus, and Giroux).

Nash, O. (1994), *Candy is Dandy: The Best of Ogden Nash*, L. Smith and I. Eberstadt (eds) (London: Carlton Books Ltd).

O'Hara, F. (2000), *Meditations in an Emergency*, 2nd edn (Avalon Travel Publishing).

Owen, W. (1983), *The Complete Poems and Fragments*, ed. J. Stallworthy, two volumes (London: Chatto and Windus).

Oxlie, M., see Greer, G. et al. (eds).

Paterson, D. (2004), *Landing Light* (London: Faber and Faber).

Pater, W. (1998), *The Renaissance: Studies in Art and Poetry*, ed. A. Phillips (Oxford: Oxford World's Classics).

Patchen, K. (1968), *The Collected Poems* (New York: W. W. Norton & Co.).

Philips, A. see Jay and Lewis (eds).

Philips, K. (1993), *The Collected Works of Katherine Philips: The Matchless Orinda*, G. Greer and R. Little (eds), three volumes (Stump Cross: Stump Cross Books).

Plath, S. (2002), *Collected Poems* (London: Faber and Faber).

Poe, E. A. (1984), *Complete Stories and Poems of Edgar Allan Poe* (London: Doubleday).

Pope, A. (2006), *The Major Works*, ed. P. Rogers (Oxford: Oxford World's Classics).

Pound, E. (2003), *Poems and Translations* (New York: Library of America).

Prior, M., see Literature Online.

Pushkin, A. (2003), *Eugene Onegin*, trans. C. Johnston, ed. M. Basker (London: Penguin Classics).

Rabinowitz, A. (2001), *Darkling: a poem* (Dorset, VT: Tupelo Press).

Raine, C. (1994), *History: the Home Movie* (London: Penguin Books).

— (2000), *Collected Poems, 1978–1998* (London: Picador).

Raleigh, W. (1972), *A Choice of Sir Walter Raleigh's Verse*, ed. R. Nye (London: Faber and Faber).

Rees-Jones, D. (2004), *Quiver* (Bridgend: Seren).

Rimbaud, A. (2005), *Complete Works, Selected Letters, a Bilingual Edition*, trans. W. Fowlie, ed. S. Whidden (Chicago, IL: University of Chicago Press).

Rochester, Earl of (J. Wilmot) (2002), *The Complete Poems*, ed. D. M. Vieth (New Haven and London: Yale University Press).

Rogers, S., see Literature Online.

Rosenberg, I. (1984), *The Collected Works of Isaac Rosenberg* (London: Chatto and Windus).

Rossetti, C. (2001), *The Complete Poems*, ed. R. W. Crump (London: Penguin Classics).

Rossetti, D. G. (2005), *Collected Writings*, ed. J. Marsh (Chicago, IL: New Amsterdam Books).

Sampson, F. (2007), *Common Prayer* (Manchester: Carcanet Press).

Sappho, various translations are in print: see, for example, (2003), *If Not, Winter: Fragments of Sappho*, trans. A. Carson (London: Virago Press Ltd).

Seth, V. (1987), *The Golden Gate* (London: Faber and Faber).

Shakespeare, W., all quotations are taken from (1988) *The Complete Works*, S. Wells and G. Taylor (eds) (Oxford: Clarendon Press).

Shelley, P. B., *The Major Works*, Z. Leader and M. O'Neill (eds) (Oxford: Oxford World's Classics).

Sidney, P. (2002), *The Major Works*, ed. K. Duncan-Jones (Oxford: Oxford World's Classics).

Smart, E. (1992), *By Grand Central Station I Sat Down and Wept* (London: Flamingo).

Smith, C. (1995), *The Poems of Charlotte Smith*, ed. S. Curran (Oxford University Press).

Southey, R., see Literature Online.

Spenser, E., (1978), *The Faerie Queene*, ed. T. P. Roche (Penguin Classics)

— (1999), *The shorter Poems*, ed. R. A. McCabe (Penguin Classics)

Steele, T., see The Poetry Foundation.

Stevens, W., (2006) *Collected Poems* (Faber and Faber).

Stewart, S., (1981) *Yellow Stars and Ice* (Princeton University Press).

Swift, J., see Representative Poetry Online.

Swinburne, A. C., (2002) *Selected Poems*, ed. L. M. Findlay (Manchester: Fyfield Books).

Symonds, J. A., see Literature Online.

Taylor, H. (1834), *Philip van Artevelde: A Dramatic Romance in Two Parts* (London: Edward Moxon).

Taylor, J., see Representative Poetry Online.

Tennyson, A. (1987), *The Poems of Tennyson*, ed. C. Ricks, 2nd edn, three volumes (London: Longman).

Thomas, D. (1995), *The Dylan Thomas Omnibus: Under Milk Wood, Poems, Stories, and Broadcasts* (London: Phoenix).

Thomas, E. (2004), *Collected Poems* (London: Faber and Faber).

Thomas, R. S. (2004), *Selected Poems* (London: Penguin Modern Classics).

Thompson, F. (1963), *Hound of Heaven and Other Poems* (Boston, Mass.: Branden Publishing Co.).

Vaughan, H., see Representative Poetry Online.

Virgil (2003), *The Aeneid*, ed. D. West (London: Penguin Classics).

Walcott, D. (1990), *Omeros* (London: Faber and Faber).

Walsh, W., see Literature Online.

Webster, A., see Leighton and Reynolds (eds).

Wesley, S., see Literature Online.

Wetzsteon, R. (1994), *Other Stars* (London: Puffin).

Whitman, W. (1981), *Leaves of Grass: The First (1855) Edition*, ed. M. Cowley (London: Penguin Classics).

Wilde, O. (2000), *Poems and Poems in Prose*, B. Fong and K. Beckson (eds) (Oxford: Oxford University Press).

Wither, G., see Grigson (ed.).

Wordsworth, W. (1994), *Selected Poems*, ed. J. O. Hayden (London: Penguin).

— (1995), *The Prelude: The Four Texts*, ed. J. Wordsworth (London: Penguin Classics).

Wroth, M. (1992), *The Poems of Lady Mary Wroth* (Baton Rouge, LA: Louisiana State University Press).

Wyatt, T. (1978), *The Complete Poems*, ed. R. A. Rebholz (London: Penguin Classics).

Yeats, W. B. (1990), *The Complete Poems*, ed. D. Albright (London: Everyman).

Young, M. L. (1997), *Casual Sex and Other Verse* (London: Bantam Books).

Guides to studying poetry

Abrams, M. H. and G. Harpham (2008), *A Glossary of Literary Terms*, 8th edn (Belmont, CA: Wadsworth Publishing).

Carper, T. and D. Attridge (2003), *Meter and Meaning: An Introduction to Rhythm in Poetry* (New York: Routledge)

Eagleton, T. (2007), *How to Read a Poem* (Oxford: Blackwell Publishing).

Easthope, A. (1983), *Poetry as Discourse* (London: Methuen).

Fenton, J. (2003), **The Strength of Poetry** (Oxford: Oxford University Press).

Fussell, P. (1979), *Poetic Meter and Poetic Form*, revised edn (McGraw-Hill).

Hollander, J. (1981), *Rhyme's Reason: A Guide to English Verse* (New Haven: Yale University Press).

Richards, I. A. (1926), *Principles of Literary Criticism*, 2nd edn (London: Routledge and Kegan Paul).

Index

Index

Index

Index